MODERN ENGLISHES

THE LANGUAGE LIBRARY

EDITED BY DAVID CRYSTAL

Loreto Todd

MODERN ENGLISHES: PIDGINS AND CREOLES

Basil Blackwell
in association with
André Deutsch

© Loreto Todd 1984

First published 1984
Basil Blackwell Publisher Limited
108 Cowley Road, Oxford OX4 1JF, England

André Deutsch Limited
105 Great Russell Street, London WC1B 3LJ, England

British Library Cataloguing in Publication Data

Todd, Loreto
   Modern Englishes.—(The Language library)
    1. Creole dialects, English
    2. Pidgin English
   I. Title   II. Series
   427'.9   PM7871
   ISBN 0-631-13655-X
   ISBN 0-631-13656-8 Pbk

Typesetting by The Camelot Press Ltd, Southampton
Printed in Great Britain by
Billing & Sons Ltd, Worcester

To the memory of
John E. Reinecke

Contents

𑌟𑌟𑌟𑌟𑌟

CONTENTS

ix

Conventions

৩৩৩৩৩৩

Phonetic symbols have been kept to a minimum in this book. Where the standard orthography is not used, the conventions employed are as follows:

Vowels

i	— similar in quality to the vowel sound in 'see'
e	— similar in quality to the first segment of the diphthong in 'say'
ɛ	— similar in quality to the vowel sound in 'get'
a	— similar in quality to the vowel sound in French 'pas'
ɔ	— similar in quality to the vowel sound in 'got'
u	— similar in quality to the vowel sound in 'moon'
ei	— similar in quality to the diphthong in 'day'
ai	— similar in quality to the diphthong in 'high'
au	— similar in quality to the diphthong in 'house'
oy	— similar in quality to the diphthong in 'boy'

Consonants

The consonants p, b, t, d, k, l, r, m, n, f, v, z, h and w have approximately the same values as in Received Pronunciation (RP). The remaining symbols are used as follows:

ch	— always has the value of the initial consonant in 'chin'
g	— always has the value of the initial consonant in 'got'
j	— always has the value of the initial consonant in 'judge'
ng	— always has the value of the final consonant in 'sing'
sh	— always has the value of the initial consonant in 'shed'
y	— always has the value of the initial consonant in 'you'
ny	— always has the value of the initial glide in RP 'new'

The normal punctuation conventions of Standard English are followed, including the use of capital letters.

Two other symbols occur:
* indicates that the structure following is unacceptable.
˜ indicates that the sound is nasalised.

When making reference in the text to books by other authors, the name of the author, date of publication and page reference are cited as follows: (Chomsky, 1972: 103). Full publication details are provided in the reading lists at the end of each chapter.

Use of Italic Script
For ease of identification the samples of pidgin and creole which occur within the text are printed in italic script and extracts in other languages such as Standard English, French and Spanish are printed in roman script.

Abbreviations and Locations of Languages Referred to in Chapters 3 and 4

🔃🔃🔃🔃🔃🔃

Bakweri	S.W. Cameroon
Carib	Caribbean
Douala	S. Cameroon
Efik	Nigeria
Eng.	English
Fante	Ghana
Fr.	French
Fula	Guinea
Gã	Upper Volta
Gaz.	Gazelle Peninsula in New Britain (Map 6, Chapter 4)
Ger.	German
Hausa	Nigeria
Igbo	Nigeria
Kikongo	Angola
Lamso	W. Cameroon
Malay	Malaya/Indonesia
Mandinka	Senegal
Mandankwe	W. Cameroon
Manus	Papua New Guinea (Map 6, Chapter 4)
Mel.	Melanesia: Crescent of islands stretching southwards from Papua New Guinea through the Solomon Islands to Vanuatu and New Caledonia
Mende	Sierra Leone
Mungaka	W. Cameroon
N. I.	New Ireland (Map 6, Chapter 4)
N'ki	Nigeria
Port.	Portuguese
Sol. I.	Solomon Islands (Map 7, Chapter 4)
Temne	Sierra Leone
Twi	Ghana
Vai	Liberia
Wolof	Senegal
Yoruba	Nigeria

Acknowledgements

ഇഇഇഇഇഇ

One learns almost everything from others, one's language, one's enthusiasms, most of one's behaviour. I have been particularly fortunate in my 'teachers' from earliest childhood onwards. From my family I learnt to understand the meaning of 'variety' in language and when it was advisable to use one form of English and not another. (Such knowledge was not just a refinement in Northern Ireland!) From friends in Cameroon and Papua New Guinea I learnt two varieties of Pidgin English and, paradoxically perhaps, learning and using pidgins caused me to think more deeply about the standard language and about the many sorts of language subsumed by such a term as 'English'.

My competence in language is a direct result of contacts with family and friends, teachers and students. Their thoughts and ideas have moulded mine. The list of people to whom I owe a debt is therefore almost infinitely long, so I shall restrict it to the people to whom I owe most: the Magees, the McCauslands and the Todds, Sister Mary Damian, Ian Hancock, Beatrice Honikman, Frans Liefrink, Tony Cowie, Teresa Wamey, Kenjo Jumbam, Bernard Fonlon, Gaman Koaggi, Lamech Tareri, and especially to Mary Penrith who helped to type and proof-read this work.

CHAPTER I

Introduction

𒀭𒀭𒀭𒀭𒀭

I.I PERSPECTIVE

IN THIS STUDY of modern Englishes, we shall travel in time and
in space to examine varieties of English which have usually been
ignored and often despised. We shall visit all areas of the world to
study the types of English that have grown up along trade routes
and which have facilitated communication among millions of
people of all races and many creeds. The focus of our attention
will be pidgin and creole Englishes and, to understand these
languages, we shall also pay attention to the people who created
them, for languages cannot be studied in isolation from people.
This claim has a corollary: we cannot despise a language or a
language variety without despising the people who use it. And the
better we learn a language, the closer we can come to its users
because language is the means by which we all express our
understanding of, and attitude towards, our individual universes.

Languages cannot be separated from people and, like people,
they defy easy classification. It is true, as many linguists claim,
that a language is an arbitrary set of signs by which members of a
speech community communicate and co-operate, but such a
definition, like the Gradgrindian view of a horse as 'Quadruped.
Graminiverous.' (*Hard Times*, Ch. 2) is essentially lifeless. It is
simply not possible to identify pidgins and creoles with the ease
that one might identify an orange. They, like all languages, are
capable of expressing the linguistic needs of a group of people,
and, since no two groups of people will ever have identical
communication needs, each language is unique. And an adequate
linguistic description must illuminate this uniqueness. The more
we study pidgins and creoles, the greater will our estimation of
them be and the more we will realise that short, facile descriptions
are, like the above two-word definition of a horse, oversimplifications. Nevertheless, we will begin with such oversimplifications
and then, in the course of our study, amplify and correct them.

We shall be able to explain much, but mysteries will remain, such as how and why peripheral trade languages in all parts of the world are so similar in structure, and how even complex communication systems can be developed so quickly by people who speak radically different languages. And even simpler mysteries cannot be fully unravelled. We know, for example, that the word 'creole' comes from a Romance word which included the meanings 'bred, brought up, reared, domestic', and that from the late sixteenth century the word was used to mean 'a person born in the colonies' and then extended to include such a person's language; but the etymology of 'pidgin' is much less clear.

In spite of much research, no one is really sure where or even when the word 'pidgin'[1] arose. It is possible, as the *Oxford English Dictionary* suggests, that 'pidgin' is a Chinese mispronunciation of 'business', that it referred to a form of English used between the Chinese and Europeans in seaports in China and the Straits Settlements in the nineteenth century and that it first appeared in print in 1850. Two other possible etymologies link 'pidgin' with trade. Charles Leland (1876: 131) suggests that it may derive from a modified form of the Portuguese word 'ocupação' meaning 'occupation, business'; and Kurt Hassert (1913: 432) relates 'pidgin' to the Hebrew word 'pidjom' meaning 'barter'.

In favour of these etymologies is the fact that pidgins have undoubtedly served as trade languages for at least five hundred years and their value in this capacity has never been disputed. Against these etymologies are the phonological difficulties of deriving 'pidgin' from either 'business' or 'ocupação', and the late appearance of 'pidjom English' in print.

D. Kleinecke (1959: 271–2) suggests that 'pidgin' comes from a Yayo word meaning 'people'. And it is certainly true that 'Pidians' does occur meaning 'local Indians' in *Purchas his Pilgrimes* (1625). Part of this book describes how the English were in contact with the Yayos in 1604–5 when they attempted to set up a South American colony. It may be that the English colonists used the phrase 'pidian English' to mean 'non-native English', but if this is where the term 'pidgin' originated it is hard to explain why there is no written reference to it between 1625 and 1850.

A further possibility is that 'pidgin' comes from Portuguese 'pequeno' meaning 'little' or 'child'. Pidginised versions of French, Dutch and Malay have been known as 'petit nègre', 'baby hollands' and 'baba Malay' and many serious writers have compared pidgins with 'baby talk' (see Section 1.5). It is also true that the Portuguese were among the first Europeans to trade in Africa, Asia and the Americas.

And finally, it is even possible that 'pidgin' is a variant form of 'pigeon' and that whilst a 'pigeon' language might be useful for carrying simple messages, it was regarded as being of little more consequence than bird-like imitations of language. That pidgins were disparaged is clear from the descriptions that have been attached to them even in this century, descriptions like 'bush English', 'bad talk', 'a macaronic jargon', 'a mongrel lingo' and 'inferiority made half articulate'.

It seems unlikely that we shall ever know precisely how 'pidgin' came into being but it is now the recognised term for a marginal or makeshift language.

1.2 PIDGINS AND CREOLES

A pidgin is a communication system that develops among people who do not share a common language. In early stages of contact, such as the first encounters between British sailors and coastal West Africans or between American soldiers and the Vietnamese, a makeshift system emerges involving a few simple structures – mostly commands – and a limited number of words, drawn almost entirely from the language of the dominant group.[2] A pidgin which derives most of its vocabulary from English is called an *English-based* or *English-related* pidgin. The type of restricted pidgin we are describing is often accompanied by gesture and mime, and it is of limited communication value. Such pidgins tend to be unstable and short-lived and they are characteristic of superficial contact between individuals or groups where only two languages are involved. If the contact is discontinued, the pidgin dies; if the contact ceases to be superficial, one or both groups will learn the other's language.

In multilingual areas of the world, however, a different fate can befall a restricted pidgin. Initially it may be used in only a limited number of situations such as trading or military operations, but it can become so useful in inter-group communications that it can be expanded into a lingua franca. This type of pidgin differs from restricted varieties in that as it expands it becomes more flexible and as it becomes more flexible it is capable of fulfilling an increasing number of the linguistic needs of its users.

A creole is a pidgin which has become the mother tongue of a group of people. This happened on a large scale at the time of the slave trade between West Africa and the Americas. Between the sixteenth and the nineteenth centuries, an estimated eight to ten and a half million[3] Africans were sold into slavery and forced by circumstances to give up their ancestral African languages and adopt a pidginised variety of a European tongue (see Chapters 3 and 5 for further details). Children born into such communities learnt to use the pidgin for all their linguistic needs. The creoles that arose under such conditions continued to make use of the simple structures and small vocabulary[4] that characterised the pidgins. But, because they were mother tongues, they had to be capable of expressing the entire linguistic needs, desires and aspirations of the speech community and so they tended to be more flexible and innovative than even the most expanded of pidgins. It is worth emphasising that creoles are the result of a language shift, whereas even if a speech community adopts an expanded pidgin as one of its mother tongues, as has happened in parts of Nigeria and in Papua New Guinea, the pidgin is usually learnt in conjunction with one or more vernacular languages.

1.3   WHAT ARE PIDGIN ENGLISHES LIKE?

To begin with, we shall concentrate on expanded pidgins related to English and we shall list the characteristics common to all those so far studied. And we shall do this to provide readers not familiar with these languages with a snapshot overview. Like any snapshot, however, our overview will be static and so it will be followed by an examination of the processes which are involved in the growth and development of pidgin languages. As will become clear from Chapter 2, there are more than sixty varieties of pidginised English in the world. All the examples cited in this section are taken from recordings of spontaneous speech in one particular pidgin, that of Cameroon, West Africa, subsequently referred to as CP.

Pidgin Englishes have a fixed word-order and they are syntactically simpler than any mother-tongue variety of English. Sentences are usually short and of the following types:

> *Wikɔp!* – Get up! (Predicate)
> *Wikɔp di pikin* – Get the child up (Predicate + Object)
> *I bin wikɔp di pikin* – She got the child up (Subject + Predicate + Object)
> *I bin wikɔp fɔ dai* – He arose from the dead (Subject + Predicate + Object + Complement)

and, although complex sentences occur:

> *A no go chɔp yam if ɔda ting dei* – I will not eat yam if there is anything else

they are less frequent and more clearly related to simple sentences than is the case in SE.[5]

Negation involves the use of one negative marker, *no* in this pidgin. It can precede the verb:

> *Go!* – Go!
> *No go!* – Don't go!
> *Dɛm fit go* – They can go
> *Dɛm no fit go* – They cannot go

or, for emphasis, it can occur before both the noun and the verb:

> *No man no go kam* – Nobody will come

or even, in very emphatic statements, it can appear before all the semantically full elements:

> *No man no laik mi no smɔl* – Nobody likes me even a little.

A negative sentence, however, must have a *no* in the preverbal slot with the result that a sentence such as:

> * *No man bin kam*

is ungrammatical, the correct form being:

> *No man no bin kam* – Nobody came.

Passive constructions do not occur, although the meanings of passives can be expressed in such ways as:

Dɛm bin kil i
Sɔm man bin kil i } He was killed.

Yes/no questions are distinguished from statements by intonation alone:

Yu no wan kam – You don't want to come

Yu no wan kam? – Do you not want to come?

and questions involving question words like when? where? and why? differ from statements only in that the question forms occur:

Yu bin go – You went
Fɔ wich taim yu bin go? – When did you go?
Usai yu bin go? – Where did you go?
Fɔ seka wɛti yu bin go? – Why did you go?

Verbs are not inflected for person or number:

A sing fɔ chɔs an ma – I sing in church and my
brɔda sing fɔ chɔs. brother sings in church.
Wi tu sing fɔ dei We both sing there

or for tense:

I bin go yɛstadei. I – He went yesterday. He
go agen tudei. Sɔmtaim goes again today. Perhaps
i no go go tumɔrɔ. he will not go tomorrow.

Instead of verbal variation such as 'go', 'goes', 'went', 'going', 'gone', pidgins make use of the base form of the verb, in this case *go*, and indicate temporal and aspectual distinctions by means of a finite set of auxiliaries (see Chapters 3 and 4 for further discussion).

It is not always easy or indeed possible to distinguish between adjectives and verbs. They can often be preceded and followed by similar items as is clear if we compare some of the structures in which *waka* < 'walk' and *big* < 'big' can occur:

I bin waka (He walked) *I bin big* (He was big)
I bin di waka (He was walking) *I bin di big* (He was getting big)

6

Sɔm waka man dei (There is a traveller there)
I go waka i kɔmbi (He'll visit his friend)

Sɔm big man dei (There is a big man there)
I go big di ting (He'll make the thing bigger)

and words derived from English adjectives are like verbs in showing no morphological variations:

> *I big* — He is big
> *I big pas mi* — He is bigger than me
> *I big pas wi ɔl* — He is the biggest of all.

Nouns are not marked for case:

> *Di dɔg dei* — The dog is there
> *A bin lɔs wi dɔg* — I lost our dog
> *Di dɔg i fut dɔn brok* — The dog's leg is broken

or, usually, for plurality:

> *Yu gɛt daso tri banana?* — Have you only three bananas?

But, if it is necessary to emphasise plurality, this can be done by the use of the third-person plural pronoun:

> *Dɛm bin kam tek ma pikin dɛm* — They came and took my children.

The set of pronouns is simpler than in Standard English (SE). Pronouns in pidgins do not reflect grammatical gender nor do they usually show case contrasts:[6]

CP			SE		
a	*mi*	*ma*	I	me	my
yu	*yu*	*yu*	you	you	your
i	*i/am*	*i*	he	him	his
i	*i/am*	*i*	she	her	her
i	*i/am*	*i*	it	it	its
wi	*wi*	*wi*	we	us	our
wuna	*wuna*	*wuna*	you	you	your
dɛm	*dɛm/am*	*dɛm*	they	them	their

Thus, we have nine distinct forms in CP and eighteen in SE. The difference is even more striking if we compare the pidgin of old, rural speakers with SE because they use only six forms, namely *mi, yu, i, wi, wuna* and *dɛm*.

Pidgins also have fewer prepositions than SE. Often a preposition has a wider range of meaning than its English cognate:

Gif di buk fɔ mi – Give the book *to* me

I dei fɔ fam – She is *at* the farm

Dɛm dei fɔ chɔs – They are *in* the church

Du dis wan fɔ mi, a bɛg – Do this *for* me, please

Di mɔni dei fɔ tebul – The money is *on* the table

Yu fit muf tɛn frangk fɔ ma kwa – You can take ten francs *from* my bag

and often, too, verbs are used where prepositions or adverbs would be required in SE:

Bring di pikin kam – Bring the child over here/to me

Tek di buk go – Take the book over there/away from me

I bin rɔn go rich di haus –He ran all the way to the house (lit. he past run go reach the house).

As far as vocabulary is concerned, pidgin speakers have learnt to make 'infinite use of finite means' (Humboldt, quoted from Chomsky, 1965: 8). Since pidgin vocabularies are small, words tend to cover a larger area of meaning. Thus *buk* < 'book' means 'a book' but also 'a letter', 'anything written', 'an education':

I tek wan pepa rait buk fɔ mi – He took a sheet of paper and wrote a letter for me

Dis ma pikin sabi buk – This child of mine is educated

and *hia* can mean 'understand', 'sense', 'notice' as well as 'hear':

A no di hia dis masa fain – I don't understand this gentleman fully

Yu go hia hɔt! – You'll suffer! (lit. you go hear hot)

A hia sɔm ting di bɔn – I smell something burning.

This lexical polysemy is less confusing than might at first appear

8

because pidgins are *spoken* languages and so context can usually clarify utterances.

Items also tend to be multifunctional, that is, they are not limited to one word class. Thus *swit* < 'sweet' can function as an adjective:

> *sɔm swit sup* – delicious stew

as a noun:

> *Dis swit go bring palava* – These sweet things (i.e. pieces of unexpected good luck) will cause trouble

as a verb, both transitive and intransitive:

> *Di sup di swit mi taim no dei* – The stew is giving me infinite pleasure
> *Di sup dɔn bigin swit* – The stew has begun to get tasty

and it can fill the role of an English adverb:

> *I sabi tɔk swit swit so* – He knows how to flatter (i.e. talk very sweetly).

Pidgin speakers also enlarge the functional power of a limited vocabulary by the use of reduplicated forms. Reduplications occur in many languages, including English, for example 'goody-goody', 'never-never', 'so-so' but they are systematically exploited by pidgin speakers for four main purposes. Firstly, reduplication cuts down on the number of homophones in the language so that we have:

san (sun) and *sansan* (sand)
wɔs (wash) and *wɔswɔs* (wasp).

Secondly, it intensifies or modifies the meaning of a simple form:

> *sɔm fain pikin* – a lovely child
> *sɔm fainfain pikin* – a really lovely child
> *bɛn* – bend
> *bɛnbɛn* – crooked
> *eni dei eni dei soso miamia* – every single day perpetual nagging.

Thirdly, it can imply a repeated or protracted action:

Pikin di krai – The child is crying
Pikin di soso kraikrai – The child is always crying.

And finally, it can be used to express the equivalent of 'one by one' and 'one each':

Di bif bin ɛnta wanwan – The animals went in one by one
Gif dɛm tutu – Give them two each.

Thus, as the above examples show, reduplication is exploited to extend a small vocabulary, reduce ambiguities and allow speakers to express subtle distinctions.

We can make one further generalisation about pidgin Englishes, a generalisation which may already be apparent from the quoted examples. Pidgins tend to be analytic. This tendency is apparent at all levels of the language. We see it in the establishment of lexical sets:

hɔs – horse
man hɔs – stallion
wuman hɔs – mare
man pikin hɔs – foal (male)
wuman pikin hɔs – filly

in the expression of complex temporal and aspectual distinctions:

kam – come
i di kam – he is coming
i bin kam – he came
i bin di kam – he was coming
i dɔng kam – he has just come
i bin dɔng di kam – he had been coming

and in the combination of simple vocabulary items to express complex or abstract ideas:

gɛt bɛlɛ – be pregnant
gɛt flawa – mature, have one's period for the first time
si mun – have one's period (lit. see moon)
wɔs bɛlɛ – last child (lit. wash stomach/womb)
man han – right (lit. man hand)
wuman han – left (lit. woman hand)

gud hat —generous, generosity (lit. good heart)
lɔng ai – greedy (for possessions) (lit. long eye)
lɔng trot – greedy (for food) (lit. long throat).

Pidgin Englishes are simpler than SE in that they are more systematic and thus easier to learn. They have jettisoned morphological and syntactic irregularities but they have not sacrificed the ability to communicate precisely and unambiguously the linguistic needs of their speakers. Pidgin Englishes have often been described as being linguistically impoverished, and, to one who does not know them well, they can certainly give this impression. It is important to remember certain facts, however. Because a pidgin is almost invariably acquired as an auxiliary language, it does not need to fill as many roles as a unique mother tongue. In addition, it is perfectly adequate to the linguistic roles in which it is used and can be expanded as the communicative needs of its users increase. Thirdly, although a pidgin's vocabulary is less extensive than that of SE, it can convey similar types of information with fewer words, often expressing abstractions by means of metaphorical extensions of basic vocabulary items like 'belly', 'eye', 'hand':

wuman i bɛlɛ – a holdall bag (lit. woman she belly)
drai ai – brave (of a man) (lit. dry eye)
drai ai – brazen (of a woman)
tai han – mean, meanness (lit. tie hand).

And finally, although SE has an extensive vocabulary, it is clear that speakers of SE use only a small part of this vocabulary in their normal day-to-day lives and, if Paul Procter is right in claiming that many speakers manage with only two thousand words (see Note 4), then the differences between speakers of SE and of a Pidgin English have probably been exaggerated.

1.4 PIDGINISATION, CREOLISATION AND DECREOLISATION

We have looked briefly at some of the characteristic features of Pidgin Englishes and are perhaps now in a better position to examine the processes which bring these languages into existence and then cause them to expand and change.

Pidginisation is a process of simplification that reduces irregularities in a language and is a natural consequence of contact between people who speak different languages or different varieties of the same language. It seems likely that the Vikings and the English communicated with each other by concentrating on shared dialect features and avoiding dissimilar structures. Almost a thousand years later, it appears that a similar type of dialect levelling was at work in Australia. Turner (1969: 10), for example, claims that in Australia in the nineteenth century dialect oddities disappeared and a common-core English evolved between speakers from different parts of Britain. The extent of linguistic simplification that occurs between speakers of mutually intelligible dialects of English is much less dramatic than the simplification that occurs in contacts between English speakers and speakers of unrelated languages, but the inspiration for both types of simplification is the same, namely the need for unambiguous communication.

Most modern pidgins are the result of colonial expansion and thus they have evolved from a master-servant type of contact between speakers of European tongues and speakers of so-called 'exotic' languages. Once again, we shall concentrate on pidgins that are lexically related to English.

A rudimentary pidgin can evolve extremely quickly, sometimes in a matter of hours. As Weinreich put it (1964: viii):

> If co-operation is a pressing necessity everyone will soon learn enough of the other man's language to establish communication even if the two mediums in contact have no genetic ties or synchronic resemblances of any sort.

Such a makeshift pidgin has a very limited vocabulary, and communication is facilitated by mime, gesture and frequent repetition, with the contactors almost certainly speaking at the tops of their voices, adding an occasional vowel as in 'muchee'[7] and possibly introducing non-English but widely-occurring words like 'savi'.[8] If the contact is sustained but keeps its non-intimate character, the Pidgin English begins to stabilise and evince some or all of the following features. Speakers of the pidgin will use the phonologies of their individual mother tongues. Thus, an Englishman may say /ɔil/ 'oil' but an African, whose mother tongue has a CVCV⁹ structure, may say /ɔja/. The former may say /spiə/ for 'spear' while the latter, whose mother tongue may not have such consonant clusters, central vowels or closing diphthongs may say /supia/; word inflections will be eliminated; stressed forms of pronouns will be used, thus 'me' in preference to 'I'; the number of prepositions will be reduced, possibly to one multipurpose preposition; and tense distinctions will not be made by modifications of the verb form although time may be indicated by such markers as 'now', 'after', 'by and by'.

The differences between mother-tongue English and the pidgins based on it can be attributed to interference and to the processes of simplification. Interference from the learner's mother tongue can be seen in two ways. He may introduce into the pidgin features that occur in his mother tongue but not in SE. Thus he may overtly distinguish between 'you (singular)' and 'you (plural)'; and he may not make distinctions which are important in English but which do not occur in his mother tongue. He may not, for example, make pronominal distinctions between 'he', 'she' and 'it'. The pidgin features which can be ascribed to simplification may come from either or both parties involved in the contact. English speakers may, as they do in telegrams, deliberately simplify their English by cutting out articles, auxiliary verbs and prepositions, and they may also reduce or eliminate irregularities. The learner may simplify the target language by overgeneralising rules, by assuming, for example, that if 'sheep' can mean 'one sheep' or 'many sheep', then 'foot' can mean 'one foot' or 'many feet'. In addition the English speaker can then imitate the learner's simplification and the learner, deprived of other models, will assume that his generalisations are correct. Like children acquiring English, pidgin speakers often overgeneralise a rule, but whereas children learn their English in a society with a ready-made communication system, pidgin speakers have to invent a language for a community which has just come into being.

In multilingual communities where modern pidgins have developed, the pidgins have been expanded by the indigenous people to facilitate inter-group contacts. The reason why pidgin speakers did not rapidly learn the full target language can be explained largely by the nature of colonial contacts, which were usually non-intimate. As soon as a pidgin developed which was sufficiently flexible to fulfil the needs of a master-servant relationship, there was little need to replace it with a variety of English closer to the mother-tongue norm. Indeed, many of the 'masters' may have preferred to encourage the use of pidgin because it helped to emphasise the status quo. But if the 'masters' found the pidgin useful, so too did the 'servants'. In areas of extreme multilingualism such as West Africa and the South Pacific,[10] the indigenous people found that the pidgins allowed more extensive inter-group contact than had previously been possible and so they employed it for more and more purposes, and each new purpose for which they used it helped to make the pidgin more adequate and more flexible.

In this period of expansion and stabilisation, the vocabulary was increased in two main ways. Firstly, words from local languages were incorporated into the pidgin. The fact that these words almost all belong to the realms of culture, food and clothing, underlines the non-intimacy of the contact between the English speakers and local people. Our examples this time will come from both West Africa (Cameroon) and the South Pacific (Papua New Guinea) to indicate the similarities in the linguistic and social contact:

CAMEROON	PAPUA NEW GUINEA
Titles	
fɔn – chief	*luluai* – headman
nchinda – chief's messenger	*tultul* – luluai's assistant
Cultural Items	
buba – blouse	*pulpul* – grass-skirt
kata – headring	*kalang* – ceremonial earrings
mbanya – co-wife	*tumbuna* – ancestors
mbombo – namesake	*birua* – enemy
ngɔmbi – spirit, god	*tambaran* – ghost, spirit

Food

akara – beancake	*abus* – meat, game
fufu – pounded yam	*kaukau* – sweet potato
kola – nut (offered to guests)	*buai* – betel nut
ntumbu – edible grub	*kindam* – crayfish.

Secondly, in addition to outright borrowing we find a high incidence of calquing; ideas borrowed from the local cultures, expressed in English words:

CAMEROON	PAPUA NEW GUINEA
gud hat – sincere (lit. good heart)	*bel klin* – sincere (lit. belly clean)
dei klin – dawn (lit. day clean)	*ai pas* – blind (lit. eye fast)
swit mɔt – flattery (lit. sweet mouth)	*wan blut* – sibling (lit. one blood)
krai dai – a wake, funeral celebration (lit. cry die)	*nek bilong singsing* – melody (lit. neck belong song)
biabia mɔt – moustache, beard (lit. hair mouth)	*maus gras* – moustache, beard (lit. mouth grass)

It seems clear that calquing was preferred to extensive borrowing from the vernaculars because a too heavy reliance on any one language would have reduced the value of the pidgin as a lingua franca. Besides that, in both West Africa and the South Pacific it is a surprising fact that the languages are much more highly differentiated than the cultures of the people who use them. Expressing this more graphically, we can point to the fact that, in adjacent valleys in Papua New Guinea, there are people who share the same beliefs, customs, music and even kinship systems, yet their languages may be as different from each other as English is from Chinese.

This period of expansion and stabilisation of the pidgin can also be regarded as a period of nativisation; a period when the local people made the pidgin serve their purposes. It is worth reflecting that, even today, Nigerian administration would be much less efficient if Pidgin English did not exist. The processes involved illustrate the human ability to create and modify language to suit changing circumstances and this is the period when creolisation may have occurred.

As far as West Africa is concerned, creolisation was forced on many Africans because of the Slave Trade. Slaves, separated from their speech communities, were forced to use a pidgin as both a work and a home language. In this way creoles became the mother tongues of millions of Africans transported to the New World. It is hard to offer accurate statistics about how and when the English creoles developed because few writers thought either the people or their languages worthy of comment, but some idea of the stability of these languages once they have been creolised can be gained by examining the Creole Englishes of Suriname in South America. Suriname, previously called Dutch Guiana, was in 1667 ceded to the Dutch by the English, who had held the territory for only seventeen years. Yet, in spite of the fact that Dutch has been the official language for over three hundred years, more than 90% of the population still speak a Creole English as a mother tongue.

There are few linguistic distinctions between a stabilised pidgin and a creole, though it is likely that a creole, as a mother tongue, has a larger vocabulary, a greater stylistic range and that it is spoken more quickly. Even where a stable pidgin becomes one of the mother tongues of a group of people, as it has in Cameroon and in Papua New Guinea, it does not have to fulfil all the linguistic purposes that a creole must for a monolingual community.

If Creole Englishes had been allowed to develop in total isolation from English, it is certain that some at least would have become distinct though related languages, as distinct from SE as SE is from Old English. But the majority of creoles and expanded pidgins have co-existed with SE because SE was, and usually still is, the official language of the countries where they are found. This co-existence has brought into being what has been called a *post-creole continuum*.[11] This term has been coined to account for the fact that nowadays in creole- or pidgin-speaking communities we do not find two distinct varieties of English exemplified by such sentences as: *di man pikin dεm bin hala* and 'the boys shouted' but an unbroken spectrum in which variants like:

di bɔi dɛm bin hala
di bɔi dɛm bin shaut
di bɔiz dɛm bin hala
di bɔiz dɛm hala
di bɔiz bin hala
di bɔiz halad

can also occur.

A post-creole continuum is often described in terms of decreolisation, the process by which the creole or expanded pidgin is modified at all linguistic levels in the direction of the status variety of the language, SE. Decreolisation is similar in cause and effect to the process of dialect levelling apparent in all mother-tongue communities, where, because of education and media influence, dialect features are becoming recessive. It is interesting to speculate about whether or not decreolisation can develop to such an extent that the extremes of the spectrum may be considered to be *stylistic* rather than *linguistic* variants. It seems possible that this may have happened in the past as empires spread and contracted, but it could only have happened if the speech communities became socially integrated. Recent history does not show this to be happening. United States Black English[12] was originally a creole and it has certainly been decreolised, especially in the last fifty years; but, in spite of the considerable overlap between BE and SE, brought about through education and prolonged contact, BE still evinces many of the features associated with Afro-American creoles.

And today there is another force at work and one which may curtail the decreolising process, at least in some parts of the world. It is a force allied to nationalism which argues that it is the pidgin or the creole which should be adopted as the official language of the country and certainly the language of education. More will be said about this in Chapters 4 and 5.

We have spoken in terms of the processes of pidginisation, creolisation and decreolisation and we have done this to stress the fact that we are dealing with dynamic and changing systems of communication and not with static standards. And yet we have probably given the impression that there is an inevitable one-two-three-ness about these processes. This is not so. Creolisation will not follow pidginisation if the speech community does not need or want the integration that a lingua franca can provide. Decreolisation need not occur if the creole remains outside the sphere of influence of its lexical source language, as it has done in Suriname. Linguistic U-turns can occur. There is some evidence that the Creole English of manumitted slaves who returned to Africa was repidginised by the people among whom the ex-slaves settled.[13] And there is even more evidence that young, disenchanted West Indians in both Britain and Jamaica are recreolising their speech as a symbol of their alienation from society (see Chapter 5).

The processes we have described are to be seen as a partial reflection of what has happened to English in the last four hundred years, but they are not to be seen as consecutive or entirely dependent on each other. Every speech community is unique and so no two varieties of English will follow identical routes of development.

1.5 THE ORIGINS OF PIDGINS AND CREOLES

So far we have considered pidgins and creoles which are lexically related to English, but these only make up a proportion of the pidginised languages in the world. In *A Bibliography of Pidgin and Creole Languages* (1975) Reinecke et al. cite over one hundred attested cases of languages which have undergone a process of pidginisation and that number is being steadily increased as more and more language-contact situations are explored. Many of the languages described by Reinecke are the direct result of colonial expansion and so we find pidgin or creole varieties of Portuguese, Spanish, French, Dutch, German and Italian as well as English. But many of the languages listed by Reinecke owe nothing to the colonial ambitions of West European nations. Each area of the world has also produced indigenous pidgins and creoles. Thus we find Anglo-Romani and Russenorsk in Europe, Baba Malay and Pidgin Hindi in Asia, Swahili and Sango in Africa, Chinook jargon in North America, Lingua Geral in South America and Hiri Motu in Papua New Guinea. All of these came into being to facilitate communication along linguistic frontiers but, in addition to the similarities in their *social* roles, these languages show marked *structural* similarities. Perhaps this can best be illustrated by a brief comparison between the West African Pidgin we have already described and Hiri Motu, a Papuan lingua franca.

In both these languages word order is fixed; word forms are uninflected; number is not indicated in nouns; gender is not marked in pronouns; there are fewer prepositions/postpositions than in the lexical source languages; there is no syntactic difference between statements and yes/no questions; and verbs and adjectives pattern in very similar ways. The comparisons overleaf (pages 20 and 21) underline the above similarities.

Such similarities are striking and we can augment them by showing, for example, how 'immediately' is expressed by the equivalent of 'now now', CP *naunau*, HM *harihari*; how 'one by one' and 'one each' are expressed by the reduplication of the numeral, CP *wanwan*, HM *tata*; and how serial verb constructions occur where SE would employ a verb + adverb/preposition:

English	Cameroon Pidgin	Hiri Motu
Take away (from speaker)	Tek go	Abia lao
		Take go
Run away	Rɔn go	Heau lao
		run go
Bring here (to speaker)	Bring kam	Abia mai
		take come

And comparable similarities are to be found in all languages which have undergone a process of pidginisation. The obvious question is *why*?

The question may be obvious but the answer is less so. Many theories have been advanced as partial explanations of why pidginised languages, created in different parts of the world by speakers of all known language-families, should evince such structural similarities. We shall mention only three theories, the

English	Cameroon Pidgin	Hiri Motu
You go	Yu go (SV)	Oi lao (SV)
You don't go	Yu no go (S neg V)	Oi lao lasi (SV neg)
I see a pig	A si swain (SVO)	Boroma lau itaia (OSV)
		Pig I see
I don't see a pig	A no si swain (S neg VO)	Boroma lau itaia lasi
		Pig I see no
He sees a pig	I si swain	Boroma ia itaia (OSV)
She sees a pig	I si swain	Boroma ia itaia
It sees a pig	I si swain	Boroma ia itaia
They see a pig	Dɛm si swain	Boroma idia itaia
The pigs are coming	Swain dɛm kam	Boroma idia mai
	Pig they come	Pig they come
The pigs aren't coming	Swain dɛm no kam	Boroma idia mai lasi
He/She/It is ill	I sik	Ia gorere
He/She/It is not ill	I no sik	Ia gorere lasi
We come from X	Wi kam fɔ X	Ai mai X dekenai
		We come X postposition
We don't come from X	Wi no kam fɔ X	Ai mai X dekenai lasi

He/She/It stays in X	I stei fɔ X	Ia noho X dekenai
You (sg) are going to X	Yu go fɔ X	Oi lao X dekenai
You (pl) are going to X	Wuna go fɔ X	Umui lao X dekenai
Is the man well?	Man i fain?	Tau ia namo?
	Man he fine	Man he well
He/She/It is well	I fain	Ia namo
He/She/It is not well	I no fain	Ia namo lasi
The man's child	Man i pikin	Tau ena natuna
	Man he child	Man he + emph. child
The woman's house	Wuman i haus	Hahine ena ruma
The child's dog	Pikin i dog	Natuna ena sisia

baby-talk theory, the relexification theory and the linguistic universals theory and we shall show that the last theory is sufficiently comprehensive to include all the others.

The Baby-Talk Theory

Many observers of pidginised languages have observed the similarities between pidgins and the early speech of children. Leland (1876: 8–9), writing about China Coast Pidgin English, claimed:

> There are in all not more than thirty altogether foreign or strange words in ordinary use, and a number of these are familiar to all persons of the least general information. What remains can present no difficulty to anyone who can understand Negro minstrelsy or baby talk

and both Jespersen (1922: Chapter XII) and Bloomfield (1933: 472) lent their weight to the notion. According to this theory the 'dominant' group in the contact situation adopted a condescending attitude to those contacted, possibly assuming that the contacted people were incapable of learning the full language, and so they spoke as if they were children, eliminating inflections and grammatical irregularities and limiting the vocabulary to a few hundred words.

It is quite probable that many European groups *did* adopt a condescending attitude to the people they contacted and that the people thus acquired a reduced form of the target language. But contacts that produced pidgins did not always involve people of markedly different status or race. Many of the indigenous pidgins and creoles referred to above evolved among people for whom the power dimension was not so obviously marked. Yet these, too, reveal structures found in the language of children between the ages of two and four. It would thus seem sensible to stress the contributions made to the pidgins by their *learners*. They, like children acquiring their mother tongue, or like anyone acquiring a second or third language, make hypotheses based on the linguistic data available. Adults, in addition, often make assumptions based on their intuitions, their mother tongues and on any strategies found useful in acquiring other languages. Children progress from their early form of language to a close approxima-

tion of the adult norm because such progress is socially sanctioned. But, at least in the early stages of contact, pidgin speakers
do not have the opportunity to expand their pidgin by reference
to the linguistic norms of the contactors.

The Relexification Theory

This suggests that most, if not all, of the pidgins and creoles which
have arisen since the fifteenth century as a direct result of
European contact stem from a fifteenth-century Portuguese-
based pidgin. It has also been suggested (Whinnom, 1965: 509–
27) that the Portuguese Pidgin may itself be descended from the
so-called *Lingua Franca* (also known as *Sabir*) which had been
employed throughout the Mediterranean as a link language at
least from the time of the Crusades. According to this theory, the
Portuguese navigators would have used a Portuguese version of
Lingua Franca in their post-fifteenth-century contacts in Africa,
Asia and the Americas. Then, as Portuguese influence began to
wane and as other European nations developed their trade, the
Portuguese vocabulary would have been replaced by the vocabularies of Spanish or French or English or Dutch, while the simple
structures would have been retained.

There is quite a bit of corroborative evidence in support of this
theory. In the first place, research suggests that the Portuguese did
develop a Portuguese-based 'reconnaissance language' in the
fifteenth century (Naro, 1973) which was specifically designed to
train Africans as interpreters. It was in no way unusual for
European traders and explorers to take local people to Europe
and train them as interpreters. A description of a 1604 English
attempt to colonise part of the coast of South America includes
the following statement:

> Then after divers conferences with the chiefe Indians, and namely with
> two of their Countrie, *which had been before in England,* and could
> speake some English, he found them very willing to have him and his
> people abide in their Countrie.
> (*Purchas his Pilgrimes,* The Fourth Part: 1250)

The Portuguese reconnaissance variety of the language contained many features associated with pidgins, namely adjective
verbs, loss of inflection, one multipurpose preposition, invariant

pronouns and one negative marker. It is not possible to prove that this modified Portuguese derived from the Mediaeval Lingua Franca but it is very likely that many navigators and traders knew the latter. Whinnom certainly feels that such an origin for fifteenth-century Portuguese Pidgin is probable. In his words:

> We do not want to suppose that such miraculous simplicity was achieved twice.
> (1965: 522)

Secondly, there is evidence that relexification, that is vocabulary replacement from Portuguese to English, has taken place. Saramaccan, an English-based creole of Suriname, derives approximately 54% of its core vocabulary from English, 38% from Portuguese, 4% from African languages and 4% from Dutch. As mentioned earlier (p. 16), the English only held Suriname from 1650 to 1667 during which time many slaves fled from the coastal plantations to the forested interior. Saramaccan is the mother tongue of the descendants of some of these runaway slaves and it seems very probable that it is a creole which derives from an incompletely relexified Pidgin Portuguese.

Thirdly, the grammars of some European-based creoles are so similar – more similar than the grammars of the standard languages – that it is hard to believe that the resemblances could be fortuitous. We shall illustrate this point by looking at part of the verb phrase in Guyanese Créole and in Krio, an English-based creole of Sierra Leone:

French	Guyanese Créole	Krio	English
Mangez	Mãʒe	Chɔp	Eat
J'ai mangé	Mo mãʒe	A chɔp	I ate
Il/Elle a mangé	Li mãʒe	I chɔp	He/She ate
Je mange/Je suis en train de manger	Mo ka mãʒe	A de chɔp	I am eating
J'avais mangé	Mo te mãʒe	A bin chɔp	I ate/had eaten
Je mangeais	Mo te ka mãʒe	A bin de chɔp	I was eating
Je mangerai	Mo ke mãʒe	A go chɔp	I shall eat
Il/Elle est plus grand que vous	Li gros pas u	I big pas yu	He/She/It is bigger than you

We could extend this comparison between the two creoles and we could also illustrate identically structured VPs from Portuguese- and Spanish-based creoles. Such similarities cannot, of course, prove that relexification has occurred but it seems a strong possibility.

Fourthly, the use of common-core structures with different vocabularies is well attested in multilingual areas. David Dalby (1970: 6) suggests that many West African languages are structurally and phonologically similar and that West African polyglots (and most West Africans *are* polyglots) can therefore minimise the linguistic load they carry by utilising the same structures with different vocabulary sets. Essentially the same conclusion was reached by Gumperz (1967: 48–57) when he studied effective bilingualism along the Maharastra-Mysore boundary in India among people who spoke two languages all day, every day. Although standard Kannada and standard Marathi differ considerably in phonology, vocabulary and syntax, Gumperz discovered that speakers along the boundary used a common-denominator grammar but manipulated two differentiated lexical sets.

And finally, students of the English language will be aware of a phenomenon similar to relexification in England after the Norman Conquest. Many French words came into the language side by side with an English equivalent:

ask	and	demand
goods	and	chattels
hearty	and	cordial
might	and	power
wish	and	desire.

Occasionally, the English word was ousted as when:

aeþele	gave way to	noble
anda	gave way to	envy
earm	gave way to	poor
leod	gave way to	people.

It is not too far-fetched to suggest that even more of the vocabulary of English would have been replaced (i.e. that English would have been in part *relexified*) if the links between England

and France had not been at least partly broken by the loss of Normandy in 1204.

Relexification certainly has occurred and probably more widely than has previously been believed. One can, for example, make a good case in support of the thesis that Gaelic was not so much replaced by English in rural areas in Northern Ireland, as that Gaelic was probably relexified towards English while the phonology, idioms and sentence patterns of the native people remained Gaelic.[14] It is even more certain that many European-related pidgins and creoles owe something to an early Portuguese Pidgin. The Portuguese were the first Europeans to forge linguistic as well as trade links outside Europe and North Africa, and every English-based pidgin and creole contains a number of Portuguese items such as the following from Sierra Leone Krio:

<blockquote>
blai – basket   *pikin* – child
palava – trouble   *savi* – know.
</blockquote>

And yet the relexification theory cannot explain why pidgins and creoles which have developed outside the influence of European languages share many of the characteristics of 'reconnaissance Portuguese'. Nor does it answer the question of how Lingua Franca evolved. A point worth emphasising here, however, is that relexification is not necessarily opposed to the baby-talk theory because, irrespective of how they arose, Lingua Franca and reconnaissance Portuguese share many features with child language.

The Theory of Linguistic Universals

In attempting to explain the evolution of pidgins, scholars have in the past come up with contradictory theories: that most pidgins arose independently (Hall, 1966) and that most pidgins derive from one proto-pidgin (Whinnom, 1965). Recently, however, scholars have become increasingly aware that pidgins resemble child language, 'foreigner talk' (Ferguson, 1971) and the language styles employed by native speakers for telegrams and headlines. The tendency now is to look for the common denominators underlying all these varieties of language and to argue that pidgins and creoles are alike because, fundamentally, languages are alike, learning processes are alike and simplification techniques are alike. It appears, therefore, that contact

26

vernaculars arise from the exploitation – albeit unwitting – of linguistic universals. We can take this further and suggest that linguists would be more likely to discover linguistic universals by concentrating on contact languages rather than on highly-formalised written standards which bear little resemblance to the varieties that people actually *speak*.

The view that all learners show a preference for common-denominator structures can, in part, be supported by our individual experiences of language acquisition. When we learn French, we have little difficulty with the structures that parallel English. Thus it is easier to learn:

J'ai une idée – I have an idea

than:

J'ai faim – I am hungry

because the second sentence runs counter to our English-influenced intuitions that one should BE hungry rather than HAVE hunger. It seems reasonable to go further and to claim that in casual contacts between speakers of English and French, the structures that would be favoured would be those which are common to both languages. Similarly, in contacts between speakers of English and non-related languages, the structures with the highest survival potential would be those which, at some level, are common to the languages of all the speakers involved in the contact.

It is not, however, easy to say what these linguistic universals are, because by the time a pidgin has stabilised sufficiently to become an effective means of communication, it has already become a complex linguisitic system and has thus modified and complicated the structures that were earlier to be found in it. Again, an example may clarify this point. In the Cameroon Pidgin of old rural speakers there are at least three respects in which their pidgin is less complex than that of young, urban Cameroon-ians. Firstly, they have a six-pronoun system only, whereas young speakers make some case distinctions (see p. 7) and have a nine-pronoun system. Secondly, apart from *dis* and *dat*, old speakers use no determiners whereas younger users of pidgin have *dis, dat, sɔm, di, ɔl, ɛni* and a much more English system of numbers, *ɛlɛvɛn* and *twɛnti*, for example, instead of *wan tali wan* and *tu tali*. Thirdly, old speakers tend to use no auxiliaries. Temporal and aspectual distinctions must be deduced from the context or from the use of a limited set of words like *nau* (now), *naunau* (immediately), *dat taim* (then), *tumɔrɔ* (in the near future) and *afta tumɔrɔ* (in the not so near future). The pidgin of even these old Cameroonians has, presumably, been modified by their own mother tongues, and so, although it may reflect an earlier form of the local pidgin, it is not to be equated with universal grammar.

Although we may never know exactly what form linguistic universals take, a wide-ranging study of pidgins, creoles and child language makes it possible to suggest that universal grammar may involve some or all of the following characteristics:

1. fixed word order, possibly with SV as the basic pattern
2. two types of words, one type being multifunctional and semantically full; the second type consisting of a very limited number (possibly only one) of prepositions or postpositions which are capable of indicating location and possession
3. a set of pronouns containing at least two items, equivalents for 'me' and 'you'
4. no inflections
5. no bound forms
6. few or no transformations, i.e. questions are the equivalent of:

         A   B

   (Question Word) + Statement + (Question Word)

   where A or B is optional, and negatives are the equivalent of:

         C   D

   (Negative Word) + Statement + (Negative Word)

   where C or D may be optional
7. temporal and aspectual distinctions are carried by context or, like interrogation and negation, by one or more word forms placed outside the statement
8. systematic use of reduplication
9. verb serialisation as a means of differentiating nominals without using case or prepositions: *Tek di buk giv i* (Take the book give he) – Give the book to him.

We have, in this chapter, looked briefly at the phenomenon of pidgins and creoles. We have illustrated their characteristics and attempted to account for their special linguistic make-up. There is still, however, a great deal that we do not know about them, partly because they have been so frequently disparaged and partly because we are only beginning to discover how languages are learned and stored and how and why they change and die. A few things do seem certain, however. Pidgins and creoles will increasingly come to the centre of linguistic argument. Since we know the entire life-cycle of some of these languages, they provide a laboratory-type framework against which linguistic theories can be tested. In addition, pidgins are examples of languages which have been acquired extremely quickly, so teachers of all languages have something to learn from the way pidgin speakers organise linguistic data. Students of pidgins and creoles are not, of course, in competition with other linguists. Their work too aims at understanding how languages work and ultimately at how the human mind works (Chomsky, 1972: 103). Whatever is learnt from their studies will be of service to all. As the Cameroonian proverb puts it:

Fut, weti a chɔp wei a no dash yu sɛf? (Foot, what do I eat that I don't give freely to you?)

NOTES

1. Fuller discussion of the etymology of 'pidgin' can be found in Todd (1974) and in Hancock (1979).
2. The following makeshift system was recorded in francophone West Africa as an African trader encouraged some American tourists to buy his goods:
    Come buy. See fine thing. Plenty fine thing. Which one you like? No dear. Small money.
    Similar exchanges can be heard wherever English-speaking tourists go.
3. This is the estimate given in James Walvin's *The Black Presence* 1971: 7.
4. The small vocabulary need not be as linguistically limiting as might first appear. Discussing his *New Generation Dictionary* (Longman, 1981) Paul Procter claimed: 'Most people use only about 2,000 words in conversation and that figure covers their reading vocabulary too.' (Quoted in the *Daily Mirror*, 25 July 1981, p. 14.)

5. This point becomes clearer when we juxtapose equivalent sentences in Standard English (SE) and in Cameroon Pidgin (CP). If we compare:

   SE: The man fell + He came in > The man who came in fell

   we have (1) the deletion of 'he' and (2) the introduction of 'who'; whereas in:

   CP: *Di man bin fɔl* + *I ɛnta* > *Di man wei i ɛnta bin fɔl* we have no deletion but only the introduction of *wei*. Similarly, if we compare:

   SE: He went   and   Where did he go?

   with:

   CP: *I bin go*   and   *Usai i bin go?*

   it is clear the CP interrogative is derived from the CP statement much more directly than the SE interrogative is from its equivalent statement.

6. Unless otherwise stated, all our examples of CP are taken from the speech of young, urbanised Cameroonians, largely because theirs is the variety which has the greatest prestige in Cameroon. Their pidgin is closer to SE than is the pidgin of older, rural speakers and their pronoun system shows some contrasts in the first and third persons whereas earlier varieties and older idiolects do not. More is said about this modification towards SE in 1.4.

7. The earliest literary sample of pidginised English occurs in Act IV of Christopher Marlowe's play *The Jew of Malta* where Barabas says:

   > Must tuna my lute for sound, twang, twang, first. . . .
   > Pardonnez-moi, be no in tune yet; so now, now all be in.

   Later, in the early eighteenth century, Defoe experimented with the use of Pidgin English in *Colonel Jack* (see Appendix A1).

8. Robertson's account of the discovery of Tahiti in 1767 gives a graphic account of the gestures and miming that occur when people need to communicate but have no shared language:

   > . . . we made all the friendly signs that we could think of, and showed them several trinkets in order to get some of them onb^d after their Counsel was over they padled all round the ship and made signs of friendship to us, by holding up Branches of Plantain trees, and making a long speech of near fifteen minutes, when the speech was over he that made it throwd the plantain branch in to the sea, then they came nearer the ship, and all of them appeard cheerful and talkt a great dale but non of us could understand them, but to pleas them we all seemd merry

   > . . . . . .

   > —by this time we hade upwards of a hundred and fifty canoes round us and a great many more still coming off from the shore,

in the canoes their was about Eight hundred men, by this time I supose they thought them selves safe, having so many of them about us, and we still making friendly signs

. . . . . .

They seemd all very peaceable for some time, and we made signs to them, to bring of Hogs, Fowls and fruit and showd them coarse cloath Knives sheers Beeds Ribons etc, and made them understand that we was willing to barter with them, the method we took to make them Understand what we wanted was this, some of the men Grunted and Cryd lyke a Hogg then pointed to the shore—oythers crowd Lyke cocks to make them understand that we wanted fowls, this the natives of the country understood and Grunted and Crowd the same as our people, and pointed to the shore and made signs that they would bring us off some—We then made signs for them to go in to their canoes and to bring us off what things we wanted—they observed what we meant and some went into their canoes. . . .   (Robertson, 1948: 136–7)

9. Many African languages have words which structure as follows:

CV (Consonant + Vowel)	ma
VCV	aba
CVCV	kaba
VCVCV	awune
CVCVCV	sunine.

Sometimes, nasals can occur in word final positions:

baŋ
kiban.

Consonant clusters are rare although homorganic nasals can occur at the beginning of a syllable:

mbam
ntufu
ɲamaŋ gɔrɔ.

10. To emphasise what such multilingualism means we shall cite two fairly extreme examples. Cameroon's population of under 8,000,000 employs over 200 mutually unintelligible languages, not counting the official languages, French and English, or the vehicular languages, Pidgin English, Ewondo Populaire and Hausa. And Papua New Guinea, with a population of under 3,000,000 includes over 700 languages within its borders.

11. The text of a speaker whose language shows clear signs of the influences of both a pidgin and SE is provided in Appendix B 7a: *Baset Toktok* – Budget Speech.

12. A very clear account of BE can be found in J. L. Dillard's *Black English* (Random House, 1972).

13. One account of this can be found in Todd (1979).

14. Such a claim is in accord with the survival of a highly-flexible and differentiated pronominal set reflected in:

I did it	Rinne mé é (Did I it)
It's myself that did it	S'é mise a rinne é
It's me myself that did it	S'é mise féin a rinne é

in such idioms as:

long head (< ceann fada)	– intelligence
poor mouth (< béal bocht)	– complaining

and in such sentences as:

Put ears on you (< Cuir cluasa ort) – Listen attentively
There was great buying on the cows – The cows sold well today.
today (<Bhí ceannacht maith ar na ba indiú)

REFERENCES AND SUGGESTIONS FOR FURTHER READING

BICKERTON, DEREK, *Roots of Language,* Ann Arbor: Karoma Publishers, Inc., 1981.

BLOOMFIELD, LEONARD, *Language,* London: Allen and Unwin, 1933.

BROWN, ROGER, *A First Language: the Early Stages,* London: Allen and Unwin, 1973.

CHOMSKY, NOAM, *Aspects of the Theory of Syntax,* Cambridge, Massachusetts: MIT Press, 1965.

CHOMSKY, NOAM, *Language and Mind* (2nd edn), New York: Harcourt Brace Jovanovich, 1972.

DALBY, DAVID, *Black through White: Patterns of Communication,* Bloomington: University of Indiana African Studies Program, 1970.

DALE, PHILIP S., *Language Development: Structure and Function* (2nd edn), New York: Holt, Rinehart and Winston, 1976.

DeCAMP, DAVID AND HANCOCK, I. F., *Pidgins and Creoles: Current Trends and Prospects,* Washington DC: Georgetown \ University Press, 1974.

DEFOE, DANIEL, *The History of the Most Remarkable Life, and Extraordinary Adventures, of the truly Honourable Colonel Jaque, vulgarly call'd Colonel Jack,* Oxford: Basil Blackwell, 1927.

DICKENS, CHARLES, *Hard Times,* Harmondsworth: Penguin, 1969.

DILLARD, J. L., *Black English,* New York: Random House, 1972.

DILLARD, J. L. (ed.), *Socio-Historical Factors in the Formation of Creoles,* The Hague and Paris: Mouton, 1976.

DUTTON, T. E. AND VOORHOEVE, C. L., *Beginning Hiri Motu,* Canberra: Pacific Linguistics, Series D, No. 24, 1974.

ELLIOT, ALISON J., *Child Language,* Cambridge: Cambridge University Press, 1981.

FERGUSON, C. A. 'Absence of Copula and the Notion of Simplicity: a Study of Normal Speech, Baby Talk, Foreigner Talk and Pidgins', in Hymes, pp. 141–50, 1971.

FERGUSON, C. A. AND D. I., *Studies of Child Language Development*, New York: Holt, Rinehart and Winston, 1973.

GRIMES, J. E. (ed.), *Languages of the Guianas*, Publication of the Summer Institute of Linguistics at the University of Oklahoma, 1972.

GUMPERZ, J. J., 'On the Linguistic Markers of Bilingual Communication', *Journal of Social Issues*, 23, 2, Cambridge, Mass., pp. 48–57, 1967.

GUMPERZ, J. J. AND WILSON, R., 'Convergence and Creolization: a Case from the Indo-Aryan/Dravidian border', in Hymes, pp. 151–67, 1971.

HALL, ROBERT A., JR, *Pidgin and Creole Languages*, Ithaca: Cornell University Press, 1966.

HANCOCK, I. F. (ed.), *Readings in Creole Studies*, Ghent: E-Story Scientia PVBA, 1979.

HASSERT, KURT E., *Allgemeine Verkehrsgeographie*, Berlin and Leipzig: G. J. Goeschen'sceh Verlagshandlung, 1913.

HYMES, DELL (ed.), *Pidginization and Creolization of Languages*, Cambridge and New York: Cambridge University Press, 1971.

JESPERSEN, OTTO, *Language: Its Nature, Development and Origin*, London: Allen and Unwin, 1922.

KLEINECKE, DAVID, 'An Etymology for "Pidgin" ', *International Journal of Applied Linguistics*, 25, pp. 271–2, 1959.

LELAND, CHARLES G., *Pidgin English Sing-Song*, London: Trübner and Co:, 1876.

NARO, ANTHONY J., 'The Origin of West African Pidgin', unpublished paper presented at the Ninth Regional Meeting of the Chicago Linguistics Society, April, 1973.

PROCTER, PAUL, *New Generation Dictionary*, London: Longman, 1981.

PURCHAS, SAMUEL, *Purchas his Pilgrimes*, London: printed by William Stansby for Henrie Fetherstone, 1625. Reprinted in 20 volumes by James MacLehose and Sons, Glasgow, 1905–7.

REINECKE, JOHN, et al., *A Bibliography of Pidgin and Creole Languages*, Honolulu: Hawaii University Press, 1975.

RIDLEY, M. R. (ed.), *Marlowe: Plays and Poems*, London: Dent Everyman's Library, 1973.

ROBERTSON, G., *The Discovery of Tahiti*, London: The Hakluyt Society, 1948.

SAINT JACQUES FAUQUENOY, MARGÚERITE, *Analyse Structurale du Créole Guyanais*, Paris: Editions Klincksieck, 1972.

SANKOFF, GILLIAN AND KAY, PAUL, 'A Language Universals Approach to Pidgins and Creoles', in DeCamp and Hancock, 1974, pp. 61–72, 1974.

SAYER, E. S., *Pidgin English*, Toronto: mimeographed, 1939.

TODD, LORETO, *Pidgins and Creoles*, London: Routledge and Kegan Paul, 1974.

TODD, LORETO, 'Cameroonian: a Consideration of "What's in a name?"' in Hancock, pp. 281–94, 1979.

TURNER, G. W., *The English Language in Australia and New Zealand*, London: Longman, 1966.

WALVIN, JAMES, *The Black Presence: a Documentary History of the Negro in England*, London: Orbach and Chambers, 1971.

WEINREICH, URIEL, *Languages in Contact*, The Hague: Mouton, 1964.

WHINNOM, KEITH, 'The Origin of the European-based Creoles and Pidgins', *Orbis* 14, pp. 509–27, 1965.

WURM, S. A. AND HARRIS, J. B., *Police Motu: an Introduction to the Trade Language of Papua*, Canberra: Linguistics Circle of Canberra, Series 1.1, 1963.

WURM, S. A., 'Pidgins, Creoles and Lingue Franche', *Current Trends in Linguistics* 8, ed. T. Sebeok, The Hague: Mouton, pp. 999–1021, 1971.

CHAPTER 2

English-related Pidgins and Creoles

🔯🔯🔯🔯🔯

2.1 HISTORICAL OVERVIEW

Less than five hundred years ago the English language was confined to one small island in Europe. Nowadays it is spoken in some form by over six hundred million people and it is rapidly becoming the lingua franca of the world. Often, when scholars discuss how the language has spread across the entire earth, they think mainly in terms of the written standard. It would, of course, be foolish to underestimate the value of the written medium. Without it, we might have seen the fulfilment of Webster's prophecy (1789: 22) that British and American Englishes would have become as different from each other:

> ... as the modern Dutch, Danish and Swedish are from the German, or from one another: like remote branches of a tree springing from the same stock, or rays of light shot from the same center, and diverging from each other in proportion to their distance from the point of separation.

In this chapter, however, we will be concentrating on pidgins and creoles; varieties of English which have been used almost exclusively in the *spoken* medium and which give us some idea of how world Englishes might have diverged if it had not been for the restraining influence of the written standard.

2.2 EUROPEAN EXPANSION: ENGLAND'S ROLE

As a result of the desire for new routes to Asia and for new trading partners, European nations began in the fifteenth century to explore the earth thoroughly and systematically. Portugal and Spain were the first to invest in maritime explorations and, by the last decade of the fifteenth century, they were already quarrelling about the ownership of the new territories. They put their dispute before the Pope and in 1494 he ruled that all lands discovered[1] anywhere in the world were to be shared between Spain and Portugal. The division was to follow the line of longitude approximately one thousand miles west of the Cape Verde Islands, West Africa. Spain was to have possession of all the discoveries to the west of the line while Portugal was to have all those to the east.

England is often thought to have entered the exploration race late and it is true that the Admiralty did not fund an expedition officially until 1699 when Dampier was sent to explore the Pacific. Nevertheless, English merchants were eager to have some part in the trade afforded by the new discoveries. As early as 1481 some English traders found their way to West Africa. The Portuguese did not approve of the English infiltrating their markets and they sent a deputation to Edward IV to insist that his subjects be restrained from trading on the Guinea Coast (Burns, 1942: 263ff). Fifty years later, in 1530, Robert Thorne, a merchant, encouraged Henry VIII to establish a trading empire in the Pacific (Hobley, 1972: 25). By 1553 English ships had sailed to Benin in Nigeria and established a trade in ivory, pepper and indigo (Blake, 1966: 6) and as early as 1555 John Lok had brought a group of African slaves to England. By 1580 Drake had circumnavigated the earth. Three years later, Sir Humphrey Gilbert took possession of Newfoundland and in 1585 a British settlement was founded in what is now North Carolina. In 1604–5 Captain Leigh tried to establish a colony near the Oyapock River on the South American Coast. Early as he was, however, he was not the first Englishman to have visited the area. According to Purchas (1625: 1264) when the Indians of the interior heard about Leigh's settlement:

> . . . one came far out of the Main from ORENOGUE to enquire of us of him [i.e. of Sir Walter Raleigh] saying he promised to have returned to them before that time.

By the beginning of the seventeenth century, then, the English had sailed and traded in every ocean and from that time on they were to extend their influence and spread their language to all parts of

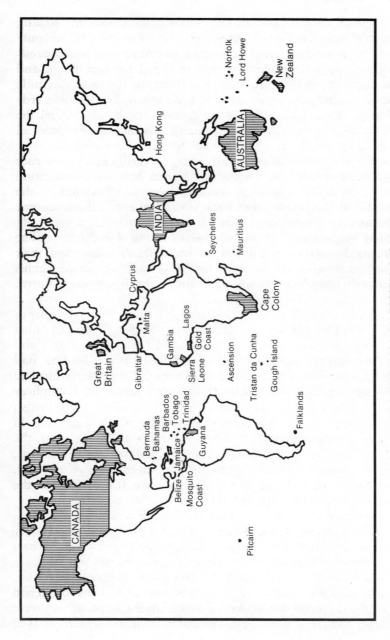

MAP 1: BRITAIN'S MAIN POSSESSIONS IN 1878

the world. By the middle of the eighteenth century the British Empire included Great Britain, the Channel Islands, Ireland, most of the east of North America, a section of the Guiana coast of South America, several islands in the Caribbean and in the Pacific, parts of West Africa and of India. By the last quarter of the nineteenth century the Empire had increased still further (see Map 1). During the nineteenth century the English language began to be spread by Americans and Australians too. Britons, Americans and Australians all made fortunes from whaling in the Pacific, and from trading with China, especially in sandalwood and bêche-de-mer sea slugs. The United States made trading treaties with China in 1846 and with Japan in 1853; and before the end of the century they took control of the Philippines and annexed the Hawaiian islands.

The spreading of English has been continued in the twentieth century by wars and by the media, with the result that the language which was once contained by a tiny European island has now been heard in every continent and probably in every seaport.

2.3 ENGLISH-RELATED PIDGINS AND CREOLES

These languages are found throughout the world (see Map 2). We shall divide them into Atlantic and Pacific varieties and examine each one briefly, providing short texts where these are available.

2.4 ATLANTIC PIDGINS AND CREOLES

All the English-derived pidgins and creoles of West Africa, the Caribbean, and the southern parts of the United States are related, not only lexically[2] through English but also in their structures, their idioms and their folklore. It is possible that they all derive from a proto-Pidgin English that developed and stabilised on the West African coast in the sixteenth and early seventeenth centuries before being transported to the Americas (Hancock, 1972: 7–8 and 52). We shall not, however, try to speculate about where or even whether such a proto-pidgin existed. The influence of West African languages on all Atlantic pidgins and creoles could account for many of the structural and

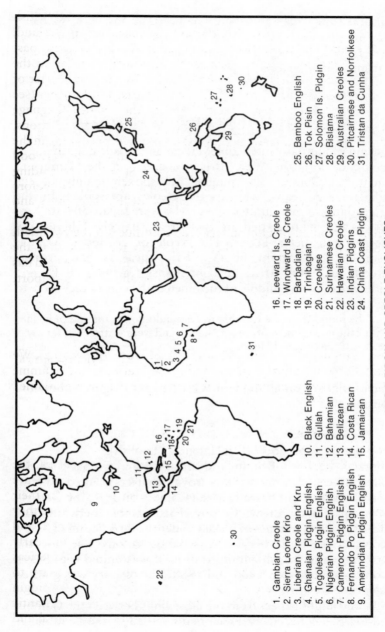

1. Gambian Creole
2. Sierra Leone Krio
3. Liberian Creole and Kru
4. Ghanaian Pidgin English
5. Togolese Pidgin English
6. Nigerian Pidgin English
7. Cameroon Pidgin English
8. Fernando Po Pidgin English
9. Amerindian Pidgin English

10. Black English
11. Gullah
12. Bahamian
13. Belizean
14. Costa Rican
15. Jamaican

16. Leeward Is. Creole
17. Windward Is. Creole
18. Barbadian
19. Trinibagian
20. Creolese
21. Surinamese Creoles
22. Hawaiian Creole
23. Indian Pidgins
24. China Coast Pidgin

25. Bamboo English
26. Tok Pisin
27. Solomon Is. Pidgin
28. Bislama
29. Australian Creoles
30. Pitcairnese and Norfolkese
31. Tristan da Cunha

MAP 2: PIDGIN AND CREOLE ENGLISHES

cultural similarities and there has been, in any case, so much inter-influencing between West African and New World varieties that it would be foolish to try to locate the points of origin and transmission too closely.

2.4.1 WEST AFRICAN PIDGINS AND CREOLES

A chain of mutually intelligible[3] Pidgin and Creole Englishes is to be found along the West African coast from the Gambia to Equatorial Guinea. The pidgins are spoken mainly by the indigenous Africans, whereas the creoles are spoken by the descendants of manumitted slaves who were repatriated to West Africa and who settled in two areas, namely Liberia and Freetown in Sierra Leone. The creole of Freetown, *Krio*, is historically important because Krio speakers had prestige throughout West Africa as Christians, teachers, clerks and middlemen. By the middle of the nineteenth century they were to

> ... be found from the Gambia to Fernando Po, by the end of it, they filled the government offices of Nigeria and were scattered as far away as the Cape of Good Hope.
>
> (Fyfe, 1956: 118)

Their influence on all modern West African pidgins is therefore considerable.[4]

1. *The Gambia*
(population 600,000;[5] official language English)
Contacts between Britain and the Gambia go back to the sixteenth century. In 1588 a royal charter granted English merchants the right to trade in the Gambia. In 1765 the Gambia formed part of the Crown Colony of Senegambia. Between 1821 and 1843 the Gambia was placed under the jurisdiction of Sierra Leone. In 1843 it became a separate colony but, for the convenience of British administration, it was united with Sierra Leone again between 1866 and 1888. The country was granted independence in 1965.

As one might expect from the close links between the Gambia and Sierra Leone, many Freetonians settled in the Gambia. A variety of Krio, called *Aku*,[6] is the mother tongue of about four thousand descendants of Freetown Krios and a related pidgin is used by many to facilitate inter-ethnic communication. Because of its geographical location, the Gambia is strongly influenced by Senegal and a pidginised Wolof is increasingly being used between francophone Senegalese and anglophone Gambians.

Samples of Gambian Aku[7]

Mi bɛlɛ de at mi —	My stomach aches (lit. My belly continuous marker hot/hurt me)
ɔkra nɛva lɔng pas im masta bɔt i de trangga —	A slave may not be as important as his master but he may be stronger in the long run (lit. Okra never long surpass him master but he continuous marker strong)
Want want no gɛt; gɛt gɛt no want —	The very needy get nothing; those who have plenty want for nothing (lit. Want want no have; have have no want).

2. *Sierra Leone*
(population 3,300,000; official language English)

Sierra Leone (Lion Mountain) was named by the Portuguese in 1460. The English traded in the Sierra Leone area from the late sixteenth century and, in 1787, this country was selected by the anti-slavery campaigner, Granville Sharp, as the home for slaves freed in England. Part of the land around modern Freetown was bought from the Temne king, Naimbana, and in 1787, 351 freed slaves sailed from Portsmouth for Sierra Leone. In 1792, these were joined by 1,131 Africans from Nova Scotia who had fought for the British in the American War of Independence. The two groups banded together and founded 'Freetown'. In 1808 the settlement became a Crown Colony and a centre for Britain's war on slavery. Many of the slaves recaptured by the British patrol boats decided to stay in Freetown and by 1834 there were 32,000

Creoles in Sierra Leone (Isichei, 1977: 129). In 1961 the country was granted independence.

The mother tongue of the returned ex-slaves was an English-based creole, subsequently called Krio, and this language undoubtedly influenced whatever pidginised English already existed on the coast. Today Krio is spoken as a mother tongue by about a quarter of a million people in and around Freetown. It is also acquired as a second language by many Sierra Leoneans and used as a lingua franca throughout the country.

Samples of Sierra Leonean Krio

a) *Arata nɔba gladi we pus bɔn — A mouse is never happy when*
pikin a cat has kittens (lit. Rat/ mouse never glad when puss born child)

Saful saful kech mɔngki — Go gently and you'll succeed

Ɔkra nɔba lɔng pas im masta — One is never better than one's master.

b) *Na im i tɛlam se, "Bɔbɔ, na yu de wit mi ɔl tɛm ɛn ɔl wetin a gɛt*
(The father said: "My son, you know you are with me always, and all that I have

na yu yon. Bɔt i gud we wi mek jɔlipati ɛn gladi, bikɔs dis yu brɔda
is yours. But it is good for us to celebrate and be glad, because your brother

ya bin dɔn dai bɔt i dɔn wek bak; i bin lɔs bɔt wi dɔn fɛnam."
here was dead and has come to life; he was lost and is found.")
(St Luke, XV, 31–32, F. G. Jones's unpublished translation, 1981)

3. *Liberia*
(population 1,700,000; official language English)
Liberia was established in 1822 for the resettlement of ex-American slaves and it and Sierra Leone are the only West African countries where some members of the population speak a variety of English as a mother tongue. By 1867, when Liberia became independent of the United States, there were over eleven thousand Afro-Americans settled in and around the capital,

Monrovia. The descendants of the original settlers (fewer than 5% of Liberia's population) monopolised government and trading until the old order was smashed by the coup of 12 April 1980, when non-commissioned soldiers, led by Master Sergeant Samuel K. Doe, killed the President, William Tolbert, with sixteen members of his entourage and then summarily executed many prominent Liberians. The coup was clearly aimed at the Afro-American élitist section of society and it seems to have had the support of the tribal communities in rural areas. The changed structure of Liberian society may, in the future, modify the type of English spoken there.

All brands of English spoken in Liberia have been strongly influenced by American varieties. Apart from the official standard language, based on US norms, we find a creole, often called *Settler English* or *Merico*, which has much in common with Black English; a pidginised English spoken mainly by the Kru tribe; and pockets of Krio.[8] The Pidgin English of the Kru is closer to Krio and to West African pidgins than to Merico because the Kru have had a long history of contact with Britain. Kru men accompanied the British on their expeditions to discover the source of the Niger and, in 1915, they declared war on Liberia 'preferring British rule and asking, in vain, for British assistance' (Isichei, 1977: 142).

Samples of a) Liberian Kru English and b) Merico

a) *Dem first time, you savvy, nothing to live. No other thing, no ground, no water for himself, all he be mixed like so so pota pota* [i.e. mud]. *Then God he begin. He part him, some place he put some ground, some place he put dem wata, but mem he no fit look him, because so so dark. By and by God he say: "Better I make some lantern."*[9]

(Crocker, 1936: 167)

b) *A gwan swit-maut dat wuman* – I'll flatter that woman
  A bin kɔtin stik – I've been cutting wood
  A ãin as hi – I haven't asked him.

c) *For de first time, noting been de only de Lawd, He be. An' de Lawd, He done go work hard for make dis ting day call 'um Earth. For six day de Lawd He work an' done make all ting – everyting He go put for Earth. Plenty beef, plenty yam, plenty*

43

*mango, plenty guinea corn, plenty ground-nut − everyting.
An' for de water He put plenty fish, an' for de air He put plenty
kinda bird.*
(Written text of unknown source. See Appendix B 6d)

4. *Ghana*
(population 11,000,000; official language English)
By 1663 Britain had established six fortified settlements on the
coast of Ghana (formerly the Gold Coast), namely Cormantine,
Cape Coast, Anashan, Egya, Kommanda and Winneba, and the
close links with Britain continued even after Ghana gained its
independence in 1957. Because of these coastal settlements where
British traders and sailors lived, often for months at a time, many
Ghanians had the opportunity to learn English as a second
language rather than as a pidgin. Ghanaians have always prided
themselves on the excellence of their English and this pride is
summed up in Professor Kofi Sey's attitude to local variants
(1973: 10):

> The linguist may be able to isolate features of Ghanaian English and
> describe them. But once these are made known to him, the educated
> Ghanaian would strive to avoid them altogether. The surest way to
> kill Ghanaian English, if it really exists, is to discover it and make it
> known.

Nevertheless, Pidgin English is used, especially by the uneducated, to aid communication in a multilingual society. It is,
however, held in very low regard and so recorded data are very
hard to acquire. The following samples were recorded on the
Legon campus in November 1978:

Samples of Ghanaian Pidgin English

Ai no de fulɔp − One's desires are rarely satisfied (lit. eye no continuous marker full + up)

A chɔp tue[10] a wan bɔs − I ate so much I almost burst (lit. I eat on-and-on I want burst)

A de go taun kam − I'm going to town but I'll be back directly (lit. I continuous marker go town come)

> *Nobi daso wan man chɔp* – Everyone is human and everyone has the right to live (lit. No + be that + so one man eat)
>
> *Wai yu wan halahala mi?* Why do you shout at me so? (lit. Why you want holler-holler me?)

5. Togo

(population 2,400,000; official language French)

Britain had close trading links with Togo throughout the nineteenth century and by the 1880s it was widely expected that Britain would absorb Togo into the Gold Coast. On 4 July 1884, however, the German flag was hoisted and treaties placing Togo under German protection were signed on 5 July. The Germans found Pidgin English already established in Togo and they used it in early contacts. In 1919, after World War 1, Togo was partitioned between France and Britain and British-mandated Togo was governed through Ghana. A referendum in the British sector in May 1956 confirmed that this part of Togo was to be permanently attached to Ghana. In 1960 Togo became a Republic and, although French is the official language, Pidgin English still flourishes on the coast and in the east.

Samples of Togolese Pidgin English

> *A de wakawaka lɛki ganaka*[11] – I'm wandering around like a person with no sense of direction (lit. I continuous marker walk walk like wanderer)
>
> *Mɔnki dai, mɔnki kam* – Nobody is irreplaceable (lit. Monkey die, monkey come)
>
> *Wan han no fit tai bandul* – Everybody needs help (lit. One hand no able/fit tie bundle/load)
>
> *Lui no lif dei* – Louis is not there (lit. Louis no live there).

(Sentences recorded by Togolese students in Leeds, 1980)

6. Nigeria

(population 80,000,000;[12] official language English)

Contacts between Britain and Nigeria have been long and

sustained. They go back to the middle of the sixteenth century when English ships reached Benin. In 1886 the Royal Niger Company officially took over control of the country around the Niger river. Eleven years later, in 1897, Yorubaland was annexed and added to the British colony of Lagos. In 1914 the various regions were amalgamated into the modern state which gained independence in 1961 and became a Federal Republic in 1963.

Nigeria is the most densely populated country in West Africa and one of the most multilingual, having approximately four hundred indigenous languages. As in other parts of West Africa, there are no statistics for the number of people who speak Pidgin English but, as the population is a young one and as more and more of it becomes urbanised (the population of Lagos in 1982, for example, was estimated at 5·3 million in Legum, 1981: B597–8), there must be at least eight million users of Pidgin English in Nigeria. Nigerian Pidgin English is widely used in ports, in towns, in the army and in the police force.

Samples of Nigerian Pidgin English

The first passage a) is taken from the *Lagos Weekend* (28 September 1979: 14) which devotes approximately half a page to its *Walkabout* feature which is written in an anglicised pidgin. The second passage b) is an Igbo speaker's translation of St Luke, XV, verses 31 and 32.

a) *Gofrument! All Our Roads Don Yamutu Finis*
    (Government! All Our Roads Are Ruined Completely)
    Biko make somebody gofument efen e fit from Kano come sef,
    (Please make someone come from the government even if it is from Kano
    anyones at all afalabulu sa, make e jus find sometins done for
    anyone who is available sir, let him just get something done for
    all dis road dem wey done wowo finish.
    all these roads are in a terrible state).

b) *Di papa bin tɔk sei: "Ma pikin, yu sabi sei yu dei wit mi eni dei eni dei, an ɔl ting wei a gɛtam na yu on. Bɔt i gud mek wi hapi, bikɔs dis yu brɔda bin dɔn dai an i dɔn wikɔp fɔ dai agɛn; i bin dɔn lɔs an wi bin luk i agɛn."*

7. *Cameroon*

(population 8,000,000; official languages French and English).
Much of coastal Cameroon was under unofficial British protection throughout the nineteenth century, but in July 1884, Germany proclaimed 'Kamerun' a German Protectorate before the British could formally annex the country. As in Togo, Pidgin English was already well established in Cameroon when the Germans took control and it still remains the most useful lingua franca in the south-west of the country, in all large urban communities, in the army and police force and in the prisons. It is almost certainly known and used by between 20% and 25% of the population.

Samples of Cameroon Pidgin English

Again, we shall illustrate the pidgin by quoting two passages, a) from a written translation of the St Luke passage that has been quoted for Sierra Leone and Nigeria and b) from a folktale.

a) *But he father he de tell he say, – "My pickin, you there with me all time, – and all my cargo i be your cargo too. – But anyhow we must chop and be glad, how your brother whe ben die, he done djorup, – and whe ben loss, he done come back again."*
(Father A. Kerkvliet, n.d. *The Sunday Gospels and Epistles*, p. 72)

b) *Sɔm dei bin dei, trɔki bin kam fɔ pig fɔ trɔs mɔni. Pig tɔk sei:*
(Once upon a time, Tortoise came to Pig to borrow money. Pig said:
"Yu tink sei mi a bi mumu? Yu go tek ma mɔni go an yu no go bakam
"Do you think I'm a fool? You'll take my money away and you'll not
agɛn."
give it back again.")

8. *Fernando Po*

(part of Equatorial Guinea; population unknown but possibly in the region of 100,000; official language Spanish)
Fernando Po was leased to the British by Spain in 1827 and it became a centre for the suppression of the Slave Trade. Between 1827 and 1840 'there grew up on the island a large colony of

freed slaves of various African tribes, but all speaking English as the lingua franca' (Gwei, 1968: 8). British missionary activity in Cameroon was launched from Fernando Po and the island has always had a large percentage of Cameroonians and Nigerians living there.

Equatorial Guinea gained independence from Spain in 1968 but under the Francisco Macias Nguema régime conditions in Equatorial Guinea deteriorated and thousands of refugees fled to Cameroon, Nigeria and Gabon. Some idea of the difficulties faced by the citizens of Equatorial Guinea may be gauged by the fact that at the time of the coup against Nguema, 3 August 1979, there was 'no money . . . in general circulation on Fernando Po island – a situation which may have lasted up to two years' (Legum, 1981: B434). With such conditions prevailing it is not surprising that there is little available information on Pidgin English in Fernando Po. When I visited the island in 1968, however, Pidgin English was widely used and was very similar to the variety used in Victoria, Cameroon.

Samples of Fernando Po Pidgin English
The sentences in a) are taken from Zarco (1938: 70–2) and the proverbs in b) were recorded in 1968.

a)
A de go na bitch –	I'm going to the beach (lit. I continuous marker go to beach)
Tu mun pas a go go Calabar –	In two months' time I'll go to Calabar (lit. Two moon pass I future marker go Calabar)
Yu go cam dis ivin? A go cam ol rait –	You'll come this evening? I'll come all right
Camerun i no faue –	Cameroon is not far away.

b)
Tit an tɔng kin jam –	Even close friends can fight (lit. Teeth and tongue can fight)
Trɔbul de kain bai kain –	There is trouble everywhere (lit. trouble there kind by kind).

2.4.2 CREOLES IN THE AMERICAS

In the Americas we find a chain of related Creole Englishes stretching from the United States, through the Caribbean to Guyana and Suriname in South America. These creoles are the mother tongues of people whose ancestors were taken as slaves from Africa. Many Asian Indians who were sent to the British West Indies as indentured labourers learnt the English creoles and for many of them also the local creole has become a mother tongue.

Apart from the creoles which developed as a direct result of the Slave Trade, there are now in the United States relics of an Amerindian Pidgin English. The Amerindians, like the Africans who remained in West Africa, did not need to creolise their Pidgin English although it was useful as a link language between them and the English-speaking settlers.

1. *United States*
(population 220,099,000[13]; official language English)
i. *Amerindian Pidgin English* was first recorded in 1641 and since then there have been many references to the type of English used between American Indians and English-speaking traders. Robert A. Hall Jr. (1966: 8) quotes a 1673 warrant:

> You, you big constable, quick you catch um Jeremiah Offscow, strong you hold um, safe you bring um afore me.

The suffix '-um', which probably indicated that the verb it followed was transitive, became a stereotyped marker of Amerindian English. Even today, in the *Beano* (a British comic for young children), one of the cartoon characters, a young Indian brave called Little Plum, uses 'um' in almost all of his utterances:

> 'On um days like this um ghostly cattle are said to appear in um sky.'
> 'Aagh! Um ghost steer!'
> 'Ahem! We knew all um time.'
> (*Beano*, 1 August 1981, p. 17)

With Little Plum, however, the 'um' is used as a type of determiner to indicate that a noun follows.

According to Dillard (1972: 143ff) Amerindian Pidgin English was probably influenced by Black Creole English, especially in the south-east of the United States.

Samples of American Indian Pidgin English
. . . white man court – court, may be one whole year! – may be two year before he marry! Well! – may be he then get very good wife – but may be not! – may be very cross! – Well now, suppose cross, scold as soon as get awake in the morning, scold all day, scold until sleep – all one; he must keep him. White people have law forbidding throwing away wife, be he ever so cross! – must keep him always . . . Indian, when he sees industrious squaw, which he like, he go to him, place his two forefingers close aside each other, make two look like one, look squaw in the face – see him smile – which is all one he say yes! so he take him home. . . . Squaw love to eat meat! No husband, no meat! Squaw do everything to please husband, he do same to please squaw; live happy.

(Leechman and Hall, 1955: 165)

Indian no fight. Indian no kill. Indian go.
Whiskey, me no take 'em, lemonade me take, cowboys wy-o-mee [i.e. home-made whiskey] *take.*

(Dillard, 1972: 154)

ii. *Gullah* is the name given to a Creole English now spoken mainly by Americans of African descent in Florida and in the Sea Islands. A related creole is spoken by Black Seminoles (i.e. Seminole Indians who inter-married with Africans who escaped from slavery) in Texas and Oklahoma (Hancock, 1981: 1–2). It is not easy to say how many speakers of Gullah there are in the United States, although it may be as many as three hundred thousand (Reinecke et al., 1975: 468). It is, however, being rapidly decreolised.

Samples of Gullah
Passage a) is taken from a written Gullah folktale while the sentences in b) are recorded utterances.

a) *Buh Elephant*, [i.e. Brother Elephant] *him bin know Buh Rooster berry well. Dem blan* [i.e. habitually] *roam togerrur*,

an Buh Rooster blan wake Buh Elephant duh mornin, so eh
kin hunt eh bittle befo de jew dry.
Dem bin a talk togerrur one day, an Buh Elephant, him bet
Buh Rooster say him kin eat longer ner him. Buh Rooster, him
tek de bet, an dem tun in nex mornin, wen de sun jis bin a git
up, fuh see who gwine win de bet.

(C. C. Jones, 1888: 41)

b)   *I ain't know se y'all bin gone* – I didn't know that you'd all
                                                gone
        You be looking, so don't say – You're usually looking, so
                        nothing   don't say anything.

(Rickford, 1974: 94 and 96)

iii. *Black English.* Since L. D. Turner's *Africanisms in the*
Gullah Dialect (1949) there has been increased recognition of the
fact that Black English (BE), the non-standard speech of many
American Blacks, derives from an American Creole English
which has much in common with Caribbean creoles and with
West African pidgins and creoles. BE has been so influenced over
the centuries by White American English that it has been
markedly decreolised. Again, there are no available figures for the
number of speakers of BE but it seems likely that at least 5% of
the total population of the United States either speak or
understand BE.

Samples of BE
Passage a) is taken from a nineteenth-century description of
'Negro English', b) is from a modern play and c) contains
sentences from live speech.

a) *Whar you bin at? Wharbouts you gwinter?* –
                        Where have you been? Where are you going to?
   Aing-got no time, chile
   Wot I done tole you?
   I'm agitten me out er ros'n piece i.e. a roasting piece.

(Harrison, 1884: 248, 256 and 259)

b) *Naw, Ah ain't no young gal no mo' but den Ah ain't no old*
   woman neither. Ah reckon Ah looks mah age too. But Ah'm
   uh woman every inch of me, and Ah knows it. Dat's uh whole

51

lot more'n you kin say. You big-bellies round here and put out a lot of brag, but 'tain't nothin' to it but yo' big voice.

(Hurston, 1969: 68)

c) *A tired right now but A don't be tired all the time*
   She waitin for me right now
   You been knowin him long?

2. The Bahamas
(population 220,000; official language English)
Geographically, and to some extent linguistically, these islands lie between the southern United States and the Caribbean. It is probable that one of the Bahamian islands was the first part of the Americas sighted by Columbus, but the Spanish took little interest in the islands. In 1629 the British granted a charter to Sir Robert Heath, allowing him territorial rights over the islands and, throughout the seventeenth century, the settlers in Carolina took a proprietorial interest in them. Many pirates took refuge in these islands and by 1713 'there were at least 1,000 active pirates on the Bahamas, outnumbering the two hundred or so settler families' (Calder, 1981: 469). After the American War of Independence, many colonists loyal to Britain left the southern states with their slaves to settle in the Bahamas. The incoming slaves far outnumbered those Blacks already working in the islands and help to account for the similarities between Bahamian and Black English. In the Bahamas, as in the Caribbean communities generally, most citizens have at least a passive knowledge of the creole.

Samples of Bahamian Creole English
Passage a) comes from an early twentieth-century recording of a folktale and b) consists of sentences recorded recently in the Bahamas.

a) *Now b'o Nanza* [i.e. the Spider Trickster] *had one trap set in de field, and b'o' Rabbit got cot. B'o' Bear say, "Ah, I cot him now. Why he stand in the field? I go see." – "B'o' Rabbit," he say, "why you stand in de field?" B'o' Rabby say, "I watch dis field for ten pence an hour, but," he say, "B'o' Bear, I want go to dance. You want dis job?" B'o' Bear say, "Done." B'o'*

Rabbit say, "You pull dis t'ing open so I can get my leg out and then you can get in."

(Cleare, 1917: 229)

b) *When she come out the room she crying she say she fall*
   I ain' go do that
   You-all ain' payin no attention
   How you go tell me she does sleep bad if you ain sleep with her?
   Dem dilly [i.e. fruit] *done ripe and rotten.*

(Shilling, 1980: 137–40)

3. The Caribbean

Virtually every island in, and every country touching, the Caribbean is the home of at least one creole (Trinidad, for example, still has relics of a Creole French and a Creole Spanish as well as having a very active Creole English). Reinecke et al. (1975: 374–77) list twenty-eight Creole Englishes in the area, many of them related, partly because of their shared history and partly also because there has been considerable movement of labour in the area. To give just one example of this movement, we can cite the case of Jamaica. Jamaican labourers have settled in and spread their creole to Nicaragua, Costa Rica, Panama, the Virgin Islands, Belize and Bermuda. We have indicated English creole-speaking areas of the Caribbean in Map 2 and we shall illustrate the diversity of these creoles by selecting seven societies which are reasonably representative of all the communities in the Caribbean.

1. Costa Rica
(population 2,190,000; official language Spanish)
West Indians, mainly from Jamaica, started emigrating to Costa Rica in search of work in the 1870s. By 1890 there were approximately forty-five thousand Creole English speakers living and working near the coast (Byfield, 1977: 3ff). To begin with, Costa Rican Creole differed little from the variety spoken in Jamaica although it began to be influenced by Standard American English as the Americans were the most influential employers in the area. The first generation of West Indian immigrants established their own church schools and so their children tended to speak only Creole English or Creole-influenced English. Gradu-

53

ally, however, and with increased momentum since the 1940s, children of West Indian origin have been attending local schools and learning through the medium of Spanish, with the result that many are becoming more proficient in Spanish than in the Creole. Nevertheless, Byfield (1977: 1) estimates that around fifty thousand Costa Ricans still make regular use of Creole English, which is, however, beginning to be influenced by Spanish.

Samples of Costa Rican Creole English
Passage a) is from the beginning of a recorded folktale and b) is a collection of sentences provided by Byfield.

a) *Wans ɔpan a taim mɔnki chu: tɔbakɔ an spit wait laim. Dis a tuori baut Brɛda Nansi an Brɛda Mɔnki. Dem wɔz alwiez a ta:k an a buɔs se wan bɛta dan di ada.*

b)   *Di mɔnki de pan di fɛns* – The monkey is on the fence
Luk pan da buɔi gwain daun di stri:t
We im tink im a go?
Dɛm chɔch pi:pul duɔn da:ns
                    Im basilarin yu – He's making fun of you (vaci-
                              lar – fool around)
                    Im goman – He has a hangover (estar de
                              goma – to be intoxicated).

2. Jamaica
(population 2,160,000; official language English)
Jamaica was captured from Spain by the British in 1655 and was more or less permanently under British rule until independence was granted in 1962. By the late seventeenth century, African slaves, in ever increasing numbers, began to be brought to Jamaica as plantation labourers and by 1690 'it was estimated that Jamaica alone needed 10,000 [i.e. slaves] a year' (Calder, 1981: 265). The death rate of the slaves was extremely high. In the first three-quarters of the eighteenth century, Jamaica imported 'close on half a million slaves' (Calder: 459), but its slave population rose by just over fifteen thousand. The slaves rebelled many times and, after a slave revolt in 1831 resulted in five hundred deaths, the call for the emancipation of slaves grew. The Emancipation Act was passed in 1833. According to this act, all slave children were to be freed by 1834 and adults were to

work three-quarters of their time for their former masters and use their wages to buy their freedom. Universal suffrage was granted to Jamaica in 1944 and this led directly to independence.

In Jamaica and in the other British-ruled islands in the Caribbean, all of the population has at least a passive knowledge of the creole.

Samples of Jamaican Creole English

Passage a) is in anglicised Jamaican Creole and is taken from a paper called: 'The Social History of Dread Talk'. The sentences in b) were recorded in Jamaica.

a) . . . *briekin fram di oul plantieshan sistim/ di rastafieran a di fers man dat staat gyaadn plaantin/ rait nou dem se bwai dem naa dipen paa no big man fi get chruu/ dem jos a du a likl selfrilaians yu nuo/*

(Pollard, 1980)

b) *Mieri bɛn kɔm yɛside* – Mary came yesterday
    Mi dɔn ta:k pan dat – I have already talked about that
  Kyari dis kɔm bak, dɛn – Take this and come back, then
      kyari dis go   take that away
  A wa:k mi wa:k mɛk – It's because I walked that I've
    mi kɔm so liɛt   arrived so late (lit. Be walk I walk make I come so late)
  Shi bakɔp di kya: nak – She reversed the car and hit the
     di wa:l   wall
 Wɛn ha:s dɛd, kau gɛt fat – When the horse is dead, the cow can get fat.

3. St Kitts
(population 70,000; official language English)
St Kitts and the neighbouring island of Nevis were discovered by Columbus in 1493 on his second voyage to the Caribbean. The first British settlers arrived there in 1622. French settlers were welcomed by the British who were glad of help against the Carib inhabitants. Shortly after 1622 African slaves and indentured Irish labourers began to be imported and the first slave revolt on an English island occurred on St Kitts in 1639. In the early eighteenth century the French settlers took control of the island but it was returned to the British by the Treaty of Utrecht in 1713.

St Kitts was recaptured by the French in 1782 but was again returned to the British and did not change hands thereafter. In 1871 the Leeward Isles (Antigua, St Kitts, Nevis, Montserrat and Anguilla) were formed into a federation. In 1967 the islands were granted internal self-government while Britain remained responsible for external affairs and defence.

Samples of St Kitts' Creole English

Mi bin a go ta:k — I was going to talk
Wai i na: wɔk? — Why does he not work?
A hu buk dat? — Whose book is that?
Mi hia hi mi tɛk sik — I heard he became ill
Mi no mi no yu a go ta:k — I didn't know you were going to talk.

4. *Barbados*
(population 250,000; official language English)
British settlement in Barbados dates from 1625. The island remained loyal to King Charles in the Civil War and was attacked and cruelly subdued by Cromwellian forces in 1652. At first there were few slaves in Barbados. In 1629, for example, there were about '1,800 Whites and 50 Blacks' on the island (Calder: 167) but, by the second half of the century, Irish rebels and African slaves had made Barbados one of the most densely populated areas on the earth. Over the two centuries of the Slave Trade, Barbados acquired 350,000 slaves but many of these died and many others were sent to other parts of the Caribbean so that by 1809 its slave population was approximately 70,000. Barbados achieved independence in 1966.

Barbados was important as a receiving depot for slaves being carried from Africa to the New World and Barbadians were renowned throughout the Caribbean for the excellence of their English. Cruickshank (1916: 63) was expressing a widely-held belief when he wrote that the 'Barbados Negro is African in hue and to a large extent in outlook, but . . . certainly not in dialect'. Thus, although creole features are to be found in Barbadian English (Bajun), they are less numerous than in other varieties of Caribbean English.

Samples of Bajun

Tu man rat kya:n liv in di: se:m ho:l	Two male rats cannot live in the same hole
Wɔ swi:t ɔn guɔt maut dɔz bɔn i: te:l	What pleases the goat's mouth burns his tail
Wa di: chail du? Hi: da ple: krikit	What's the child doing? He's playing cricket
Chikin mɛri, ha:k de nia	When the chicken is happy, the hawk is already close by.

5. *Trinidad and Tobago*
(population 1,130,000; official language English)
In 1595 Sir Walter Raleigh defeated the Spanish who had colonised Trinidad and formally annexed the island for Britain. British sovereignty was not, however, effectively established until 1763 for Tobago and 1779 for Trinidad. Before then the islands changed hands several times and knew Spanish, French, Dutch and British rule. At the time of Emancipation there were 9,000 slaves in Tobago and 17,000 in Trinidad. Trinidad found that it needed more labour for its growing sugar industry and so freed slaves from other parts of the Caribbean and from the United States were encouraged to settle there. In addition, approximately 145,000 indentured labourers from the Indian subcontinent were brought in. Trinidad and Tobago united in 1889 and gained their independence in 1962. Most of the population of both islands know and use Creole English.

Many of the Indians who moved to Trinidad worked side by side with creole-speaking Africans from whom they learnt the creole. Their influence on the creole has yet to be assessed in full, although they certainly expanded the vocabulary by the introduction of such lexical items as:

choli – an Indian blouse	*masala* – a type of curry
choti – a plait	*roti* – a type of bread.

Samples of Trinibagianese
There are three samples of Trinibagianese. Passage a) consists of proverbs taken from Ottley's *Sayings of Trinidad and Tobago*; b) contains examples of the creole spoken by Indians in Trinidad

and Tobago; and c) is an extract from a novel by a Trinidadian novelist now living in London.

a) *Man dead grass grow ah he door-mouth*
   Pickney a nyam muma – The child may eat the mother
   but muma na nyam but the mother won't eat the
   pickney child
   Behind back is Dog, before face is Mister Dog
   Is betta belly buss than good food waste
   One one does full basket.

(Ottley, 1966: 5, 6, 11)

b) *If yu mi:t sɔm indian* – If you meet some Indians and
    pipul, an yu kyã ta:k you can't talk your language
    yu langwij, dei dɔz (i.e. Bhojpuri) they laugh at
    laf yu daun bikɔz dei you because they say you don't
    sei yu ẽ no yu rilijɔn know your religion
    Shi ri:chin di: ej nau – She's reaching the age now
    tu ta:k wi ta:k gud when she should be able to
    speak our language well
  Shi:sik an shi dei in bɛd – She's sick and she's in bed.

c) "Girl, I in big trouble. Big, big trouble. If you know what Tiger go and do! He go and invite two Americans he does work with to come for Indian food tonight!"
   "Is wat happen to him at all? He crack? He is ah damn fool in truth. He bringing wite people to eat in dat hut? Tiger must be really going out of he head, yes. Gul, yuh making joke!"
   "Man, Rita, I tell you is true! My head hot! I don't know what to do."
   "Well, yes," Rita mused, "Ah did know he chupid, but not so chupid! Well, all you have to do is do yuh best, gul."
   "Rita, you go have to help me, girl."
   "But sure, man. Wat yuh want me to do?"
   "Yuh have to lend me plenty thing. I want glass. Plate. Cup. Spoon. Knife. Fork. Tablecloth –"
   "Take ease, keep cool! Between the two ah we we go fix up everyting good. Don't look so frighten. Why de hell yuh fraid Tiger so? Allyuh Indian people have some funny ways, oui."

(Selvon, 1952: 161)

6. Guyana

(population 860,000; official language English)
Sir Walter Raleigh visited Guyana in 1595 and there were a number of attempts by the British to colonise the area in the early seventeenth century. The Dutch, French and British all held parts of the South American coast in the seventeenth and eighteenth centuries but Guyana came under unequivocal British rule in 1814. From the sixteenth century onwards Guyana shared in the Slave Trading economy practised throughout the Caribbean and, like Trinidad and Tobago, was in the second half of the nineteenth century the recipient of large numbers of indentured Indian labourers. The population is made up as follows: East Indians approximately 50%, Africans 33%, Amerindians 16% and Europeans 1%. All the Guyanese living on the coast and in main towns have at least a passive knowledge of the creole. Guyana gained its independence from Britain in 1966.

Samples of Creolese

Passages a) and b) represent the same information in two types of creolese: a) is an example of basilectal creole, that is a form of creole which has not been markedly affected by SE; b) shows the influence of SE in vocabulary and in syntax. Both passages were provided by George Cave in a lecture on Guyanese English in Leeds, 1975.

a) *Maanin suun abi bina gu bakdam said fu gye waata pan di swiit waata trench kaaz abi na bin gat non stan paip a iisteet dem taim. Mi bina tek di tuu big bokit fram bakpaat abi hows an mi lil sisii di nada pinii wan. Abi giit owt kwik taim an ron, ron, ron sutee abi miit kaaz nof badii an dem bai an gyal piknii bin ga fo dip waata an ker am ahows fo dem muuma mek dem tii.*

b) *Suun marnin wii yusiz tu gu dong bakdam said fu gyet waata from di swiit waata trench biikaaz wii din gyet noo stan paip pun di esteet den. A yusiz tu tek di tuu big bokit from biihain wii hows an mi lil sista di oda lil wun. Wii yusiz tu gyet owt kwik an ron till wii miit biikaaz nof piipl an de chiren had woz tu dip waata an kyar um hoom fu de muda mek de tii.*

(Early in the morning we used to go to the back of the estate to get water from the sweet water trench because we didn't have any stand pipes on the estate in those days. I used to take the two big buckets from behind our house, and my little sister the other little one. We used to get out quickly and run until we reached because many people and their boys and girls used to have to dip water and take it home for their mother to make their breakfast.)

7. Suriname
(population 440,000; official language Dutch)
Suriname (formerly Dutch Guiana) shared with Guyana a history of changing European rulers. In 1651 the coast of Suriname was colonised by the British from Barbados. Many of the English settlers left because of illness and because of the attacks from the Dutch who formally took over control in 1667. By 1680 only thirty-nine Englishmen were left (Voorhoeve, 1970: 55) although their exodus was in part compensated for by the arrival of two hundred Portuguese-Jewish planters in 1665. Suriname, like Guyana, evolved a plantation economy and thus imported many African slaves and indentured Indians. There are several related English-based creoles in Suriname, all of them deriving from seventeenth-century plantation speech. The three most important of these are Sranan, Saramaccan and Djuka. Reinecke et al. estimate that 98% of the population speak one or other of the English-derived creoles (1975: 432). Suriname gained its independence from Holland in 1975.

Samples of Surinamese Creolese
Passage a) offers comparable sentences in Sranan, Saramaccan and Djuka and b) is a brief extract from the first original work in Sranan, *Life at Maripaston*, written in the second half of the nineteenth century by King.

a) Sranan   Saramaccan
   A go na oso   *A go a wosu*
   A waka kon   *A waka ko*
   A waka go na oso   *A waka go a wosu*
   A tyari den fisi kon   *A tya dee fisi ko*

Djuka	English
A go a osu	He went home
A waka kon	He walked here
A waka go a osu	He walked to the house
A tyai den fisi kon	He brought the fish here.

(Huttar, 1974)

b)   *Now disi de na tori* – This is the story of the start of
      foe na bigin foe na Johannes King's life with his
   libi foe Johannes King wife Magdalena.
 nanga hen wefi Magdarena

(ed. H. F. De Ziel, 1973: 113)

2.5 PIDGINS AND CREOLES IN THE PACIFIC

Most of the Pacific pidgins and creoles came into being later than their Atlantic counterparts because the trading which began to affect the linguistic behaviour of the South Pacific islanders did not start until the late eighteenth century.[14] The exact origin of the English-derived pidgins and creoles in the Pacific and their relation to each other and to non-Pacific varieties are still not fully established but their lexical patterning and structural similarities help us to co-classify them. All of them, for example, use (or have used) 'by and by' as a marker of futurity and 'suppose' to indicate conditionality. But some Pacific pidgins are very closely related and should be regarded as dialectal variants rather than as separate developments.[15]

1. *China Coast*

We shall treat China Coast Pidgin English first because, although it is now virtually extinct, it was an important lingua franca in the eighteenth and nineteenth centuries and may well have had a seminal influence on South Pacific varieties. China Coast Pidgin English originated in Canton, possibly as early as the seventeenth century since the English established a trading post there in 1664 (Hall, 1966: 8). The pidgin became more widely used in Canton and Macao in the eighteenth century as the European demand for tea grew. CCPE spread along the coast and was used in many of the ports between Canton and Shanghai as well as into the

Yang-Tze valley. It reached its peak of usefulness in the second half of the nineteenth century.

CCPE's decline began about 1890 and although relics of it can still be found in Hong Kong, it has almost completely died out. Its link with South Pacific varieties stems from trade. The European and American demand for tea and silk grew in the eighteenth and nineteenth centuries. The Chinese did not want European merchandise (Hobley, 1972: 54) but were happy to take sandalwood, pearl shells and bêche-de-mer sea slugs, all of which were available in the South Pacific.

Samples of China Coast Pidgin English

Passage a) is taken from Leland's *Pidgin English Sing-Song* (1876); b) contains sentences from Hall (1944); and c) offers two sentences recorded in Hong Kong in 1977.

a) *Captin Jones nother-tim make fightee China-side, muchee big bobbely* [i.e. noise, disorder, quarrel] *make he. Chinaman blongey war-junk he shootee too muchee allow, Chinaman he holla', "Hwan-na-kon!" (t'hat talkee, "Foleign dog!") Captin Jones talkee, "Dam!" By'mby one piecee allow come t'his side, he allow stick in one China boy blongey Captin he boat. Captin he wailo* [i.e. went away] *chop-chop, he wantchee pullee allow outside that China boy; he pullee, pullee velly muchee; no can do.*

('Captain Jones and the Arrow': 89)

b)   *hi plenti sik* – he was very sick
    hi fes luk-si olsem chiken – his face looks like a chicken
        maski, maj kæn du – never mind, I can do it
 maj blong nəmbər-wan boj – I am the chief boy.

(Hall, 1944: 103–5)

c) *Shuga ken, wan dala wan luk* – Sugar cane, one dollar per section
    ðis a nɔmba wan gud buk – This is excellent book.

(Tsang, 1977)

2. *Hawaii*
(population 770,000; official language English)
Captain Cook discovered the Sandwich Islands (later Hawaii) in

1778 and they soon became a popular port of call for traders in the Pacific. As early as 1786 these islands were regularly visited by American ships which were trading in fur with the Chinese and 'some took Hawaiian crewmen on board' (Clark, 1979b: 5). This may have helped to introduce some China Coast Pidgin English into Hawaii because, according to Carr (1972: 4), by 1791 at least two words from CCPE, namely *chowchow* (eat) and *pickaninny* (child), had currency in Hawaii. United States missionaries worked in the islands from 1820 and the United States government annexed them in 1898.

From the 1850s the Hawaiian islands began to be developed as sugar plantations and large numbers of workers were brought in. By 1897 46,000 Chinese worked in Hawaii and these labourers were later augmented by 17,500 Portuguese from Madeira and the Azores, 61,000 Japanese, 6,000 Puerto Ricans, 8,000 Koreans, 8,000 Spanish and 120,000 Philippinos (Carr, 1972: 5–6). With such linguistic diversity on the islands, pidginised English flourished and many children born on the plantations used creolised English as a mother tongue. Hawaii became one of the United States of America in 1959 and today many varieties of English are heard on the islands, all of them being increasingly influenced by American Standard English.

Samples of Hawaiian English

Three passages are provided: a) comes from an 1840 novel, *Two Years Before the Mast*; b) contains sentences from Carr's *Da Kine Talk*; and c) is taken from the *Honolulu Advertiser* of 12 March 1980.

a) *New Zealand kanaka* [i.e. native] *eatee white man; Sandwich Island kanaka – no. Sandwich Island kanaka ua like pu na haole* [i.e. are just like Europeans] *– all 'e same a' you.*

(Dana, 1840, Chapter 19)

b)   *Where you stay go?* – Where are you going? (150)
We goin meet Jane-guys at the – We're going to meet Jane and
      movie her friends at the movies (132)

Him numba one pilau – He's the very worst overseer
[rotten] *luna* [foreman] in the plantation (141).

(Carr, 1972: 132, 141 and 150)

c) *Dear Maili:*

> *Howyu? Auwe, hea we ah third month in 1980. Aloha no!*
> *You made some nu'ea resolushuns, eia nei? Not me*
> *nowadays, I tell yu.*
>
> *Erry ea I used to say . . . I going huhu all those cement*
> *mixahs and fellas like dig up all'a coconut trees . . . but I no get*
> *noplace, so poho. Wasetime.*
>
> *Now I only shut my makas and waha and stay countryside*
> *and enjoy ovah hea . . .*
>
> *Anyway, sorry you not home when I call, so I shake up ole*
> *Aleka-ma foa go Honolulu shopping.*
>
> *Us two makules hop on the bus, show the passes and sit*
> *down comfy and enjoy the free ride. I took plenty kala*
> *wrapped up in my red bandana inside my muumuu, cuz I hea*
> *all about those snatchas.*
>
> *(Maili Yardley Column, Honolulu Advertiser, 12 March 1980)*

3. *Papua New Guinea*

(population 3,080,000; official language English)

The island that is now Papua New Guinea and Irian Jaya was
sighted by a Portuguese navigator, Antonio d'Abreu, in 1512. In
1545 a Spanish navigator named the island 'Nueva Guinea'. The
Dutch visited the island in 1606, the English in 1670 and the
French in 1768, but none of these people attempted a permanent
settlement. In 1793, the British East India Company started a
settlement in New Guinea but it failed and the British showed
relatively little interest in the area for the next century. In 1883
the Queensland government, worried by the growing German
presence in the region, annexed the entire island and the offshore
islands on behalf of Britain. Britain, however, repudiated the
annexation and came to an agreement with Germany by which
the north-eastern part of the island became a German Protectorate and the south-eastern part (known as Papua) a British
Protectorate. (Holland had already annexed the western part of
the island in 1828.) In the First World War, an Australian force
attacked German installations and German New Guinea came
under Australian rule in September 1914. In 1920 Australia was
granted a mandate to govern German New Guinea and the two
sections of the island were known as 'The Territories of Papua

and New Guinea'. In 1975 the two sections united and became independent as 'Papua New Guinea'.

Pidgin English, known locally as 'Tok Pisin', was spread in Papua New Guinea by migrant labourers who had worked with other South Pacific islanders in Samoa, Fiji and Queensland. Today it is the most widely-used language in the country, being spoken or understood by at least one million people.

Samples of Tok Pisin

Passage a) is from a government publication on 'Government and Independence'; b) is taken from a booklet on 'Road Safety'; and c) is from St Luke XV, 31–32.

a) *Gavman na Independens* (The Government and Independence)
Bilong wanem yumi i mas get ol lo? (Why do we have laws?)
Long olgeta hap long dispela graun sapos manmeri i sindaun
(Everywhere in this world where men and women live)
wantaim i mas get ol lo. Sapos nogat, orait
(together there must be laws. Suppose there weren't any, all right)
i nogat rot long tambuim pasin bilong stil.
(there would be no way to forbid stealing.)
(Gwyther-Jones, 1972: 1)

b) *Sapos yu kisim bagarap, kisim namba bilong narapela draiva,*
(If you have an accident, get the other driver's number,)
sapos yu ken, kisim naim bilong em na adres tu,
(if possible, get his name and address too,)
na tokim polis long em. Noken paitim em o tok nogut long em.
(and report it to the police. Don't fight or abuse him.)
Rot Sefti Long Niugini, 1972: 10)

c) *Na papa i tokim em, i spik, 'Pikinini, oltaim oltaim yumi tupela i save stap wantaim. Na olgeta samting bilong mi em bilong yu. Tasol nau yumi mas amamas, na bel bilong yumi mas gutpela. Dispela brata bilong yu em i dai pinis, tasol nau em i kamap laip gen. Em i lus pinis, tasol nau yumi painim bek.'*
(*Nupela Testamen*, 1969: 263)

4. *Solomon Islands*
(population 210,000; official language English)
The Solomon Islands have a history similar to Papua New
Guinea's in that they were sighted several times in the sixteenth
century, visited by the British in 1699 and turned into a British
Protectorate in the nineteenth century, in 1893 in this case. In
addition, Solomon Islanders were from the 1860s persuaded to
work on plantations, mainly in Queensland. These islands are,
like Papua New Guinea, multilingual and the returning plantation workers helped to spread their Plantation Pidgin English as a
lingua franca throughout the island group. The Solomon Islands
achieved independence in 1978.

Samples of Solomon Island Pidgin English
Passage a) is a recording of a version of 'The North Wind and the
Sun'; b) is an extract from a book to encourage adult literacy; and
c) is again St Luke XV.

a) *Tupela san en bumburu tupela pait. San em i se: "Man, mi*
   gatim
   (Both the sun and the wind had a fight. The sun said: "Man, I
   have
   paua tumas. Mi pitim spoilim man hia." Bumburu em i se:
   "Woswe
   a lot of strength. I can destroy people." Bumburu said: "How
   man? Bai mi strong tumas. Mi savi spoilim everi samting, vilis,
   man? I will be stronger. I can destroy everything, villages
   kokonas tri, san, kanu. Everiwan mi savi bagarap pinis."
   coconut trees, sand, canoes. I can utterly destroy everything.")

b) *Hao fo iusim disfala buk* (How to use this book)
   Iu save lukim eni wod olsem hemi saon long ia blong iu. Sapos
   hemi garem wanfala sta (olsem) long fran blong hem, diswan*
   hemi minim iu mas lukluk long bihaen fo gudfala wei fo
   *raetam. Olsem iu save lukim *abaut abaot long mekwan pej.*
   **Abaut hemi no nambawan wei fo raetem bat abaot hemi*
   nambawan wei fo raetem.
(*Buk Blong Wei Fo Raetem Olgeta Wod Long Pijin*, Honiara,
                                                         1961, i)

c) *Papa i tokim, em i se: "Pikinini bilong mi, yu stap long ples bilong mi oltaim oltaim en everi samting bilong mi em i bilong yu. Olsem yumi mas amamas tumas en bel bilong yumi mas glad: bipo, brata bilong yu em i dai pinis, bot nau em i kamap laip agen. Em i lus pinis, bot nau yumi painim em agen."*

(J. Richards, 1971, unpublished translation)

5. *Vanuatu*

(formerly the New Hebrides; population 97,000; official languages French and English; unofficial lingua franca Bislama)

Vanuatu consists of an archipelago of small islands, all of which had been charted by the time of Cook's third voyage to the Pacific in 1776. In 1906 France and England agreed to govern the islands as a condominium and this rule lasted until 1980 when Vanuatu gained its independence. Vanuatuans may well have been influential in helping to stabilise and spread the type of Pidgin English already illustrated for Papua New Guinea and the Solomons because, in the 1860s, many Vanuatuans were taken to Queensland, Fiji and Samoa as indentured labourers on sugar and cotton plantations and, on most of these plantations, a South Pacific Pidgin English became the lingua franca. The name applied by Vanuatuans to their pidgin is *Bislama*, a term derived from 'bêche-de-mer', a sea slug found throughout the South Pacific. Bêche-de-mer trading flourished from the 1840s and it seems likely that a pidginised English was used to facilitate the trade.

Samples of Bislama

Passage a) illustrates Vanuatuan Pidgin English of the nineteenth century; passage b) offers two versions of the St Luke verses; and passage c) is the beginning of the Vanuatuan constitution (see Appendix B7b).

a) *'You see ... no good missionary stop Tanna. Suppose missionary stop here, by and by he speak, "Very good, all Tanna man make a work." you see that no good: Tanna man he no too much like work. By-and-bye missionary speak, "No good woman make a work: very good, all man he only get one woman." You see Tanna man no like that; he speak, "Very good plenty woman: very good woman make all work." Tanna man no savé work ... he too much lazy; he too much gentleman!'*

'You see . . . suppose missionary stop here, he tell all man,
"Very good, get a clothes." That no good; very good, white
man get a clothes; very good, black man make a paint.
Suppose black fellow get a clothes he no look well: you look
this fellow, he no look well!'

(McFarlane, 1873: 106)

b) i.   *Papa bilong em i ansa long em, i se "pikinini bilong mi,*
oltaem yu yu stap long ples bilong mi, mo olgeta samting we
oli bilong mi, oli bilong yu. Be i stret nomo bilong yumi
mekem lafet ia, yumi glad. From we brata ia bilong yu, bifo em
i ded, be nao em i laev bakegen. Bifo em i lus, be nao yumi
faenem em."

(Bible Society, 1971)

ii.   *Nao papa blong hem i ansa long hem, i se "Pikinini blong*
mi, oltaem yu yu stap kolosap long mi, mo olgeta samting
blong mi oli blong yu. Be i stret nomo blong yumi mekim lafet
ya, yumi glad, from we brata blong yu we bifo i olsem we hem
i ded, naoia hem i laef bakegen. Bifo hem i lus, be naoia yumi
faenem hem bakegen."

(Nyutesteman, 1980: 158)

c) *Konstitusin Blong Ripablik Blong Vanuatu (Niu Hebrides)*
1980
Ripablick blong Nyuhebrides, hem i wan kantri we olgeta
man ples blong hem i holem paoa blong gavman, nao gavman
blong olgeta nomo i rul long hem.
(The Republic of the New Hebrides is a sovereign democratic
state.)

6. *Australia*

(population 14,420,000; official language English)
The Dutch began to explore the Australian coast in the 1640s.
Forty years later, in 1688, an English buccaneer, William
Dampier, sailed along the eastern coast of Australia but it was not
until 1770 that Australia was charted and officially claimed for
Britain by Cook. By 1788 a convict settlement was established at
Port Jackson, near Sydney, and a large proportion of the convicts
were from Ireland. Eastern Australia remained a convict settle-
ment until 1840, after which time the continent began to be
colonised by free, and mainly British, settlers. Gold was disco-

vered in 1851 and this led to an increase in the population as prospectors from America, Europe and China moved in. Although gold helped to stimulate immigration and to improve communication networks in Australia, much of the later wealth of the country was based on farming. In 1901 the six states of Australia proclaimed the 'Commonwealth of Australia' with a federal parliament in Canberra, but this was merely formalising an unwritten constitution because the states had had virtual autonomy from Britain since the middle of the nineteenth century.

Between the eighteenth and the twentieth centuries three types of Pidgin English have been heard in Australia:

a) Aboriginal Pidgin English, probably dating back to the earliest contacts between Aborigines and English speakers and, at one time, quite widely spoken throughout the continent.

b) South Pacific Pidgin, confined mainly to Queensland and the Torres Straits. This variety probably derived from a trade English, almost certainly related to CCPE and used by traders dealing mainly in bêche-de-mer and sandalwood. Between 1863 and 1904, 61,160 labourers were shipped from South Pacific islands to work as plantation labourers in Queensland (Parnaby, 1964: 203). This process of using indentured labour was known as 'blackbirding'. On the multilingual, multiethnic plantations Pidgin English flourished.

c) Chinese Pidgin English. By 1861 there were about 39,000 Chinese workers in Australia (Ramson, 1966: 153), most of whom worked in the goldfields. The Pidgin English they employed derived from CCPE and it died out in Australia early in the twentieth century.

Samples of Australian Pidgin English
Passage a) contains samples of nineteenth-century Pidgin English; b) illustrates the pidgin in the Torres Straits; and c) offers sentences from a Creole English in the Northern Territories.

a) 1828 *All gammon white fellow pai-alla* [i.e. talk] *cabon gunya* [i.e. big house] *me tumble down white fellow.* (It was all false that the white fellows said in the Court-house that I killed the white fellow.)

(Ramson, 1966: 111)

1832 *What for you jerran budgerry whitefellow? White-*
fellow brother belongit to blackfellow. (Why are you
afraid of the very good white man? The white man is
the brother of the black man.)

(Ramson, 1970: 43)

c. 1870   Commandments
1. *Man take one fellow God; no more*
2. *Man like him God first time, everything else behind*
3. *Man no swear*
4. *Man keep Sunday good fellow day belong big fellow*
   master
5. *Man be good fellow longa father mother belonga him.*

(Fussel, 1871: 48–9)

b)   *Ai tok lo yu* – I'm talking to you
       Im bin hitim mi long aan – He hit me with his hand
     Plenti maan i kech-im fish – Some men catch fish down at
              daun lo riva   the river
       I gat manggo lo det tri – There are mangoes on that
                             tree
          Mait i kam fa luk mi – He might come to see me
          Pikanini i go krai. – The child will cry.

(Sandefur, 1983)

c) *Ay bin jiden la im* (I been sit – I camped at his place
        down long him)
     Yu gin wed la mi lilbid? – Can you wait for me a little?
        Im bin megim ginu – He made a canoe
            Yu gu jilib – Go to sleep
        Yu jabi? Namu. – Do you understand? No.

(Sharp, 1975: 7–8)

7. *Pitcairn*
(population in 1978, 68; official language English)
Pitcairn was an uninhabited island when it was taken over by the
men who had mutinied against Captain Bligh of the *Bounty* in
April 1789. Pitcairn provides an interesting case-study for
language use and change because we know the names, numbers
and places of origin of all the people who settled on the island in
January 1790. There were nine English-speaking mutineers,
twelve Tahitian women, six South Pacific men from Tahiti,

Raiata and Tupuai and one child, a little girl from Tahiti (Danielsson, 1963: 208–10).

In 1856, because of overcrowding, the Pitcairnese were taken off their island and all 194 of them resettled on Norfolk Island which had previously been a convict settlement. Between 1859 and 1864, forty-three of the Pitcairnese returned to their island while the others remained on Norfolk Island where they were gradually outnumbered by settlers of Australian origin.

Samples of Pitcairnese and Norfolkese

Passage a) is in Pitcairnese, and dates back to 1821; b) is a sample of Norfolkese.

a) *I like much hear you talk – that very good – Capt Raine very funny man – we like to do well but we not know how – no good in doing wrong.*

(Quoted from Ross and Moverley, 1964: 119)

b) *I gwen down Farder's morler fa see dar Pe ar lee boy fa dems; he fall out one tree & he sa boo hoo both his shin & dem tull he sa Hute Hute his ballay. I wish I gut some gothy fa carlay down fa hem, semes thing he gwen ar car go narway fa long time; but I gwener come back & larner yorlya what a way hem.*

(I'm going down to Father's place to-morrow to see that little boy of theirs. He fell out of a tree and he's got lumps on both his shins; and they say he has scratched and cut his stomach. I wish I had some roasted young whale-birds to take down for him, for it looks as if he won't be able to go swimming for a long time. But I'll come back and tell you how he is.)

(Collected by Flint in 1957, published in Ross and Moverley, 1964: 200–201)

2.6 PIDGINS IN ASIA

Apart from China Coast Pidgin English which we have considered with Pacific varieties, there are two categories of 'Pidgin English' in Asia. The first types are found in India and derive from contacts between the Indians and the British and the second, which may be referred to collectively as 'Bamboo English', owe their origin to contacts between people from Japan, Korea, Vietnam and Thailand with soldiers from the United States.

1. *India*
(population c. 650,980,000; fourteen languages, not including English which is still a useful link language)
It is not certain whether or not Pidgin Englishes do exist or ever have existed in India. It seems very probable that marginal Pidgin Englishes arose between the British and their servants, and in order to facilitate trade, but it is unlikely that they became stabilised as efficient lingua francas. Schuchardt (1891: 286–305) describes three non-standard Englishes, namely 'Butler English', 'Baboo/Babu English' and 'Chee-chee English'. The first bears the closest resemblance to Pidgin Englishes found in other parts of the world. 'Butler English' is a simplified transaction English used in trade and in master-servant relationships. This variety continues to exist (personal communication, Mehrotra) as a trade language between Indians and tourists and between Indians who do not share a common Indian language. 'Babu English' is a term applied derogatively to an Indian-influenced English which is satirised by a number of Indian poets including Nissim Ezekiel, from whom one of our samples is taken. The third type, 'Chee-chee English', was not a pidgin at all, but the name applied to the English of the Anglo-Indian population.

Samples of Indian Englishes
Passage a) is taken from Schuchardt and is an illustration of Butler English; b) is part of a letter which could be described as Babu English; c) is a poem satirising Indian English; and d) illustrates modern 'Pidgin English'.

a) i *Butler's yevery day taking one ollock for own-self, and giving servants all half half ollock; when I am telling that shame for him, he is telling, Master's strictly order all servants for the little milk give it – what can I say mam, I poor ayah woman?*

ii *Yes, sare, all done gone finished whole*
I all right now, ma'am
Missus want amah for the baby?
I speaking English-same as missus.
             (Schuchardt, 1891: 292–3)

72

b) *Sir,*

I beg to invite your kind attention to the insatiable thirst for knowledge of an obscure bibliophil that compels him to be a suppliant for your munificence. To get down to brass tacks, I have a good mind to be enlightened by your book but my chronic financial stringency obfuscates the lofty idea.

Might I therefore request you to furnish the poor student languishing in the icy quagmire of despondency with a copy of the gem of knowledge gratis.

c) *Goodbye Party for Miss Pushpa T.S.*
Friends,
our dear sister
is departing for foreign
in two three days,
and
we are meeting today
to wish her bon-voyage.
. . . . . .
Miss Pushpa is coming
from very high family.
Her father was renowned advocate
in Bulsar or Surat,
I am not remembering now which place.
                    (Nissim Ezekiel, 1976: 23)

d) *Burning place. Dead body burning place. Twenty four hour burn. Holy man not body burn. The small boy not body burn. Children not burn. They put* [i.e. are put] *the Gang* [i.e. in the Ganges].
I am here waiter. Any tourist any time any eating any evening.
            (R. R. Mehrotra, 1981, personal communication)

2. Bamboo English

This is the term given to the varieties of simplified English which developed in Asia as a result of the American involvement in Japan, Korea, Vietnam and Thailand since the end of the Second World War. Since these contacts were relatively superficial and involved speakers of only two languages, they tended to produce marginal, unstable pidgins. It is impossible to say how many Asians and Americans used such simplified exchange systems but, at present, Bamboo English is probably not used by more than a few hundred people.

Samples of Bamboo English
Sample a) is from Japan; sample b) from Thailand.

a) *Tell him to hayaku the hell over here*
   (hayaku = quick)
   This beer is ichiban
   (ichiban = number one)
   Hey GI, you want short-time – only five dollars!

   (Norman, 1955: 46–7)

b) *They have girlfriend right? But stay all together. They have*
   children. Can do like that – huh? In Thailand can not do same
   like that. Much different Thailand and America.
   I no have home. Now I no want stay mamson you know. I no
   like stay home. I come back leo leo [immediately] *you know.*

   (Gebhard, 1975)

2.7 MARGINAL CASES

As we have seen in Chapter 1, it is not always easy to distinguish linguistically between a pidgin and a creole. Nor is it easy to draw sharp distinctions between English-related creoles and dialects of English like Hiberno-English, where a form of English has displaced an indigenous mother tongue and where substratal influences from the ancestral mother tongue continue to be apparent. In our survey of world pidgins and creoles we have found four English-related languages which do not quite fit the pidgin-creole categories we have described and yet which show pidginisation features. Two of these, St Helena English and Tristan da Cunha English, are mother-tongue varieties which differ from SE, but the differences are due to early isolation from mainstream English as well as to influences from non-mother-tongue speakers of English. The third language, Anglo-Romani, is a type of English spoken by many Romanies and it shows the influences of both English and Romani. Some dialects of Anglo-Romani retain many of the Romani inflections while other dialects have lost these inflections and replaced them with English prepositions and inflections. The fourth language, Shelta, is the most complex and marginal of all. According to Hancock (1974: 130) it is spoken by about 30,000 people in Ireland, Britain, Canada, the United States and possibly also in Australia and South Africa. It is a 'secret' language, sometimes called 'Tinkers' Talk' and it is used by itinerants, usually of Irish origin, and their descendants. Shelta differs from pidginised languages in two main ways. Firstly, it was created to *impede* communication, that is, it was meant to be incomprehensible to speakers of both Gaelic and English and secondly, the type of modifications that occur suggest that the originators of Shelta (possibly dispossessed Irish nobility) were literate. The word order and syntax of Shelta are essentially English whereas much of the vocabulary is modified Gaelic, the modifications taking the form of full inversions such as *kam* from *mac* (son), *gop* from *póg* (kiss); partial inversion such as *tarpog* from *bratach* (rag) or from *brat* (rag) + *óg* (young); change of vowel such as *graig* from *gruaig* (hair) and the addition of affixes such as *grula* from gr + *ubhal*/ual/(apple) + a.

Samples of the Marginal Cases

1. St Helena English

   Do you belong to this cabin?   (Are you from this cabin?)
   So us was carry on singing   (We carried on singing)
   I hear Jenny's done dead   (I hear Jenny has died)
   I's fine. You's welcome.
   He do it real good like.

                                           (Ryan, 1980: 1–24)

2. Tristan da Cunha English

   I didn't was want to went in the dark
   But we-all doesn't mind. We doesn't get run over by no motor cars on Tristan
   I done went to the Doctor and he gave me a hinjection and I'se better now
   I'se done tell her she must be married before Lent
   Where you was yesterday?

                                           (Zettersten, 1969: 82–7)

3. Anglo–Romani

Passage a) is a 1973 translation of Luke XV, 31–32 and b) is a set of sentences taken from Leland's nineteenth-century study of Anglo-Romani.

a) *But his dadrus penned: 'My chavvi, tuti's with mandi sor the cherus, and tuti can have sor of my kovels. So it was kushti for us to be losheno, because tiro pral was mulo, ta he's jivdo again. Lesti shavved, but akno he's latchered.'*

(BFBS, 1973)

b) *When there's a boro bavol, huller the tan parl the naver rikk pauli the bor*
(When the wind is high, move the tent to the other side of the hedge)
Yeck mush can lel a grai ta panni, but twenty cant kair him pi
(One man can take a horse to water, but twenty can't make him drink)
He's too boot of a mush to rakker a pauver chavo
(He's too proud to speak to a poor man)
Yeckorus a mush chored a gry and jalled him avree adree a waver tem, and
(Once a man stole a horse and ran him away into an other country, and
the gry and the mush jalled kushi bak kettenus. Penned the gry to his mush,
the horse and the man became very intimate. Said the horse to the man,
"I kaums your covvas to wearus kushtier than mandy's, for there's kek chucknee
"I like your things to wear better than mine, for there's no whip
or mellicus adree them."
or spur among them.")

(Leland, 1873, 102–3 and 216)

4. Shelta
Muilsha's gather swurth a munniath, munni-graua-kradyi dhuilsha's munnik.
(I's father up in goodness, good-luck at stand(ing) thou's name.

Gra be gredhi'd shedhi ladhu, as aswurth in munniath. Bug muilsha thalosk-minurth
Love be made upon earth, as up in goodness. Give I day now
goshta dhurra. Gretul our shaku, araik muilsha getyas nidyas gredhi gamiath muilsha.
enough bread. Forgiveness our sin, like I forgives persons to do badness I.)
Mwilsha bog'd Sheldru swurth nadherum's miskon (I learnt Shelta at mother's breast)
Muilsha's kam grankes od luba (My son knows two words)
Niyesh kradyi a simaja (Don't stay a minute)
Glox nidesh a glox raks aburth od grifin (A man's no man without two coats.)

(Macalister, 1937: 139–40)

2.8 CONCLUSION

We have looked at English-based pidgins and creoles around the world and seen that they fall into two main families: the Atlantic varieties which probably arose in West African ports and were transported to the Americas where they became the only mother tongue of children born into slavery; and the Pacific varieties which are found in Australia, Papua New Guinea, the Solomon Islands and Vanuatu, which may be the remnants of a dialect continuum which flourished throughout the South Pacific in the nineteenth century and which may have derived from China Coast Pidgin English. There are many similarities between the two main families, similarities that are due to linguistic universals, to the fact that sailors may have introduced the same features into contact varieties in all parts of the world[16] and to similar sociological conditions. Pidgins and creoles were spread in the Atlantic by slavery and in the Pacific by blackbirding. The descriptive labels are different but the practices had essentially the same results: the rupturing of small but coherent societies, and the creation of the need for a lingua franca.

NOTES

1. Chinua Achebe often makes the point that a land is said to be 'discovered' when a white man, and preferably an Englishman, first puts his foot upon it.

2. Ian Hancock has done most work on the lexical similarities of Atlantic pidgins and creoles. His articles of 1971 and 1977 are particularly valuable in this respect.

3. 'Mutual intelligibility' is not easily defined because intelligibility need not work equally in both directions. A speaker of SE and a speaker of a rural dialect in Northern Ireland are said to speak mutually intelligible dialects but the Northern Ireland speaker will have less difficulty understanding the speaker of SE than vice versa, largely because the Northern Ireland speaker has, through education and the media, also been exposed to SE. Thus it is unlikely that the SE speaker would understand:

   > *Thon baygle broke our Bridie wild* – That ill-mannered young man embarrassed my sister terribly (lit. Yon beagle broke our Bridie wild)

   even though all the lexical items and the syntactic patterns are English. Mafeni (Spencer, 1971: 111) has claimed that he, a Nigerian, could not always understand Cameroon Pidgin English but I have witnessed a long conversation between women from Cameroon, Nigeria, Togo and Sierra Leone where each used her own pidgin/creole variant of English, where all were aware of the variations but where there were no problems of inter-intelligibility.

4. See Todd (1979) for an examination of the possible influence of Krio on Cameroon Pidgin, an influence which is hardly surprising in view of the fact that 29% of the early Christian missionaries to Cameroon were Krios (Gwei, 1966: 140–4).

5. All figures for West African populations are taken from Legum (1981).

6. Mbassy-Njie (1976: 4) writes: 'Le mot "aku" est une transformation de "oku", nom donné par des Sierra Leonais aux descendants d'esclaves d'origine Yoruba.' (The word 'aku' is a transformation of 'oku', a name given by the Sierra Leoneans to the descendants of slaves of Yoruba origin.)

7. In all the samples provided in this chapter, written texts are presented in the same orthography as that used by the individual writers. All spoken samples are transcribed systematically according to the conventions described on p. xi. Where a sample is not ascribed to a particular author, it means that the recording was made by me.

8. In July 1981 a Liberian was being repatriated from Manchester. She asked for a Krio speaker to translate for her at her hearing and a Freetown student, Freddie Jones, agreed to act in this capacity. I asked the student if her Krio was very different from his own and he said that it was perfectly comprehensible but a little old-fashioned.

9. This is a highly-anglicised version of Genesis and possibly owes more to mother-tongue English speakers than to the Kru. Other similar versions are found in other parts of the world. (See Appendix B 6b)

10. The more usual form of this word in West African pidgins is *sotei*. It can be the equivalent of 'until':

    A bin chop sotei i kam – I ate until he came
    or 'on and on and on':
    A bin chɔp sotei : : : :

    The form *sotei* may derive from 'so' = '(s)tay' or it may be a blend of English 'so' and Portuguese 'até' which means 'until', 'up to'.

11. I asked for an explanation of *ganaka* because the word was unknown to me and was told that it meant 'a disoriented bushman'. The form *kanaka* meaning 'native' occurs in Pacific Pidgin English and is said to derive possibly from 'cane+hacker'. It is possible that the term was spread in both West Africa and the Pacific by the Germans. This claim gains some support from the fact that some Cameroon speakers knew the form *ganakɔ*, meaning 'bushman' and, in Cameroon, the form *meri* meaning 'woman' is known by older speakers although it occurs in no other Atlantic variety, but is the accepted form in Papua New Guinea.

12. Nigeria's population is only an estimate. Many observers believe that the last Nigerian census did not produce an accurate population figure. It is also an over-simplification to list 'English' as the 'official language'. In the state assemblies, the main local Nigerian language also has official status.

13. Population figures for the Americas and the Pacific are taken from Webster's *New World Atlas* (1982).

14. Evidence suggests that the first Europeans tried to learn the local languages. Captain Bligh, for example, had followed Captain Cook's example in trying to learn enough Tonga to communicate with the local people. It was sometimes difficult, as Bligh reports of his 1789 visit to Tonga, but then an islander called Tepa was found and he was 'accustomed to our manner of speaking their language' (Bligh, 1792: 149). The first real impact on the islanders' language use came in the nineteenth century as the South Pacific was used for whaling purposes. Many islanders joined whaling crews and often one whaling venture lasted for three years. Whaling increased

sharply after 1820 so that there were often hundreds of whaling ships in the area at any one time. By the 1860s whaling began to decline, but this decline coincided with the growth of plantations on which islanders from many linguistic backgrounds came together and found Pidgin English an essential tool in inter-group communication.

15. Several other Pidgin Englishes existed in the Pacific in the nineteenth and early twentieth centuries, including varieties in New Caledonia, Fiji, Tonga, Tahiti, Samoa and New Zealand. Because New Caledonian and New Zealand varieties were of seminal importance in the spread of Pidgin English we provide brief samples:

New Caledonia – *Boat belong you?* Is this your boat?
Allsame man ouioui belong boat mate mate kaikai. (All the French who were on the boat are dead and eaten.)

(Quoted in Clark, 1979: 37)

New Zealand

THURSDAY EVENING—My natives went up to Mr Marsden to inform him of their determination to go to England with me. Mr Marsden was very angry with them, and said they must not go on any account. The natives' reply was, "We love Mr Butler and mother, and wish to go with them." Mr Marsden then asked them if they did not like Port Jackson. They replied. "No, this land is no good for the New Zealand men. New Zealand men all die. You bury our countrymen all the same as (kararehe) a beast; you no cry, nor pray, when you bury New Zealand man! Pakeha die, plenty karakia; New Zealand man die, no karakia!" That is, when white people die, there are many prayers said; but when a New Zealander dies, there is no prayer offered for him, but he is buried like a beast – without ceremony.

"Mr Butler go back to New Zealand, very good; no Mr Butler go back New Zealand, very bad. No New Zealand man stop at Port Jackson; go back, go back. . . . By and by Mr Butler come back to New Zealand, (kapai) good; No Mr Butler come back, (ka pouri te ngakau) the heart will be distressed for him."

(Butler, 1927: 372)

16. Items such as *savi, pikin(ini), olsem, baimbai* were probably used by sailors in their contacts with all non-English speakers since they tend to occur throughout the world. Other items like *skin* meaning 'body' and *slak/slek* meaning 'tired' and *wei* as a relative pronoun also occur in both Atlantic and Pacific varieties although not in SE and may owe their spread to a nautical jargon.

REFERENCES AND SUGGESTIONS FOR FURTHER READING

ACHEBE, CHINUA, *Morning Yet on Creation Day*, London: Heinemann, 1975.

BAKER, S. J., *New Zealand Slang*, Christchurch, etc.: Whitcombe and Tombs Ltd, 1941.

BAKER, S. J., *The Australian Language*, Sydney: Currawong Publishing Co., 1966.

BEECHING, JACK (ed.), *Richard Hakluyt Voyages and Discoveries*, Harmondsworth: Penguin, 1972.

BERRY, J. AND GREENBERG, J. H., *Current Trends in Linguistics 7*, The Hague: Mouton, 1971

BLAKE, J. W., *Europeans in West Africa Vols 1 and 2*, London: Hakluyt Society, 1942.

BLIGH, WILLIAM, *A Voyage to the South Seas*, London: George Nicol, 1792.

BRITISH AND FOREIGN BIBLE SOCIETY, *Nupela Testamen*, Canberra and Port Moresby: BFBS in Australia, 1969.

BRITISH AND FOREIGN BIBLE SOCIETY, *Gud Nyus Bilong Jisas Krais*, Auckland: Bible Society in New Zealand, 1971.

BRITISH AND FOREIGN BIBLE SOCIETY, *Nyutestem Long Bislama*, Suva, Fiji: Baebol Sosaete Blong Saot Pasifik, 1980.

BURNS, ALAN, *The History of Nigeria*, London: Allen and Unwin, 1964.

BYFIELD, CLARENCE, *The Verb Phrase In Costa Rican Creole*, unpublished MA dissertation, University of Leeds, 1977.

CALDER, ANGUS, *Revolutionary Empire*, London: Jonathan Cape, 1981.

CASSIDY, F. G. AND LEPAGE, R. B., *Dictionary of Jamaican English*, Cambridge: Cambridge University Press, 1980.

CARPENTIER, J.-M., *Le Pidgin Bislama(n)*, Paris: SELAF, 1979.

CARR, ELIZABETH BALL, *Da Kine Talk From Pidgin to Standard English in Hawaii*, Honolulu: Hawaii University Press, 1972.

CAVE, GEORGE, 'The English Language in Guyana', unpublished lecture, Leeds, 13 February 1975.

CLARK, ROSS, 'A Further Note on "Beach-la-Mar"', *Te Reo 21*, pp. 83–5, 1978.

CLARK, ROSS, 'The Rise and Fall of New Zealand Pidgin', paper presented at the second New Zealand Linguistic Conference, Wellington, 1978.

CLARK, ROSS, 'In Search of Beach-la-Mar', *Te Reo 22*, pp. 3–64, 1979.

CLARK, ROSS, 'On the Origin and Usage of the Term *Beach-la-Mar*', *Te Reo 20*, Auckland: Proceedings of the Linguistic Society of New Zealand, pp. 71–82, 1979.

CLEARE, W. T., 'Four Folk-tales from Fortune Islands, Bahamas', *Journal of American Folklore 30*, pp. 228–9, 1917.

CROCKER, W. R., *Nigeria, a Critique of British Colonial Administration*, London: Allen and Unwin, 1936.

CRUICKSHANK, J. G., *Black Talk*, Georgetown: Argosy Co., 1916.

DANA, R. H., *Two Years Before the Mast*, New York: Harper, 1840.

DANIELSSON, BENGT, *What Happened on the Bounty*, London: Allen and Unwin, 1963.

DAY, R. R. (ed.), *Issues in English Creoles*, Heidelberg: Julius Groos Verlag, 1980.

DILLARD, J. L., *Black English*, New York: Vintage Books, Random House, 1972.

DUTTON, T. E., 'Informal English in the Torres Straits', in RAMSON, 1970, pp. 137–60, 1970.

ESCURE, G., 'Copula Variability in the Creole Continuum of Belize', unpublished paper presented at the Third Biennial Conference of the Society for Caribbean Linguistics, Aruba, September 1980.

EZEKIEL, NISSIM, *Hymns in Darkness*, Delhi: Oxford University Press, 1976.

FISHMAN, J. A. et al., *The Spread of English*, Rowley, Mass.: Newbury Press, 1978.

FLINT, E. M., 'The Language of Norfolk Island' in Ross and Moverley, 1957, pp. 189–211, 1957.

FLINT, E. M., 'Aboriginal English', *English in Australia 6*, Melbourne: Association for the Teaching of English, pp. 3–21, 1968.

FORBES, JACK D., *Nevada Indians Speak*, Reno: University of Nevada Press, 1967.

FUSSEL, J., *A Kanaka Slave*, London: Stockwell, 1871.

FYFE, C. H., 'European and Creole Influence in the Hinterland of Sierra Leone before 1896', *Sierra Leone Studies, New Series, No. 6*, pp. 113–23, 1956.

FYLE, C. N. AND JONES, E., *A Krio English Dictionary*, Oxford: Oxford University Press and Sierra Leone University Press, 1980.

GEBHARD, J. G., 'Variation in Thai Adaptation of English Language Features: A Study of Thai English', unpublished paper presented at the International Conference on Pidgins and Creoles, Hawaii, January 1975.

GWEI, SOLOMON, *History of the British Baptist Mission in Cameroon, with Beginnings in Fernando Po*, unpublished BD thesis, Ruschlikon-Zurich, Switzerland, 1966.

GWYTHER-JONES, R. E., *Gavman Na Independans*, Port Moresby: Department of Information, 1972.

HALL, ROBERT A. JR., *Melanesian Pidgin English Grammar, Texts, Vocabulary*, Baltimore: Linguistic Society of America, 1943.

HALL, ROBERT A., JR., 'Notes on Australian Pidgin English', *Language* *19*, pp. 293–7, 1943.

HALL, ROBERT A., JR., 'Chinese Pidgin English Grammar and Texts', *Journal of the American Oriental Society 64*, pp. 95–113, 1944.

HALL, ROBERT A., JR., *Pidgin and Creole Languages*, Ithaca: Cornell University Press, 1966.

HANCOCK, IAN F., 'Some Aspects of English in Liberia', *Liberian Studies Journal*, Greencastle, Indiana, pp. 207–13, 1970.

HANCOCK, IAN F., 'A Provisional Comparison of the English-derived Atlantic Creoles', Dell Hymes (ed.) *Pidginization and Creolization of Languages*, Cambridge: Cambridge University Press, 1971.

HANCOCK, IAN F., 'A Domestic Origin for the English-derived Atlantic Creoles', *The Florida FL Reporter*, Spring/Fall, pp. 7–8 and 52, 1972.

HANCOCK, IAN F., 'Shelta: A Problem of Classification' in David DeCamp and I. F. Hancock (eds) *Pidgins and Creoles: Current Trends and Practices*, pp. 130–7, 1974.

HANCOCK, IAN F., 'Appendix: Repertory of Pidgin and Creole Languages', in A. Valdman (ed.) *Pidgin and Creole Linguistics*, Bloomington: Indiana University Press, 1977.

HANCOCK, IAN F., 'Seminole Reunion', *UT News*, Austin, Texas: News and Information Service, prepared by Nancy Neff, 1981.

HARRISON, J. A., 'Negro English', *Anglia 7*, pp. 232–79, 1884.

HOBLEY, L. F., *Exploring the Pacific*, London: Methuen, 1972.

HOYOS, F. A., *Barbados: A History from the Amerindians to Independence*, London: Macmillan Caribbean, 1978.

HOYT, E. P., *African Slavery*, New York and London: Abelard-Schuman, 1973.

HUGO, HOWARD, Translation of 'To be or not to be' in British Solomon Islands Pidgin English, mimeographed, 1970.

HURSTON, ZORA NEALE, *Their Eyes were Watching God*, New York: Fawcett Premier Books, 1969.

HUTTAR, GEORGE, 'Some Kwa-like Features of Djuka Syntax', unpublished paper presented at the International Conference on Pidgins and Creoles in Hawaii, 1975.

ISICHEI, ELIZABETH, *History of West Africa Since 1800*, London: Macmillan, 1977.

JONES, C. C., *Negro Myths from the Georgia Coast*, Boston and New York: Houghton, Mifflin and Company, 1888. Reissued Detroit: Singing Tree Press, Book Tower, 1969.

KERKVLIET, A., *The Sunday Gospels and Epistles with short explanations in Pidgin-English*, Buea: Catholic Mission Press, n.d.

LEECHMAN, DOUGLAS AND HALL, R. A., JR., 'American Indian Pidgin English: Attestations and Grammatical Peculiarities', *American Speech XXX 3*, pp. 163–71, 1955.

Legum, Colin (ed.), *Africa Contemporary Record*, New York and London: Africana Publishing Co., 1981.
Leland, C. G., *English Gypsies and their Language*, London: Trübner and Co., 1873.
Leland, C. G., *English Gypsy-Songs*, London: Trübner and Co., 1875.
Leland, C. G., *Pidgin English Sing-Song*, London: Trübner and Co., 1876.
Leland, C. G., 'Shelta, the Tinkers' Talk', *New Quarterly Magazine 3*, London, pp. 136–41, 1880.
Leland, C. G., 'The Tinkers' Talk', *Journal of the Gypsy Lore Society 1*, pp. 168–80, 1907.
LePage, R. B. and DeCamp, David, *Jamaican Creole*, London: Macmillan, 1960.
Macalister, R. A., *The Secret Languages of Ireland*. Cambridge: Cambridge University Press, 1937.
Mafeni, B., 'Nigerian Pidgin' in Spencer (ed.) *The English Language in West Africa*, pp. 95–112, 1971.
Markey, T. L. (ed. and translator), *Hugo Schuchardt: The Ethnography of Variation Selected Writings on Pidgins and Creoles*, Ann Arbor: Karoma Publishers Inc., 1979.
Mazrui, Ali A., *The Political Sociology of the English Language: An African Perspective*, The Hague: Mouton, 1975.
McFarlane, S., *The Story of the Lifu Mission*, London: James Nisbet, 1873.
Mbassy-Njie, C., *Etude Comparative des Systèmes Phonologique et Grammatical de l'Aku et l'Anglais*, unpublished Master's thesis, University of Dakar, Senegal, 1976.
Melville, H., *Typee*, London: John Murray, 1846.
Melville, H., *Omoo*, New York: Harper and Brothers, 1847.
Mihalic, F., *The Jacaranda Dictionary and Grammar of Melanesian Pidgin*, Brisbane: Jacaranda Press, 1971.
Mühlhäusler, P., *Growth and Structure of the Lexicon of New Guinea Pidgin*, Canberra: Pacific Linguistics Series C, No. 52, 1976.
Mühlhäusler, P., 'Samoan Plantation Pidgin English and the Origin of New Guinea Pidgin', in *Papers in Pidgin and Creole Linguistics 1*, Canberra: Pacific Linguistic Series A, No. 54, pp. 67–119, 1978.
Nelson, H., *Papua New Guinea*, Harmondsworth: Penguin Books, 1972.
Nicholas, J. L., *Narrative of a Voyage to New Zealand*, London: James Black and Son, 1817.
Nihalani, P. et al., *Indian and British English: A Handbook of Usage and Pronunciation*, New Delhi: Oxford University Press, 1978.
Norman, A. M. Z., 'Bamboo English: The Japanese Influence upon American Speech in Japan', *American Speech XXX*, 1, pp. 44–8, 1955.

OTTLEY, C. R., *Sayings of Trinidad and Tobago*, Port of Spain: compiled and published by C. R. Ottley, 1966.

OTTLEY, C. R., *The Story of Trinidad and Tobago in a Nutshell*, Port of Spain: Horsford Printerie, 1972.

PARNABY, O. W., *Britain and the Labor Trade in the Southwest Pacific*, Durham, N.C.: Duke University Press, 1964.

PEEK, BASIL, *Bahamian Proverbs*, London: John Culmer Ltd, 1949.

POLLARD, VELMA, 'The Social History of Dread Talk', unpublished paper presented at the Third Biennial Conference of the Society for Caribbean Linguistics, Aruba, September 1980.

PRIDE, JOHN (ed.), *The New Englishes*, Rowley: Newbury House, 1982.

PURCHAS, SAMUEL, *Purchas his Pilgrimes*, London: printed by William Stansby for Henrie Fetherstone, 1625.

RAMSON, W. S., *Australian English*, Canberra: Australian National University Press, 1966.

RAMSON, W. S. (ed.), *English Transported*, Canberra: ANU Press, 1970.

RAY, S. H., 'The Jargon English of the Torres Straits', *Reports of the Cambridge Anthropological Expedition to Torres Straits, Vol. 3*, Cambridge University Press, pp. 251–4, 1907.

REINECKE, J. E., *Marginal Languages: A Sociological Survey of the Creole Languages*, unpublished PhD thesis, University of Yale, 1937.

REINECKE, J. E., *Language and Dialect in Hawaii*, Honolulu: University Press of Hawaii, 1969.

REINECKE, J. E. et al., *A Bibliography of Pidgin and Creole Languages*, Honolulu: University Press of Hawaii, 1975.

RICKFORD, JOHN R., 'The Insights of the Mesolect' in *Pidgins and Creoles: Current Trends and Prospects*, eds David DeCamp and I. F. Hancock, Washington, DC: Georgetown University Press, pp. 92–117, 1974.

ROSS, A. S. C. AND MOVERLEY, A. W., *The Pitcairnese Language*, London: André Deutsch, 1964.

RYAN, JAMES, *A Saint Helena (South Atlantic Ocean) Vocabulary*, mimeographed, 1980.

SANDEFUR, J. R., 'Modern Australian Aboriginal Languages: The Present State of Knowledge', *English World-Wide*, Heidelberg: Julius Groos Verlag, 1983.

SANKOFF, DAVID (ed.), *Linguistic Variation: Models and Methods*, New York: Academic Press, 1978.

SAYER, E. S., *Pidgin English*, Toronto: mimeographed, 1939.

SCHUCHARDT, H., *Kreolische Studien, I–IX*, Vienna: Carl Gerold's Sohn for Vols I–VI and Vienna: K. Tempsky for Vols VII–IX, 1882–91.

SELVON, S., *A Brighter Sun*, London: Longman Caribbean, 1952.

SEY, KOFI A., *Ghanaian English*, London: Macmillan, 1973.

SHARPE, M. C., 'Notes on the "Pidgin English" Creole of Roper River', *Papers in Australian Linguistics 8*, Canberra: Pacific Linguistics A39, pp. 1–20, 1975.

SHARPE, M. C., AND SANDEFUR, J. R., 'The Creole Language of the Katherine and Roper Areas, Northern Territory' in M. Clyne (ed.) *Australia Talks: Essays on the Sociology of Australian Immigrant and Aboriginal Languages*, Canberra: Pacific Linguistics D23, pp. 63–77, 1976.

SHILLING, ALISON, 'Bahamian English: A Non-Continuum?', in D. Day (ed.) *Issues in English Creoles*, Heidelberg: Julius Groos Verlag, 1980.

SMITH, LARRY (ed.), *English for Cross-Cultural Communication*, London: Macmillan, 1980.

SPENCER, JOHN, 'The Anglo-Indians and their Speech: A Socio-linguistic Essay', *Lingua 16*, pp. 57–70, 1966.

SPENCER, JOHN (ed.), *The English Language in West Africa*, London: Longman, 1971.

STEVENSON, R. L., *In the South Seas*, London: Chatto and Windus, 1900.

TODD, LORETO, 'Cameroonian: A Consideration of "What's in a name?"' in I. F. Hancock (ed.) *Readings in Creole Studies*, Ghent: E Story Scientia, pp. 281–94, 1979.

TODD, LORETO, *Some Day Been Dey: West African Pidgin Folktales*, London: Routledge and Kegan Paul, 1979.

TODD, LORETO, *Varieties of English around the World: Cameroon*, Heidelberg: Julius Groos Verlag, 1982.

TURNER, L. D., *Africanisms in the Gullah Dialect*, Chicago: University of Chicago Press; repr. New York: Arno Press, 1969, 1949.

TSANG, ISABELLE, 'English in Hong Kong', unpublished essay, University of Leeds, 1977.

VOORHOEVE, JAN, *Sranan Syntax*, Amsterdam: North Holland Publishing Co., 1962.

VOORHOEVE, JAN, *Den Toe Boekoe di Lukas skrifi. Lucas en Handelingen in oude en nieuwe Surinamse vertaling*, Amsterdam: Bijbelgenootschap Suriname en Nederland, 1966.

VOORHOEVE, JAN, 'The Regularity of Sound Correspondences in a Creole Language (Sranan)', *Journal of African Languages, 9*, pp. 51–69, 1970.

'WALKABOUT', 'Gofrument! All Our Roads Don Yamutu Finis', *Lagos Weekend*, 28 September, p. 14, 1979.

WANG, PEGGY, *Chinese Pidgin English and Theories of Pidginization*, unpublished MA thesis, McGill University, Canada, 1979.

WARD, R. G. *American Activities in the Central Pacific 1798–1870*, Ridgewood, New Jersey: Gregg Press, 1966.

WEBSTER, NOAH, *Dissertation on the English Language*, Boston: Isaiah Thomas and Co., 1789.

WEBSTER'S, *Webster's New World Atlas*, Miami: Kimberley Press, 1982.

Wurm, S. A., 'Pidgins, Creoles and Lingue Franche', *Current Trends in Linguistics 8*, The Hague: Mouton, pp. 999–1021, 1970.

Yardley, Maili, 'Us Two Makules', *Honolulu Advertiser*, 12 March 1980.

Yule, Henry and Burnell, A. C., *Hobson Jobson: Being a glossary of Anglo-Indian words and phrases, and of kindred terms, etymological, geographical and discursive*, London: J. Murray, 1886; repr. London: Routledge and Kegan Paul, 1968.

Zarco, Mariano de, *Dialecto ingles-africano; o Broken-English de la colonia española del Golfo de Guinea*, Turnhout: H. Proost, 1938.

Zettersten, Arne, *The English of Tristan da Cunha*, Lund: C. W. K. Gleerup, 1969.

de Ziel, H. F., *Life At Maripaston*, The Hague: Martinus Nijhoff, 1973.

CHAPTER 3

Case Study One: Cameroon Pidgin English

🔕🔕🔕🔕🔕

3.1 HISTORICAL BACKGROUND

Recent studies of Cameroon[1] suggest that the people in this area may have had commercial dealings with Mediterranean countries two thousand five hundred years ago and it appears likely that the Carthaginian navigator, Hannon, witnessed an erupting Mount Cameroon as he sailed down the West African coast at the beginning of the fifth century BC (Mveng and Belinga Nkoumba, 1978: 41–48). Little is known about this period, however, and it is not until thirteen hundred years later that information became available.

About the eighth century AD the Kanem-Bornu Empire arose and spread from Lake Chad through northern Nigeria and Cameroon, eventually reaching as far south as Foumban (see Maps 3 and 4). In the eleventh century the ruler of Kanem-Bornu, Houmé, was converted to Islam and soon this religion had spread throughout the Empire. The Empire reached its peak of greatness during the reign of Idriss Alaoma (1580–1617), but although it began to decline after Idriss was assassinated in Northern Cameroon, many of the key centres of the Empire survived until the nineteenth century.

European maritime exploration began in the early fifteenth century. By 1472 the island of Fernando Po and the Cameroon coastline were explored by Fernão do Poo. The Portuguese called the river that flowed into the sea near Douala 'Rio dos Camarões' (River of Shrimps) because of the migrating shrimps they encountered in the bay. The name 'Camarões' occurs in 1500 in Juan de la Cosa's map of the area. At first it applied only to the river and the bay, then to the Douala settlement and gradually, by extension, to the whole country. The Portuguese did not settle in

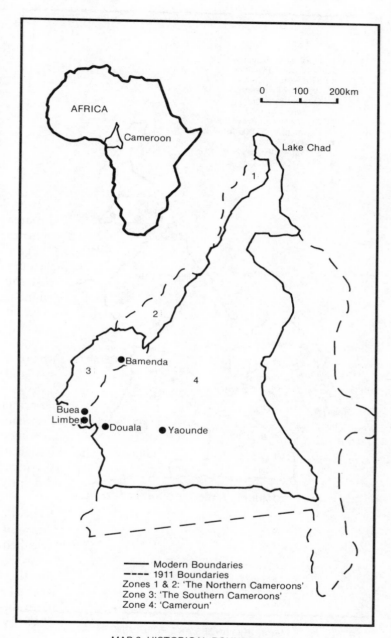

MAP 3: HISTORICAL BOUNDARIES

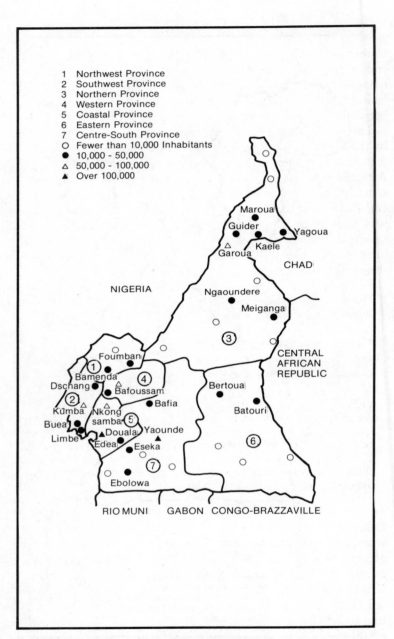

Maroua
Guider   Yagoua
            Kaele
Garoua   CHAD

NIGERIA   Ngaoundere
                    Meiganga
                ③
                        CENTRAL
                        AFRICAN
        Foumban   REPUBLIC
    ①
    Bamenda   ④
Dschang   Bertoua
    ②   Bafoussam
Kumba   Bafia   Batouri
Buea   Nkong
Limbe   samba   ⑤   ⑥
        Douala Yaounde
        Edea   Eseka
                    ⑦
            Ebolowa

RIO MUNI   GABON CONGO-BRAZZAVILLE

MAP 4: PROVINCES AND POPULATION

Cameroon although they traded with the coastal people until the end of the fifteenth century. From 1498, however, the Portuguese navigators tended to go directly from Portugal to the Cape Verde Islands, to the Cape of Good Hope and on to India and so trading between Portugal and Cameroon virtually ceased.

The Portuguese traders were followed by the Dutch and then by the French and the British. It is not easy to say when English was first heard on the Cameroon coast but John Hawkins sold Africans into slavery in 1563 and the influence of the British steadily increased along the entire West African coast until, at the end of the eighteenth century, it could be claimed that English was spoken in all coastal areas thus giving English-speaking sailors a trading advantage (Labarthe, 1803: 70). It is equally hard to be certain about what type of English was being spoken in the area. In 1734 Moore (297) could claim:

> The English have in the River Gambia much corrupted the English language, by Words or Literal translations from the Portuguese . . .

but a form of English was sufficiently well established in Calabar (a Nigerian coastal town with close links with Douala²) to enable a local Efik chief to keep a diary in it from 1785 to 1788:

> 31.1.1788
> about 5 am in aqua Landing with great fog morning so Igoin Down for Landing and I·have send my son on bord Hughes [i.e. SS Hughes] to call his ashor [i.e. ashore] and give him slave [i.e. possibly slaves] and after that I & Egbo Young and Eshen Duk agoin on bord Rogers at 1 clock noon I have send two my father son for mimbo market [i.e. to the market where local alcohol was sold].
>
> (Forde, 1956:115)

English was certainly heard in the north of Cameroon in 1823 when a British team discovered and explored Lake Chad. Shortly after this, in 1827, the British Baptist Missionary Society established a mission in Fernando Po, using some Jamaicans and Krios as catechists. In 1843 Pastor Joseph Merrick, a Jamaican, left Fernando Po and set up a mission station near Douala. This had to be closed down in 1849 but by 1858 Alfred Saker had established a permanent missionary settlement at Victoria (renamed Limbe).

At the same time as the missionaries were active in Fernando Po, British traders from Liverpool and Bristol were encouraged to set up floating hulks as trading posts close to Douala. In 1861 these traders were joined by the German firm of Woermann but by this time a form of English was so well established in the Douala area that Woermann and his employees had to use it in their dealings with the coastal people.

During the last quarter of the nineteenth century the coastal chiefs became increasingly anxious to have Cameroon annexed by the British government,[3] but, to begin with, Britain was not eager to acquire further African colonies. By 1884 Britain had decided to annex Cameroon but even as Edward Hyde Hewett was on his way to sign the treaty with Cameroon chiefs, Nachtigal forestalled him and on 14 July 1884 'Kamerun' became part of the German Empire.

In April 1885 Germany and Britain agreed that the missionary territory in the region of Limbe should remain British. German, however, became the official language of the rest of the country although English in a pidginised form was used by both Germans and Cameroonians, especially on the large coastal plantations. These plantations were established by the Germans and drew their labour force from many different tribal groups and even, in part, from Togo and Benin (formerly Dahomey). Many of the German troops were already conversant with a form of Pidgin English since it was sometimes used as a link language between them and their West African soldiers. By the late nineteenth century Pidgin English had also become the lingua franca of the people of the Bamenda area. Harry Rudin (1938: 358) claims that they clung to it in preference to German or a vernacular language:

In the grasslands of North Western Cameroons there were so many dialects that the various tribes spoke and still speak Pidgin English, to make themselves understood by others in their periodic market days.

In 1911 the boundaries of German Kamerun were drawn when France ceded 275,000 square kilometres of Equatorial Africa to Germany (see Map 3). Germany was not to hold this long, however, because in 1916 the Allies drove the Germans out of Cameroon and the country was partitioned between France and

England (see Map 3) and this partition was ratified by the peace treaty of June 1919. Francophone Cameroon gained its independence on 1 July 1960 and a year later a plebiscite was held in anglophone Cameroon so that people in the 'British Cameroons' could decide whether to unite with 'French Cameroun' or Nigeria. The southern section voted to join their francophone neighbours and the northern section voted for unification with Nigeria. On 1 October 1961, the Federal Republic of Cameroon came into being with French and English as its official languages. In 1972 a referendum was held to allow all Cameroonians to vote on turning the federation into a United Republic. The vote was overwhelmingly in favour and on 2 June 1972, the Federal Republic was replaced by the United Republic of Cameroon.

3.2 SOCIOLINGUISTIC BACKGROUND

Cameroon is a multilingual, multiethnic society. According to the officially sanctioned *Cameroon Today* (1977: 42):

> The geographical variety of Cameroon is matched by the richness of its cultural diversity, which springs from an amazing ethnic patchwork comprising some 200 different groups.

It is not yet certain how many vernacular languages exist in Cameroon although the number cannot be lower than two hundred for a population of under eight million. A sociolinguistic survey carried out by the University of Cameroon in 1977–8 revealed that eighty-nine languages (Koenig: 20) were spoken in urban communities alone, and this figure did not include English, French or Cameroon Pidgin (CP) or the 185 dialects also recorded by the survey (Koenig: Appendix C: 2–4).

As one might expect in such a country, monolingualism is rare but facts on who speaks what language to whom and on what occasions are, as yet, unobtainable. As far as usage of CP goes, Koenig's report suggests that between 30% and 100% of the inhabitants of ten major cities, namely Douala, Yaounde, Bafoussam, Garoua, Ngaoundere (all officially francophone[4]), Limbe, Buea, Kumba, Bamenda and Mamfe (all anglophone), have some command of the language, with the highest percentages of fluent speakers being found in Limbe, Kumba, Bafoussam and Douala.

Four-fifths of the country's population is classified as franco-phone (see Map 5) and so it is French which is the dominant language. The dominance has affected both English and CP in that both are susceptible to influence from French, especially with respect to their vocabularies. Thus Cameroon English has adopted terms like:

baguette – French bread
gendarme – policeman
lycée – secondary school
stage – paid leave of absence

and the CP heard in francophone towns, while similar in phonology and syntax to the CP of anglophone areas, has absorbed a large number of French items including:

bɔngbɔng – sweet (<bonbon)
dantite – identity card (<carte d'identité)
didɔng – I say! Really! (<Dis donc!)
esans – petrol (<essence)
gasɔng! – boy! (<garçon)
patrɔng – boss (<patron)
shef – sir (<chef)
talɔng – high-heeled shoes (<talon).

It is, however, fair to say that French has not, as yet, altered CP's core vocabulary.

It is impossible to be certain when CP established itself in Cameroon but it seems very probable that it was stabilised, expanded and given prestige by the Baptist missionaries who began to evangelise Cameroon from the middle of the nineteenth century. Among these missionaries were eighteen Krio speakers from Sierra Leone, four Krio speakers from Fernando Po, and six speakers of Jamaican English. Thus creole speakers formed over 36% of the expatriate missionaries to Cameroon between 1845 and 1887 (Gwei, 1966: 140ff). Catholic missionaries began to establish themselves in Cameroon from 1890 onwards. They were German speakers but as their prime concern was the spiritual welfare of the Cameroonians on the large coastal plantations, they found that CP was the most useful language for

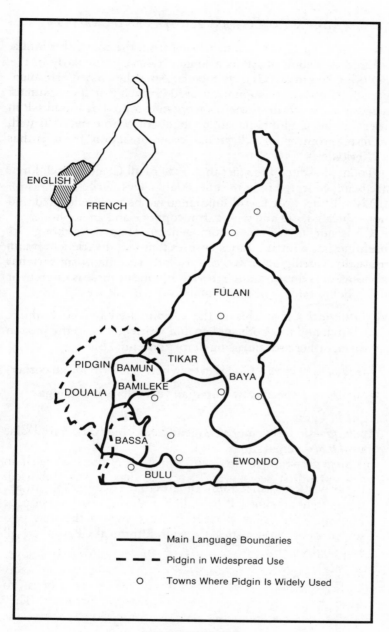

MAP 5: LANGUAGES

instruction. Later, when they moved from the coast, they again realised the value of CP as a lingua franca, particularly in the multilingual grasslands of Bamenda. After the First World War, French Catholic missionaries used French for purposes of religious instruction in the francophone zone, but the missionaries in the anglophone zone, many of whom were Dutch, preferred to use CP. (Personal communication from Father A. Kerkvliet.)

Today, in spite of the fact that 90% of all Cameroon children are being educated in both official languages (Debel, 1977: 66), CP is still the most useful link language between educated and non-educated, old and young, francophone and anglophone.

CP is not, of course, a homogeneous language although its usefulness as a lingua franca ensures that its subvarieties remain mutually intelligible. We can isolate six main subvarieties although it is important to stress that none of these is discrete or easily delimitable. The main subdivisions of CP are:

1. *Liturgical CP* – This is the variant used by the Catholic Church and it is both spoken and written. It is, in the spoken form, rather archaic, using *lif* for existential BE:

   Gɔd lif fɔ ɔl kɔna – God is everywhere (God BE for all corner)

   and it has a specifically Christian vocabulary including:

   grasia – grace
   pekata – sin (now, more frequently, *bad, big bad* – mortal sin, *smɔl bad* – venial sin)
   jɔrɔp fɔ dai –resurrection.

   In the written form it approximates to the orthography of SE, thus often making CP look like a substandard version of English. This point is clear if we compare the first two sentences of the Apostles' Creed in Liturgical CP, spoken CP and English:

Apostles' Belief	A bilif fɔ Gɔd	Apostles' Creed
I believe for God, – the Father whe he get all strong, whe he been make heaven and ground. And for Jesus Christ his only son, we Master, whe he been conceive by the Holy Ghost, and born for the Virgin Maria.	A bilif fɔ wan Gɔd, di Fada wei i gɛt ɔl trɔng, wei i mek hɛvɛn an grɔng. An a bilif fɔ Jisas Kraist wi masa, di wan pikin fɔ God, wei i bɔn fɔ di Holi Gost, an tek man i skin fɔ di smɔl wuman pikin, Maria.	I believe in God, the Father almighty, creator of heaven and earth and in Jesus Christ his only son, Our Lord, who was conceived by the Holy Ghost, and born of the Virgin Mary.

Other Christian groups make use of CP, but none of them as consistently as the Catholic Church.

2. *Coastal CP* – This is the variety used in the Limbe area. It is an almost exclusively unwritten variety and is closer to Sierra Leone Krio than any other variety of CP. In particular, many Coastal\CP speakers use *na* rather than *fɔ* as a locative preposition:

> Coastal CP: *i dei na haus* – He is in the house
> Non-coastal CP: *i dei fɔ haus* – He is in the house
> Krio: *i de na ɔs* – He is in the house.

3. *Grafi CP* – This is the CP of the Bamenda 'Grassfields' (from which the term 'grafi' i.e. 'grasslander' derives). It has many features in common with Liturgical CP and has become the basis for the most widely-used variety of CP in Cameroon today. The Société Biblique used the Grafi CP of old Christians as the basis for its translation of St Mark's Gospel. This translation uses a consistent, phonetically-based orthography

and yet most Cameroonians find it much harder to read than the inconsistent orthography in Catholic translations:

Di fos tok fo di gud nyus fo Jesus Christ God yi Pikin. 2. I bi sem as i di tok fo di buk fo Isaiah, God yi nchinda (Prophet), "Lukam, mi a di sen ma nchinda fo bifo yoa fes weh yi go fix yoa rud fan."

(St Mark, I, 1–2)

4. *Francophone CP* – This CP is found in Douala and in parts of the francophone zone, including several towns, like Bafoussam and Nkongsamba. Like Liturgical CP it tends to be somewhat archaic in structure and vocabulary and it is the only subvariety of CP which still uses German-derived *mitwɔk dei* for 'Wednesday'. Francophone CP is, again, mainly a spoken language, but it has been used in the written medium in a small grammar:

You ouan ouork for mi? – Do you want to work for me?
Yes, a ouanam – Yes, I do
Oui go kouik, you di waka – We will go quickly, you are
sofri plenti walking too slowly

(Aubry, n.d. 54–5)

and for humorous and satirical purposes in French-medium papers:

King fo Toly (The King of Storytelling)
Sista dis tam mared fo solja swit pass mack! (Sister at the moment to be married to a soldier is best of all!) *Tou young woman weh dem sabiam longtam, dem mitam fo market*: (Two young women who had known each other for a long time, met in the market:) *Wéè . . . sista. Wussai you de commot soh. Longtam a noba sy you aguen, wussai you bin go?* (Wei . . . my dear. Where have you come from? It's a long time since I saw you, where have you been?)

(*Courrier Sportif du Bénin*, 28 January 1974)

5. *Bororo CP* – This is the pidgin used by the Cattle Fulani, a nomadic tribe. It differs from the other varieties in its method of indicating possession:

CP generally: *ma wuman, ma pikin* ⎱
Bororo CP: *wuman fɔ mi, pikin fɔ mi* ⎰ my wife, my child.

6. *Makro CP* – This variety is used by young urban dwellers who do not wish to be understood by other CP speakers. It is perhaps best described as an argot based on CP but with lexical items from French, Douala and other local languages and with many CP items modified to make them unrecognisable:

kas	< *kasanggu* (Kaiser+ ngu=hide)	whip
pal	< *palava*	trouble
damji	< gendarme	police, law
reme	< mère	mother, old woman.

3.3 THE PHONOLOGY OF CAMEROON PIDGIN ENGLISH

As we have seen in 3.2, CP is not a homogeneous language. It has not been standardised, has no official orthography and, as a language which is learnt in conjunction with at least one Cameroon vernacular, it tends to reflect the phonology of its speakers' mother tongue. Thus, Douala speakers may use an implosive / ɓ/ in words like ɓoma (boa-constrictor) and ɓrɔda (brother) whereas Bamenda speakers may prefix a homorganic nasal resulting in *mboma* and *mbrɔda*. In addition, phonemic distinctions reflect mother-tongue usage so that, for example, /l/ and /r/ will only tend to occur as distinct phonemes in the CP of speakers whose mother tongues make this distinction, and vowel counts can vary between five and ten, as in the vernaculars. Nevertheless, the phonologies of the vernacular languages in the pidgin-speaking areas of Cameroon are relatively similar and, in addition, all types of CP are being influenced by Cameroon SE.

The description that follows reflects the usage of fluent, articulate, literate anglophones between the ages of twenty and thirty-five because their variety of CP has the greatest prestige. The phonology of this group does not differ radically from that of fluent speakers in other groups because their mobility militates against regional retentions, and the all-pervasive pressure for effective communication with other Cameroonians tends to reduce the number of non-shared characteristics. In addition, the phonology of this variety of CP closely resembles the phonology of Igbo speakers of Nigerian Pidgin, and so is of use across national boundaries.

3.3.1 *Phonemes*

CP has eleven vowel phonemes, seven monophthongs and four diphthongs:

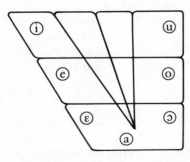 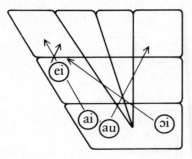

It has twenty-two consonants, although the bracketed phonemes have a very light phonemic load:

	Bilabial	Labio-Dental	Dental	Palato-Alveolar	Palatal	Velar	Glottal
PLOSIVE	p b		t d			k g	
NASAL	m		n		ny	ng	
AFFRICATE				ch (j)			
LATERAL			l r				
FRICATIVE		f (v)	s	sh (ʒ)			h
SEMI-VOWEL	w				y		

3.3.2 *General Comments on CP's Phonology – Vowels*

In CP all syllables are approximately the same length. Length is never phonemic but long allophones may occur in final syllables:

> *a bin chɔp sotei : : :* – I ate and ate and ate.

A type of vowel harmony exists, especially in the speech of older Cameroonians, in that one rarely finds /i/ and /e/, /u/ and /o/, /e/ and /ɛ/ or /o/ and /ɔ/ in consecutive syllables or polysyllabic words:

> *bɛlɛ* – stomach
> *palava* – trouble
> *kaiman* – crocodile
> *nyamangɔrɔ* – snail.

Vowels tend to be nasalised when they occur in the vicinity of a nasal consonant, the nasality often being a feature of the entire syllable:

> *mãtutu* – type of palmwine
> *nĩngã* – slave, inferior person.

In CP the initial segment of a diphthong tends to be more prominent than the second with the result that, in rapid speech, the second element is occasionally lost:

> *bɔi / bɔ^i / bɔ* – boy
> *daiman / da^{i}man / daman* – corpse
> *teik / te^{i}k / tek* – take
> *taun / ta^{u}n / tan* – town

and when diphthongs occur finally in a word, they are marginally longer than when they occur initially or medially.

3.3.3 *Consonants*

In CP we can establish twenty-two consonantal phonemes by means of minimal pairs. In some idiolects /r/ and /l/ are not distinguished but a sound /ʌ/ is used for both. With increased education, however, most speakers distinguish the sounds in words which come from either English or French. Thus they may still use /ʌ/ in words like *makala*, a local food, but they would aim at /l/ in *lait* and *lise* ('light' and 'school') and /r/ in *rait* ('right').

Although twenty-two consonantal phonemes can be established for CP, /v, j, and ʒ/ seldom occur. In addition, voiced plosives tend to be devoiced when they occur in word final position, and thus there is very little auditory difference between:

bak (back) and *bag* (bag)

hat (heart) and *haḍ* (hard)

bap (slap) and *baḅ* (cut hair).

It is possible that this tendency to devoice was established due to the influence of German speakers of CP but, in practice, it rarely, if ever, causes any confusion.

There are two other main differences between SE consonantal patterns and those of CP. Consonant clusters (other than homorganic nasal+consonant) are rare in CP. When clusters beginning with /s/ occur there is a strong tendency to insert a vowel between the /s/ and the following consonant, a vowel which may differ according to the vowel in adjacent syllables:

s"mɔl – small

sⁱtik – tree, stick, guava.

Two periods of lexical borrowing can, indeed, be seen in items derived from English words beginning with s + 1/2 consonants, thus:

EARLY	RECENT
kwis – squeeze	*s"kwanda* – squander
krash – scratch	*s"kru* – screw
trenja – visitor	*sⁱtraik* – strike
tanap – stand	*s"tadiɔm* – stadium
tei – stay	*sⁱtim* – steam.

And secondly, /ng/ can occur initially in CP:

ngɔngngɔng – tin for measuring quantities of rice, etc.

ngkanda   – hide, skin.

3.4. CP'S LEXICON

CP's vocabulary is derived largely from English (although it seems likely that many items were reinforced by German cognates) and all items of the lexicon of international English are potential CP material. In addition to items from English, however, we also find lexical contributions from the local vernaculars, from Krio, Portuguese, Yoruba, Kongo, Twi, Ewe, German, Latin and increasingly from French. Words borrowed recently into CP are from English and French and all such borrowings have been made to fit CP's phonology:

fɛdɛrɛshɔn – federation
yunivasiti – university
konje – holiday (<congé)
sangkant – fifty francs (<cinquante).

Many calques occur in CP, as will be indicated in the following vocabulary study, and circumlocutions exist:

jus dɛm gɔd haus – synagogue (Jews they God House)

although these are less common in CP than in other pidginised languages and even the quoted example is a coinage of missionaries, rather than of local people.

The following sections (3.4.1–12) set out the core vocabulary of CP. All the items occur regularly in spontaneous conversations, and Swadesh's wordlist,[5] modified to take account of CP's individuality, has been the basis of my selection. Illustrative sentences, taken from recordings made in Cameroon, are provided.

3.4.1 CP's Core Vocabulary – Numbers
The numbers all derive from English, thus:

wan, tu, tri, foa, faiv, siks, sɛven, et, nain, tɛn, ɛlɛvɛn, twɛf, tɛtin, twɛnti, tɛti, fɔti, fifti, wan hɔndrɛd, wan tausan.

In the speech of older anglophones and of uneducated francophones, there is evidence of a different number system, based on *tali*, 'ten':

wan tali – 10
wan tali wan – 11
wan tali foa – 14
tu tali – 20
tu tali nain – 29
faiv tali – 50
tɛn tali – 100

but this system is rapidly losing ground to the English system.

3.4.2 *Body Parts and Functions*

ai – eye (< Eng. 'eye')
　　1. *Ai no di shut bif* (eye no cont. marker shoot animal) – It
does no harm to look.

anus – anus (< English 'anus')
　　2. *Man no fit luk fɔ ɔda man i anus if i no sho i on* (man no fit
look for other man he anus if he no show he own) – A person
cannot look at another's shortcomings without revealing his
own.

bɛlɛ – stomach, seat of the emotions (< Eng. 'belly')
　　3. *I bin vɛks fɔ i bɛlɛ* (he past time marker vex for his belly) –
He was annoyed.
Bɛlɛ frequently occurs in idiomatic expressions and calques:
gɛt bɛlɛ – become pregnant
bɛlɛ bait – stomach pain, cancer (belly bite)
was bɛlɛ – last child (wash belly).

biabia – hair (< ? Eng. 'beard-beard', ? Port. 'barba')
　　4. *Man wei i bɔn i biabia na i go fɔs hia di smɛl* (man who he
burn he hair BE he go first hear the smell) – We are likely to
notice things which affect our comfort.

blɔd – blood (< Eng. 'blood' reinforced perhaps by Ger. 'Blut')
　　5. *Hau i blɔd blak so?* (how he blood black/dark so?) – How is
it that the blood is so dark?

bɔbi – breast (< ? Eng. dialect 'bubby', ? N'ki 'bobei' – 'breast')[6]
　　6. *Bɔbi dɛm laik dɔg i on* (breast they like dog he own) – Your
breasts hang! (An insult to a woman.)
bɔbi-mɔt – nipple, is a calque.

bon – bone (< Eng. 'bone')
　　7. *Awuf i no gɛt bon* (something-for-nothing he no get bone) –
What we get without effort will be of little value.

chuk – have intercourse with, pierce, prick, thorn (< Fula 'chuk'
　　– 'pierce, prick', Eng. dial. 'chook' – 'prick')
　　8. *Chuk yu mami!* – Have intercourse with your mother! (This
is perhaps the strongest insult in CP. Sometimes it is reduced to
Yu mami and accompanied with the gesture of a cupped right
hand with the palm facing the man who is being insulted.)

fes– face (<Eng. 'face')
  9. *I fes lɔng* – She has a long face (literal, not metaphorical).
'*Fes*' only occurs in educated speakers' usage. Uneducated
speakers would prefer:
I hɛd lɔng – She has a long head/face.

fut – foot, leg, trouser leg (<Eng. 'foot' and Ger. 'Fuss')
  10. *A wan brok ma fut* (I inceptive aspect break my foot) – I
almost broke my leg.
  11. *Bai mi trausa wei i gɛt pɛnsɛl fut* (Buy me trousers which
he get pencil foot) – Buy me slacks which taper.

han – hand, arm, sleeve (<Eng. 'hand' and Ger. 'Hand')
  12. *A laik gaun wei i gɛt lɔng han* – I like dresses with long
sleeves.
Han also occurs in the calques   *manhan* – right
                                      wuman han – left.

hɛd – head, skull, face (< Eng. 'head')
  13. *I hɛd bin bigin gro* – His head began to grow.

las – buttocks, bottom part, dregs (<Eng. 'last' reinforced by
  Eng. 'your ass' segmented as 'you rass' and Fula 'ras' –
  buttocks)
  14. *Dres las smɔl* (Dress buttocks small) – Move up a bit.
(CP 'dress' probably derives from military 'Dress!' meaning
'Get into the correct place in line!')

maut – mouth (<Eng. 'mouth')
  15. *Wɛti dei fɔ pikin i maut?* – What's in the child's mouth?
Two common calques occur using /mɔt/, the earlier form of
maut:
bɔbi mɔt – nipple (breast mouth)
doa mɔt – door.

mbanja – rib (<Bakweri 'mbandʒoa' – 'ribs')
  16. *Dɛm bin mek Ifa fɔ Adam i mbanja* – Eve was made out of
Adam's rib.

mblakɔt – penis (< ? Eng. 'black out')
  17. *Dɛm bin kɔt pikin i mblakɔt* – They circumcised the child.

nkanda – hide, skin, occasionally bark of tree (<Kikongo
  'kanda' – skin, rind, peel, bark)

18. *Hau ma nkanda trɔng so?* – Why is my skin so coarse and rough?

nos – nose (<Eng. 'nose' possibly reinforced by Ger. 'Nase')
  19. *Waitman i nos shap plenti* – European noses are very pointed.
  The calque *nos hol* – nostril – occurs.

ɔnda-han – armpit (<Eng. 'under hand')
  20. *I bin putam fɔ iɔnda han* – She put it in her armpit.

pima – vagina (<Twi 'ε-pim' – clitoris)
  21. *Yu mami i pima!* – This is another CP insult, usually levelled at a man, and meaning 'Your mother was promiscuous.'

pis – urine, urinate (<Eng. 'piss')
  22. *Wuman fit pis fɔ bɔtul?* – Can a woman urinate into a bottle? This is the refrain of a worksong, often sung to annoy a passing woman.

si mun – menstruate (<Eng. 'see moon' calqued from local vernaculars)
  23. *I dɔn finish fɔ si mun* – She has stopped menstruating.
  The expression for 'menstruating for the first time' is *gεt flaua* (get flower) and the equivalent expression in Cameroon English is 'germinate'.

skin – body (<Eng. 'skin', calqued from vernacular usage)
  24. *I gεt fat skin* – She is fat (This is meant as a compliment).

shit – excrement, excrete (<Eng. 'shit')
  25. *Εlεfan di shit hawe i di chɔp* (elephant cont. marker shit how it cont. marker eat) – By their fruits shall ye know them.

tit – tooth, teeth (<Eng. 'teeth')
  26. *Tit an tɔng sabi fait* – Even close friends can quarrel.

tɔng – tongue (<Eng. 'tongue')
  In CP, *tɔng* is never used as a synonym for 'language' which would be translated by 'tɔk', for example:
  kɔntri tɔk – vernacular language.

3.4.3 Family/Kinship

ba/baba/pa/papa – father, senior male relative, old man (<Eng. 'pa/papa', Cameroon vernaculars 'pa/papa/ba/baba')
   27. *Ba, yu wɛl?* – Are you all right, Father?

bo – name greeting to a friend of the same sex (<Eng. dial. 'bo' – term of address, Mende 'bo' – term of address, and perhaps French 'beau')
   28. *A sei, bo, a bɛg, blo mi wan tausan* – I say, friend, lend me 1,000 francs, please.

brɔda – brother, close male relative, man from the same village (<Eng. 'brother' influenced by vernacular usage)
   29. *Dis na ma brɔda* – This is my brother (i.e. we are from the same village).

fɔlɔ bak – younger sibling (<Eng. 'follow back' calqued from local vernaculars):
   30. *A no gɛt fɔlɔ bak. A bi was bɛlɛ.* – I have no younger brothers or sisters. I'm the last child.

ma/mami/mama – mother, close senior female relative, respectful term of address to an older woman or to a woman with children (<Eng. 'ma/mama/mami', and Cameroonian vernaculars 'ma/mami/mama')
   31. *Usai mama dei?* – Where is the lady of the house?

man pikin – boy, son, young male (<Eng. 'man' + Port. 'pequeno', calqued on vernacular usage)
   32. *Tek dis man pikin gɔt, kɔmbi* – Take this young male goat, friend.

mbanya – a co-wife (<Bakweri 'mbaɲa' – 'co-wife')
   33. *A dɔn tɛl papa pikin mek wi tek mbanya wan taim* – I have told my husband (the father of children) that we should take a co-wife as soon as possible.

mbombo – namesake, a close relationship (<? Temne 'a-bombo' – 'vagina') Mbombos often address each other as 'nem' (<Eng. 'name')
   34. *Trisa na ma mbombo* – Teresa is my namesake.
   35. *Nem, usai yu di go?* – Namesake, where are you going?

miyɔ – in-law (<Bakweri 'muyɔ' – 'in-law')
36. *I bi dat king i miyɔ* – He was that king's son-in-law.

pikin – child, young of an animal (<Port. 'pequeno' – 'little')
37. *Yu gɛt hau mɛni pikin?* – How many children have you?

sisi/sista/titi – sister, especially younger sister, close female relative, female from the same village of approximately the same age (<Eng. 'sister' and Douala 'titi' – 'little girl' reinforced by vernacular usage)
38. *Sisi, yu dɔng kam!* – Welcome, Sister.

was/wɔs bɛlɛ – last child (<Eng. 'wash belly' calqued on vernacular usage). See 30.

wuman pikin – daughter, female child, young female (<Eng. 'woman' reinforced by Efik 'uman' – 'woman' + Port. 'pequeno' – 'little', calqued on vernacular usage)
39. *I tek dat king i wuman pikin* – He took (in marriage) that king's daughter.

yawɔ – concubine, 'country' wife (<Yoruba 'yàwɔ́' – 'wife, concubine')
40. *I bin lɛf dat i yawɔ an i tek sɔm ɔda man i njumba* – He left his country wife and took (in marriage) another man's lover.

3.4.4. *People/Professions*

dɔkta – doctor (<Eng. 'doctor')
41. *Dɔkta no bin hɛlɛp so a bin go si malam* – The doctor didn't help so I went to see the medicine man.

draiva – driver (bus, train, taxi, mammy-waggon) (<Eng. 'driver')
42. *Sing trɔng, a bɛg, mek draiva no slip* – Sing loudly, please, so that the driver won't fall asleep.

fɔn – chief (<Bamenda vernaculars 'fɔn' – 'chief')
43. *Fɔn bin gi ɔda sei mek i shidɔng* – The Fon gave the order that he should sit down/stay.

hɔntaman – hunter (<Eng. 'hunter' + 'man')
44. *Bad lɔk bif no di si hɔntaman* – A doomed animal doesn't see the hunter.

kapɛnta – carpenter (< Eng. 'carpenter')
45. *Yu ting sei na kapɛnta klin mi?* – Do you think I was made by a carpenter? i.e. Do you think I have no feelings?

karia – carrier, bearer (< Eng. 'carrier')
46. *Karia go totam fɔ hɛd* – The bearer will carry it on his head.

kɔmbi – close friend (< Eng. 'company'). See 32.

malam – one with magical powers, one skilled in traditional medicine, love potions (< Arabic (via Hausa) 'mallam' – 'a priest'). See 41.

man – man, male, person (< Eng. 'man' reinforced by German 'Mann'). See 2.

mukala – white person, person with light-coloured skin (< Douala 'mukara' – 'white-skinned person'). Other terms used for 'white person' are, *waitman*, *bakra* and *beke*, the latter two being most common in Igbo settlements.
47. *Di pikin rɛd laik mukala* – The child is the colour of a European (i.e. reddish/yellow like a European).

mumu – mute, a fool (< Twi 'múmú' – 'mute', 'deaf and dumb')
48. *I bin tɔk laik sei a bi mumu* – He spoke as if I were a fool.

nchinda – messenger of the fon (< Bamenda vernaculars 'nchinda')
49. *I bin sɛn nchinda mek i as sei na wɛti* – He sent his messenger to ask what was going on.

nggɔmbi – ghost, spirit, more recently 'false God' (< Bakweri 'ngambi' 'sorcerer, diviner' reinforced by Kikongo 'nzumbi' – 'ghost')
50. *I sabi tɔk fɔ nggɔmbi* – He can communicate with spirits.

ningga – slave, subservient person (< ? Eng. 'nigger')
51. *I bi ningga fɔ mi* – As far as I am concerned he is worthless.

njumba – lover, often a male lover (< Bakweri 'jumba' – 'lover'). See 40.

nɔs – nurse (< Eng. 'nurse')
52. *Dis na ma bebi-nɔs* – This is my 'nursemaid', i.e. my child's

minder. (*Bebi* is becoming increasingly common in CP but it is not replacing *pikin*, except in the speech of more affluent CP users.)

tifman – thief (< Eng. 'thief' + 'man')
53. *Tifman i haus na soso mɛdɛsɛn* – A thief's house is well protected. (*Mɛdɛsɛn* can be used for a 'talisman' and for 'mechanical gadgetry' as well as for 'health cures'.)

ticha – teacher (< Eng. 'teacher')
54. *Ticha tɔk sei pikin gɛt sɛns* – The teacher says the child is intelligent.

treda – trader (< Eng. 'trader')
55. *Treda bin tek tɛn tausan an chenji-chenji* – The trader accepted 10,000 francs and some things in exchange.

trenja – visitor, guest (< Eng. 'stranger' influenced by vernacular usage)
56. *Trenja no di kuk nkanda* – A visitor does not cook hide/tough meat, i.e. visitors do not have time for prolonged activities.

wuman – woman, female (< Eng. 'woman' reinforced by Efik 'uman' – 'woman, female')
57. *Mɔni had, wuman no sabi* – Money is hard to get but women don't understand that.

3.4.5. *Animals*
More and more animal names are being adopted by CP speakers, names like *frɔg, laiɔn, lisad, taiga, vɔlcha* but the following list gives only those items which could occur in all varieties of CP.

alata / arata – mouse, rat, rodent (< Eng. 'rat')
58. *Arata nɛva hapi wɛn pusi bɔn pikin* – Mice are never happy when cats have kittens.

ans – ant (< Eng. 'ants')
59. *I go fain wan smɔl ans* – He went to look for one little ant.

babu – baboon (< Eng. 'baboon')
60. *Mɔnki tɔk sei babu wowo* – The monkey says the baboon is ugly.

bɛd / bɔd – bird (< Eng. 'bird')

61. *Trɔki tek wan fɛda fɔ ɛni bɛd* – Tortoise takes one feather from each bird.

bif – animal, meat (< Eng. 'beef')
62. *Dɛn i bin mek ɔl kain ting; i mek bush; i mek bif tu* – Then he created everything; he created the forest; he created animals too.

bushbif – undomesticated animal, game meat (< Eng. 'bush' + 'beef')
63. *Bushbif swit pas ɔda wan dɛm* – Bush-meat is more delicious than other kinds of meat.

chiga / jiga – jigger, sand-fly (< Carib 'sikë' – 'sandfly')
64. *Chiga dei fɔ i fut, chiga dei fɔ i han, chiga dei fɔ i maut sɛf* – There were jiggers in his feet, in his hands and even in his mouth.

chukuchukubif – porcupine (< Eng. dial. 'chook' – 'pierce' reinforced by Fula 'chuk' – 'pierce, prick' + Eng. 'beef')
65. *Stik bin fɔl fɔ rod kil chukuchukubif* – A tree fell across the road and killed a porcupine.

dɔg – dog(< Eng. 'dog')
66. *I gɛt dɔg bɔt i no gɛt wuman* – He has a dog but he hasn't got a wife.

ɛlɛfan – elephant (< Eng. 'elephant'). See 25.

fawul – fowl, chicken (< Eng. 'fowl')
67. *Hɔk tek wan smɔl fawul dasham fɔ i pikin* – The hawk took one little chicken and gave it to her children.
Many words are built on *fawul*:
  man fawul – cock
  bush fawul – guinea fowl
  dɔk fawul – duck.

got – goat (< Eng. 'goat')
68. *A gɛt sɔm fain tori fɔ tɔk. Diswan i bi fɔ sɔm tu fulish got* – I have a good story to tell. This one is about two foolish goats.
As with *fawul*, *got* can be used as a building block for related words, thus:
wuman pikin got – female kid
    ship got – sheep.

hɔk – hawk (< Eng. 'hawk') (The hawk, like the tortoise, is a common character in folktales.) See 67.

hɔnibi – bee (<Eng. 'honeybee')
  69. *I bin chɔp daso hɔnibi an nggumsi* – He ate only bees and locusts.

hɔs – horse (< Eng. 'horse') This word is hardly ever heard near the coast because horses could not live there. In the early part of this century, horses were often used by missionaries in the Bamenda area.
  70. *Fada no laik dat hɔs agen* – Father (i.e. a priest) does not like that horse any more.

kaiman – crocodile, alligator (<Carib. 'kaiman' – 'crocodile')
  71. *Yu no gɛt diskain kwa. Diswan kaiman* – You haven't got this kind of bag. This one is crocodile skin.

karanggwa – lice, fleas (<Mandinka 'garangwa' – 'flea, louse')
  72. *Karanggwa di hambag mi taim no dei* – The lice are really tormenting me.

kau – cow (<Eng. 'cow') This word is very rarely heard in CP, but *bush kau* meaning a type of 'buffalo' is quite common:
  73. *Dɛm di glad fɔseka dɛm dɔn kil man pikin bush kau* – They are happy because they've just killed a bull calf buffalo.

kɔting gras – type of edible rodent somewhat bigger than a buck rabbit (<Eng. 'cutting' + 'grass' calqued on vernacular usage)
  74. *Di chɔp bin tu fain! ɔl kain ting dei fɔ tebu; kɔting gras dei dei; mimbo dei dei . . .* – The food was exceptionally good. There were all kinds of things on the table; there was cutting-grass there and alcohol . . .

mboma – boaconstrictor (<Kikongo 'mboma' – 'python')
  75. *Mboma bin tɔk sei: 'Dei no bi wan'* – Boaconstrictor has said: 'There will always be another day.'

mɔnki – monkey (<Eng. 'monkey'). See 60.

mɔskito – mosquito (<Eng. 'mosquito')
  76. *Mɔskito laik ia taim no dei bɔt ia no bin gri mariam* – The mosquito loved the ear dearly but the ear would not agree to marry him.

nggumsi – locusts – a delicacy in Cameroon (<Mandankwe 'ŋgumsi' – locusts). See 69.

njangga – crayfish, smallfish (<Bakweri 'janga' – 'small crayfish') 77. *Di sup no swit. Njangga no dei* – The stew is not tasty. There are no crayfish in it.

nyamangɔrɔ – snail (<Bakweri 'ɲamaŋgɔrɔ' – 'snail') 78. *Trɔki laik fɔ mek palava so i disaid sei i go mek kɔni fɔ nyamangɔrɔ* – Tortoise loved stirring things up so he decided to play a trick on Snail.

pusi – cat (<Eng. 'pussy'). See 58.

trɔki – tortoise, the trickster hero of Cameroon folktales (<Eng. dial. 'torkle' reinforced by Port. 'tartaruga'). See 78.

3.4.6. *Objects/Natural Phenomena*

aiɔn – iron (<Eng. 'iron') 79. *Aiɔn no fit hɔt if yu no putam fɔ faia* – Iron cannot get hot if you do not put it into the fire.

akis – axe (<Eng. 'axe') 80. *I tek akis kɔt stik* – He takes his axe to cut down a tree.

ashis – ash, ashes (< Eng. 'ashes') 81. *Fɔ seka wɛti dɛm bin put ashis fɔ dat man i hɛd?* – Why did they put ash on that man's head?

bris – breeze, wind, air (<Eng. 'breeze') 82. *Trɔki bin go waka tek smɔl bris* – Tortoise went out for a walk to get some fresh air.

bush – uncultivated area, forest, wild, uncivilised (<Eng. 'bush') 83. *Bush dɔn opɛn, grafiman di sabi buk!* – The wilderness has opened, now that a grasslander is literate!

(m)bundu – camwood (<Mende 'bundui' – 'camwood') 84. *Dɛm put mbundu plenti fɔ dɛm skin* – They cover their bodies with camwood colouring.

chukuchuku – thorn (<Eng. dial. 'chook' – 'pierce' reinforced by Fula 'chuk' – 'pierce, prick')

85. *Dɛm bin put chukuchuku kap fɔ Jisɔs i hɛd* – They put a crown of thorns on the head of Jesus.

deiklin – dawn (<Eng. 'day' + 'clean' calqued on vernacular usage)
86. *Deiklin an a wikɔp fɔ shapshap mɔning* – Dawn came and I got up very early in the morning.

doamɔt – door, doorway (<Eng. 'door' + 'mouth' calqued on vernacular usage)
87. *I di soso tanap fɔ doamɔt* – She's always standing at the door.

dɔti – dirt, dust, earth (<Eng. 'dirty' reinforced by Twi 'dɔté' – 'soil, earth, clay')
88. *I tek dɔti fɔ i han; i masham; i mekam tɔn laik man* – He took earth into his hands; he squeezed it; he made it turn into the shape of a man.

ɛg – egg (<Eng. 'egg')
89. *Bɛlɛ wuman no gɛt fɔ chɔp ɛg* – A pregnant woman must not eat eggs.

faia – fire (<Eng. 'fire'). See 79.

fam – farm (<Eng. 'farm')
90. *Mami di wɔk fam* – My mother cultivates the farm.

fɛda – feather (<Eng. 'feather'). See 61.

flaua – flower (<Eng. 'flower')
91. *Dat shipgot di soso chɔp man i flaua* – That sheep is always eating people's flowers.

frut – fruit (<Eng. 'fruit')
92. *ɛni kain frut dei* – There were all kinds of fruit there.

gras – grass (<Eng. 'grass')
93. *Mek yu giam gud gras* – Give it good grass to eat.

grɔng/graun – ground, world, earth (< Eng. 'ground')
94. *Trɔbul go kam fɔ dis graun* – Suffering will come to the world.

hama – hammer (< Eng. 'hammer' reinforced by Ger. 'Hammer')
  95. *Dɛn i bin tek hama brok ston* – Then he took a hammer to break some stones.
(The adjectival *hama-hama* meaning 'enormous' as in *sɔm hama hama ɛlɛfan* may derive from a reduplicated form of 'hammer'.)

haus – house (< Eng. 'house')
  96. *Mek wi tai tri haus fɔ hia* – Let us build three houses/huts here.

hil/mauntɛn – hill, mountain (< Eng. 'hill, mountain')
  97. *Datwan na hil, ɔ na maunten ɔ na wɛti?* – Is that a hill or a mountain or what?

kɔbɔ/kɔpɔ – copper, money (< Eng. 'copper')
  98. *Kɔpɔ di tɔk* – Money talks.

kɔntri – home area, maternal village (< Eng. 'country' influenced by vernacular usage)
  99. *Lamso man di soso tɔk kɔntri tɔk* – Lamso people invariably speak their vernacular, i.e. Lamso.

laitning – lightning (< Eng. 'lightning')
  100. *Ren fɔl, tɔnda kam, laitning tu* – The rain fell, the thunder started and the lightning as well.

mbanda – attic, space between rafters and roof, used for drying fish, corn or other food (< Hausa 'baandaa' – 'drying fish or meat over fire')
  101. *I bin put dat kɔn fɔ i mbanda* – He put that corn in his loft.

mun – moon, month (< Eng. 'moon')
  102. *Dat hafhaf mun dei* – There's a crescent moon.

nait/nɛt tam – night (< Eng. 'night/night + time')
  103. *A no laik waka fɔ nɛt tam* – I don't like being out when it is dark.
The most usual divisions of the day are:
  dei klin – dawn
  san tam – hours of daylight
  nɛt tam – hours of darkness

but *mɔning taim, iwining taim* are becoming more widespread as are the *sɔn* and *nait* pronunciations of 'sun' and 'night'.

palava – trouble, controversy, problem (< Portuguese 'palavra' – 'word, speech'). See 78.

pɔtɔpɔtɔ – mud, slime (< Kikongo 'pɔtɔpɔtɔ' – 'mud')
104. *Dat pɔtɔpɔtɔ di soso kɛrɛng kɛrɛng* – That mud is terribly slippery.

ren – rain (< Eng. 'rain'). See 100.

rod – road, path, way (< Eng. 'road'). See 65.

ruf – roof (< Eng. 'roof')
104a. *Dɛm no di yus gras agɛn fɔ ruf* – They no longer use thatching for roofs.
(In many idiolects *zinc* is used to mean 'roof'.)

shado – shadow, soul, reflection (< Eng. 'shadow' influenced by vernacular usage)
105. *Di dɔg si sɔm shado fɔ wata* – The dog saw his reflection in the water.

sid – seed (< Eng. 'seed')
106. *An sɔm sid bin fɔl fɔ sɔm graun wei i gɛt ston plenti* – And some seed fell on stony ground.

skai – sky (< Eng. 'sky')
107. *Wɛti dei fɔ ɔp, fɔ skai?* – What's up there, in the sky?
(Often the phrase *fɔ ɔp* is used instead of *fɔ skai*.)

smok – smoke (< Eng. 'smoke')
108. *Wɛn i bin dɔn bɔn dat i haus, smok bin dei fɔ ɔl kɔna* – When he had burnt his house, there was smoke everywhere.

spia – spear (< Eng. 'spear')
109. *Di spia no bin gri kil mami wata* – The spear was unable (did not agree) to kill the female water spirit.

stik – tree, stick, guava (< Eng. 'stick' influenced by vernacular usage). See 65.

sta – star (< Eng. 'star')
110. *Mi, a no laik nɛt tam wei i blak plenti, wei sta i no dei an*

mun tu i no dei – I don't like the nights that are very dark, when there are no stars and no moon either.

ston / ton – stone (< Eng. 'stone'). See 106.

tɔnda – thunder (< Eng. 'thunder'). See 100.

wata – water, lake, river, spring, tear (< Eng. 'water' influenced by vernacular usage)
111. *Smɔl wata di rɔn go fɔ big wata* – Small rivers flow into bigger ones.
Wata occurs in the calques:
> *ai wata* – tears
> *hɔnggri wata* – thirst
> *maut wata* – saliva.

yia – year, age (< Eng. 'year' perhaps reinforced by Ger. 'Jahr')
112. *Hau mɛni yia yu gɛt?* – How old are you?

3.4.7. Food[7]

akara – a type of pancake made from bean flour (< Yoruba 'akara' – 'cake made of beans, ground and fried')
113. *Na daso akara witi ashu ɔ witi banana i sabi chɔp* – It's only akara and either ashu or bananas that he likes to eat.

ashu – a type of vegetable paste (< Mungaka 'ashu' – 'paste'). See 113.

banana – banana, plantain (< Kikongo 'banana' – 'type of banana'). See 113.

bif – meat, animal (< Eng. 'beef')
114. *Dɛm di kɔl i sei 'nyam-bofe' fɔseka sei i sabi chɔp bif taim no dei* – They call her 'beef-master' because she eats a lot of meat.

bins – bean, beans (< Eng. 'beans')
115. *I tek bins grainam mek akara* – She took beans, ground them and made akara.

chichi – small fritters made from cornflour (< Igbo 'chīchī' – 'fritter')
116. *Di chichi fain* – The chichi are delicious.

egusi – ground melon seeds used in cooking (< Yoruba 'ɛgusi' – 'food made from melon seeds')
117. *A bɛg, gif mi egusi fɔ tɛn frank* – Please give me ten francs worth of egusi.

fis / fish – fish (< Eng. 'fish' perhaps influenced by Ger. 'Fisch')
118. *Fish di kɔs plenti naunau* – Fish is very expensive at the moment.

fufu – pounded yam/cocoyam/tuber (< Yoruba 'fufu' – 'pounded yam')
119. *Dat sup di mek fufu pas laik krismas* – That stew makes it extremely easy to eat fufu (That soup cont. marker make fufu pass like Christmas).

gari – grated cassava (< Yoruba 'gari' – 'grated cassava')
120. *Ibo dɛm sabi chɔp gari* – Igbos love gari (Igbo they know eat gari).

grɔnɔt / graunɔt – ground nut, peanut (< Eng. 'ground' + 'nut')
121. *Dat i grɔnɔt chɔp fain bad* – Her meal in which she used groundnuts (as a sauce) was really delicious.

jakatɔ – garden egg (< Wolof 'jakato' – 'garden egg')
122. *Jam pas dai mɔnki chɔp pepe tɔk sei na jakatɔ* – In a severe famine a monkey will eat pepper and call it garden eggs. (Extremity pass death monkey eat pepper talk say be garden egg).

kasava – vegetable with starchy roots (< Eng. 'cassava' probably through Portuguese. The origin of the word may lie in the Taino language of Haiti.) The following is a children's chant:
123. *Hu bin du? Hu bin du dat kaina man man ting?*
Hu bin shit? Hu bin shit fɔ mami kasava?
Hu bin du . . .
Who did it? Who did that terrible thing?
Who excreted? Who excreted on Mami's cassava?

kɔki – type of food made from nuts or cɔrn and wrapped in banana leaves (< Bamenda vernaculars 'kɔki' – as above)
124. *Kɔki kɔn fain pas kɔki grɔnɔt* – Cocky corn is nicer than cocky groundnut.

koko – cocoyam (< Twi 'kooko' – 'edible root')

125. *Koko no di pas fain if njamanjama no dei* – Cocoyams are not easily eaten if there are no greens.

kola – type of nut, offered and eaten as a sign of friendship and also to keep people awake (< Temne 'k-ɔla' – 'cola nut')
126. *Yu no go chɔp kola witi mi?* – Aren't we going to eat kola together?

kɔn – corn (< Eng. 'corn'). See 125.

mbɔngga – type of flat fish (< Bakweri 'bɔnga' – 'flat fish')
127. *A bin di soso fain mbɔngga bɔt a no siam* – I looked everywhere for mbonga but I couldn't see any.

mbɔr – a groundnut ball like *kɔki grɔnɔt* (< Lamso 'mbɔr' – 'groundnut delicacy')
128. *Dat pikin sabi chɔp mbɔr witi miɔndɔ* – That child loves eating mbor and miyondo.

milik – milk (< Eng. 'milk' possibly reinforced by Ger. 'Milch')
129. *Di pikin drai fɔseka i no gri drink milik* – The child is thin because he won't drink milk.

mimbo – palmwine, alcohol (< ? Bakweri 'mimbo' – 'wine')
130. *Mimbo di kul hat* – Alcohol consoles (mimbo cont. marker cool heart).
There are other words for types of palmwine such as *matutu* 'sweet palmwine' but *mimbo* is widely used for all types of local and imported drinks, including, occasionally, soft drinks.

miɔndɔ – type of paste made with grated cassava and shaped like a stick before being wrapped in a leaf (< Douala '*miɔndɔ*' – as above). See 128.

njamanjama – greens, spinach-type vegetable (< Lamso 'njaman-jama' – 'greens'). See 126.

njangga – small crustacean, dried and used in cooking (< Bakweri 'janga' – as above)
131. *I drai laik njangga* – She's as thin as a dried crayfish.

nɔnɔ – buttermilk (< Mandinka 'nɔnɔ' – 'cow's milk')
132. *Na daso mi wan sabi drink nɔnɔ* – I'm the only one (in the family) who drinks buttermilk.

MODERN ENGLISHES: PIDGINS AND CREOLES

ntumbu – edible maggots, regarded by some as a delicacy
(< Mandinka 'tumbu' – 'edible grub')
   133. *Di ting swit bad. Yu no sabi sei frenshman dɛm di glad fɔ
   bai ntumbu?* – They are really delicious. Don't you know that
   the French are eager to buy ntumbu?

ɔkrɔ – okra (< Igbo 'ɔkurɔ' – 'okra')
   134. *ɔkrɔ di kɛrɛng kɛrɛng smɔl* – Okra is somewhat slippery
   when cooked.

ɔnyɔn – onion (< Eng. 'onion')
   135. *A no go bai dat i ɔnyɔn ɔ i ɔranj agɛn* – I won't buy his
   onions or oranges any more.

ɔranj – orange (< Eng. 'orange'). See 135.

ɔya – oil (< Eng. 'oil')
   136. *Wishkain ɔya yu gɛt? A wan daso pamɔya* – What kind of
   oil have you? I only want palmoil.

pepe – pepper (< Eng. 'pepper'). See 122.

planti – plantain (< Eng. 'plaintain'; reinforced by Port. 'plan-
tano')
   137. *I fit chɔp planti? I fit chɔp banana ɔ weti i fit chɔp?* – Can
   she eat plantains? Can she eat bananas or what can she eat?

sɔl – salt (< Eng. 'salt' possibly reinforced by Ger. 'Salz')
   138. *Waitman laik sɔl tumɔch* – Europeans like salt very
   much.

sup – stew, sauce, side-dish containing meat and/or vegetables
(< Eng. 'soup' possibly reinforced by Ger. 'Suppe'). See 77.

yam / yams / nyams – ɣam (< Twi 'anyinam' – 'yam')
   139. *Wuman no sabi gro nyams* – Women can't grow yams.

3.4.8 *Dress*

abada – long overshirt, often embroidered (< Yoruba 'agbada' –
'type of gown worn by men')
   140. *Fɔ krismas i bin bai abada, danshigi witi trɔsis* – For
   Christmas he bought a complete outfit, abada, danshigi and
   trousers.

bata – sandals (< Eng./Fr. 'Bata' – brand name)
 141. *A gɛt fɔ bai wan pia bata* – I must buy a pair of sandals. (The word *sandal* is beginning to replace *bata*.)

buba – blouse with long, wide sleeves (< Yoruba 'buba' – 'blouse')
 142. *A no gɛt buba fɔ wia witi dis ma fain fain lapa* – I have no buba to wear with this lovely lapa.

danshigi – type of shirt (< Hausa 'dantshiki' – 'gown for men which reaches to the knee'). See 140.

drɛs / gaun – clothing, outfit (< Eng. 'dress/gown')
 143. *Pita gɛt sɔm fain drɛs, sɔm prɔpa gaun* – Peter got a lovely outfit, a really terrific one.

hat – hat (< Eng. 'hat')
 144. *Na waitman blakman! Na soso hat i di wia!* – He's a black European! Always wearing hats!

hɛdtai – scarf, headdress, an essential part of a woman's dress (< Eng. 'head' + 'tie' influenced by vernacular usage)
 145. *Kɛntɛ no go du. Hɛdtai no dei* – The Kente cloth won't be enough. There won't be enough for a headtie.

kata – a headpad used for carrying heavy loads. (< Kikongo 'ŋkata' – headpad)
 146. *Dat kata dɔn chakara ɔlɔl* – That headpad is all broken.

kɛntɛ – type of Ghanaian cloth popular for special occasions (< Twi 'kente' – 'country cloth'). See 145.

kɛp – local headwear for men (< Eng. 'cap')
 147. *Wuman no fit wia bamɛnda kɛp* – Women can't wear a Bamenda cap.

klos / kros – clothes (< Eng. 'clothes')
 148. *I hɛd no kɔrɛk. I no di put klos fɔ i skin agen* – His head is not right. He no longer wears clothes.

lapa / rapa – material worn by women. It is wrapped round the lower half of the body, tucks in at the waist and reaches to the ankles (< Eng. 'wrap'/ Eng. dial. 'lap' – 'fold round'). See 142.

shu – shoe (< Eng. 'shoe')
149. *'Talɔng' bi sei shu wei dɛm gɛt lɔng hil* – 'Talongs' are high-heeled shoes.

trɔsa/trɔsis – trousers (< Eng. 'trouser/trousers'). See 140.

3.4.9 *Exclamations*[8]
Although there are not many widely-used exclamations in CP, the following are known throughout the country:

ashia – empathy formula (< ? Arabic 'asiya' – 'be sad, console' or ? Eng. 'hush ya')
150. *Ashia fɔ wɔk/sik!* – Good luck with your work/Sorry you are ill!
If someone falls or breaks something, an onlooker automatically says:
Ashia! – I empathise with you.
The person consoled may retort:
Ashia no di hɛlɛp – Saying 'ashia' doesn't help
only to be told:
Ashia di kul hat – Ashia consoles (i.e. cools the heart).

a – This exclamation is slightly disapproving. It tends to be added to a sentence, as a questioning emphatic:
151. *Yu no di hia, a?* – Are you not listening?
or added to a word to suggest disapproval:
Mɔni a! – Money is not all it's supposed to be!
Pita a! – Don't talk to me about Peter!

o – often accompanies and reinforces *ashia* as in:
152. *Ashia o, ma pikin!* – I'm really sorry, child.
It also follows and emphasises the warmth of a greeting:
Mɔning o! – A very good morning to you!
or of any word or sentence:
Mɔni o! – You can do anything with money!
Na palava dis o! – There'll be trouble over this!

wandaful – amazing, terrible (< Eng. 'wonderful')
153. *ɛni man dai fɔ dat ples! Wandaful!* – Everybody died there! How terrible!

4.4.3 Family/Kinship

b(a)rata – sibling/close relative of the same sex (<Eng. 'brother' modified by vernacular usage)

30. *Maria, yu lukim brata bilong yu?* – Mary, can you see your sister?
31. *Jon, yu lukim brata bilong yu?* – John, can you see your brother?

kandere – a relative on the mother's side, aunt, uncle, cousin, nephew, niece (<Eng. 'kindred' possibly influenced by Ger. 'Kinder' and modified by vernacular usage)

32. *Asde, mi lukim wanpela kandere i stap long Mosbi* – Yesterday, I saw an aunt who lives in Port Moresby.

Compounds involving *kandere* are common:

    kandereman – male relative on the mother's side
    kanderemeri – female relative on the mother's side
  kandere pikinini man – male child relative on the mother's side.

mama – mother, grandmother, close female relative of mother's age (<Eng. 'mama' + vernacular usage of 'mama')

33. *Mama save wokim haus olsem papa* – Mama can build a house just as well as papa.

Mama occurs in compounds including:

  lapun mama – grandmother (usually on the father's side)
  smol mama – paternal aunt.

manmeri – people (<Eng. 'man' + 'Mary')

34. *Dispela manmeri i no inap liptimapim dispela ston* – These people cannot lift this stone:

Man and *meri* represent 'male' and 'female' as well as 'man' and 'woman':

    pikinini man – boy
    pikinini meri – girl
   bulmakau man – bull
   bulmakau meri – cow.

papa – father, paternal uncle, guardian (<Eng. 'papa' + vernacular usage of 'papa')

35. *Papa, bai mi rausim em?* – Papa, shall I throw it out?

Like *mama*, it can occur in many compounds including:

> *lapun papa* – grandfather
> *smol papa* – paternal uncle
> *was papa* – foster father (wash + papa)
> *papa tru* – real father
> *papamama* – parents, foreparents.

pikinini – child, young person, offspring, seed (< Port. 'pequeninho' – 'very small')
36. *Doktaboi i givim sut long pikinini* – The orderly is giving an injection to the child.

susa (occasionally *sista*) – sibling of the opposite sex, age-mate of the opposite sex (< Eng. 'sister' modified by vernacular usage)
37. *O susa, bilum bilong mi i hevi moa, na het i pen . . .* – O sibling of the opposite sex, my bag is very heavy and my head aches . . . (part of an advertisement for Aspro).
There is a tendency for *brata/susa* to be used to mean 'brother/sister' in the English sense among young, educated speakers. The compound *bratasusa* can be used for siblings or closely related children.

tambaran – spirits of one's ancestors (< Gaz. 'tambaran' – 'spirits')
38. *Ol i go long singsing tambaran* – They (i.e. the men) are going to the ceremony in honour of their ancestors.

tambu – in-law (< Gaz. 'tambu' – 'taboo')
39. *Tambu bilongen i no gat wok* – His in-law is unemployed.

tumbuna – remote ancestors and descendants (< Gaz. 'tumbuna' – relatives before one's grandparents and after one's grandchildren)
40. *Ol i harim stori bilong tumbuna* – They are listening to a folktale (i.e. a story of our ancestors).

wanlain – age-mate (< Eng. 'one + line' calqued on vernacular usage)
41. *Mitripela i wanlain* – The three of us are age-mates.
Wan occurs in many compounds which are calques from the vernaculars:
> *wanpis* – orphan (one piece)
> *wanpisin* – member(s) of the same tribe (one bird/business)

3.4.10 Verbals

The lexical items in Sections 3.4.1 to 3.4.8 can all function as nominals and yet it should be stressed that, since multifunctionality is a marked feature of the CP lexicon, many of them are not exclusively nominal. CP verbals are similarly multifunctional. Thus *waka* from English 'walk' can function in all of the following contexts:

> *sɔm waka man* – a traveller
> *sɔm lɔng waka* – a long walk
> *A bin waka sotei a taia* – I walked until I was tired
> *A bin go waka ma kɔmbi* – I went to visit my friend.

The most frequently used verbals in CP can be divided into two types:

a. verbals which can modify a noun or noun phrase (NP):

> *Di pikin dɔn[9] big / sɔm big pikin* – The child has got big / a big child

b. verbals which cannot modify a noun phrase:

> *Di pikin dɔn go   * sɔm go pikin* – The child has just gone.

The former will be identified as AV (adjective verb) and the latter as V (verb). One further distinction can be made with regard to verbals. Some can take the third person bound pronoun '-am' in such constructions as:

> *Na X a go X-am* – I'll really X it/him/her/them

and:

> *Mek yu X-am* – X it/him/her/them (This is a polite form of *X-am*).

A verbal will be given the marker 'T' (transitive) if it can occur in such constructions. Four examples will illustrate how the system works.

1. *hɔt* < English 'hot' is *AVT:*
> *sɔm hɔt faia* – a warm fire
> *Di faia di hɔt* – The fire is getting warmer
> *Na hɔt a go hɔtam* – I'll really heat it
> *Mek yu hɔtam* – Heat it (please).

2. *kam* < English 'come' is V:
   > *Di man di kam* – The man is coming.

3. *tek* < English 'take' is VT:
   > *Di man go tek di chɔp* – The man will take the food
   > *Na tek a go tekam* – I'll really take it
   > *Mek yu tekam* – Take it.

4. *waka* < English 'walk' is AV:
   > *sɔm waka man* – a traveller
   > *Di man di waka* – The man is walking
   > ?*Na waka a go wakaam* – I'll really walk it
   > ?*Mek yu wakaam* – Walk it.

The last two sentences are unusual and are rejected by many CP speakers but they are not absolutely impossible. CP, like English, can frequently use words in non-normal contexts. In English, for example, 'hear' is usually classified as a stative verb which does not appear in progressive structures, yet:

> I can't hear you. That's better. I'm hearing you now.

is acceptable. And finally, verbals which are multifunctional (that is which can also function as nominals) are given the marker 'M', thus *hɔt* and *waka* would take 'M' because the following sentences are acceptable:

> *Yu go hia hɔt* – You'll suffer (You go hear hot)
> *A bin waka sɔm lɔng lɔng waka* - I went for a very long walk.

3.4.11 *Verbals in CP's core vocabulary*

ansa	VTM	< Eng. 'answer'	– answer, reply
as(k)	VT	< Eng. 'ask'	– ask
bad	AVM	< Eng. 'bad'	– (be) bad, evil, 'very much'
bai	VT	< Eng. 'buy'	– buy
bak	AVTM	< Eng. 'back'	– back, give back, return
bait	VTM	< Eng. 'bite'	– bite, sample, taste
bɛri	VT	< Eng. 'bury'	– bury. (This word is in free variation with the phrase *putam fɔ graun*.)
big	AVTM	< Eng. 'big'	– big, increase, be important
bigin	VT	< Eng. 'begin'	– begin. (This word nor-

			mally co-occurs with *stat* from 'start': *Dɛn i go bigin stat duam* – Then he set about doing it.)
bita	AVM	< Eng. 'bitter'	– bitter, sharp-tasting
blak	AVTM	< Eng. 'black'	– black, dark, blacken, darken
blo	VTM	< Eng. 'blow', 'borrow'	– blow, blast, lend
blu	AVTM	< Eng. 'blue'	– blue, make blue
bɔil	VT	< Eng. 'boil'	– boil
bɔn	VTM	< Eng. 'burn'	– burn, roast, grill
bɔn	VT	< Eng. 'born'	– give birth to
bring	VT	< Eng. 'bring'	– bring, take, carry towards
brok	VT	< Eng. 'broke'	– break. (*Brok* only occurs adjectivally in the fixed phrase *brok marach*, a fish with many bones and so, reputedly, the cause of many rows between husbands and wives.)
chakara	VT	< Ewe 'tsaka'	– 'be mixed'
			– scatter, break into small pieces, shatter
chip	AVT	< Eng. 'cheap'	– cheap, be cheap, cheapen
chɔp	VTM	< Eng. 'chop'	– eat, food
		< ?China Coast PE	– (cf. 'chopsticks')
dai	AVTM	< Eng. 'die'	– die, dead, death
dans	VTM	< Eng. 'dance'	– dance, be joyful
dash	VTM	< Gã 'dase'	– 'thank you'
		< Port. 'dar'	– 'give'
			– tip, give something extra
dia	AV	< Eng. 'dear'	– expensive, be dear
dig	VTM	< Eng. 'dig'	– dig, digging
dinai	VT	< Eng. 'deny'	– refuse, reject, deny
drai	AV	< Eng. 'dry'	– thin (of people, etc.) empty (of purse, etc.)
drai	AVTM	< Eng. 'dry'	– dry, parched, drought
draiv	VTM	< Eng. 'drive'	– drive, send away

drim	VTM	<Eng. 'dream'	— dream, daydream
drink	VTM	<Eng. 'drink'	— drink (it occurs in pre-nominal slot in the set phrase *drink-masa* — a heavy drinker)
drɔm	AVTM	<Eng. 'drum'	— drum, drumming
du	VT	<Eng. 'du'	— do
du	V	<Eng. 'du'	— be sufficient
ɛnta	VT	<Eng. 'enter'	— come in
fain	AVT	<Eng. 'fine'	— fine, lovely, beautify
fain	VTM	<Eng. 'find'	— look for, find
fait	VTM	<Eng. 'fight'	— fight, quarrel, war
fawe	AV	<Eng. 'faraway'	— be far away, distant
fiba/va	VM	<Eng. 'fever'	— be feverish, fever
fiba/va	VT	<Eng. 'favour'	— resemble
finis	VTM	<Eng. 'finish'	— finish, end
flai	VT	<Eng. 'fly'	— fly
fɔgɛt	VT	<Eng. 'forget'	— forget
fɔl (dɔng)	VTM	<Eng. 'fall (down)'	— fall, fall down
fɔlɔ	AVT	<Eng. 'follow'	— follow, go with, following
ful	AV	<Eng. 'full'	— full
fulɔp	VT	<Eng. 'full-up'	— fill
gada	VT	<Eng. 'gather'	— gather up, collect
gɛt	VT	<Eng. 'get'	— have, get, obtain
gif/gi	VT	<Eng. 'give'	— give
go	V	<Eng. 'go'	— go
grin	AVTM	<Eng. 'green'	— green, make green
gud	AVM	<Eng. 'good'	— good, be good, goodness
had	AVM	<Eng. 'hard'	— hard, be hard, hardness
haid	VT	<Eng. 'hide'	— hide
hala	VTM	<Eng. 'holler'	— call out, shout
hambag	VTM	<Eng. 'humbug'	— annoy, infuriate
hɛlɛp	VTM	<Eng. 'help'	— help, assist
hɛv(i)	AV	<Eng. 'heavy'	— heavy
hia	VT	<Eng. 'hear'	— understand, hear, sense
hɔngri	AVM	<Eng. 'hungry'	— hunger, hungry
hɔt	AVTM	<Eng. 'hot'	— hot, heat, hurt
jagajaga	AVT	<Ewe 'jagajaga'	— 'sprawling, spread all over' — shabby, untidy, sprawl

jɔm	VTM	<Eng. 'jump'	– jump, leap
kɛrɛng-kɛrɛng	AVM	<Fante 'kyerɛn-kye'	– 'basket' then 'plant held in basket' then 'muci-lagenous plant' then 'slip-pery' slippery
kil	VTM	<Eng. 'kill'	– kill
klaim	VTM	<Eng. 'climb'	– climb, go up
klos	VT	<Eng. 'close'	– close, shut
kɔf	VTM	<Eng. 'cough'	– cough. (When one coughs or sneezes a sympathy formula is used in CP. This may be 'kɔsu' in Lamso-speaking areas or the more widespread 'ashia'.)
kol	AVTM	<Eng. 'cold'	– cold, cool, coldness
kɔl	VTM	<Eng. 'call'	– call
kɔm/kam	V	<Eng. 'come'	– come
kɔmɔt	V	<Eng. 'come+out'	– come out, go out
kɔnk	VTM	<Mandinka 'kɔ̃'	– 'knock' – pound (as of a headache), throb *Ma hɛd di kɔngk* – My head is throbbing.
kɔnggɔsa	VM	<Fante 'ngkong-konsa'	– 'lying, duplicity' – gossip
kɔs	VTM	<Eng. 'curse'	– insult
kɔt	VTM	<Eng. 'cut'	– cut
krai	AVM	<Eng. 'cry'	– cry, weep
krɔkrɔ	AVM	<Vai 'kirikiri'	– 'scabies', scabby, have scabies, sca-bies
laf	AVTM	<Eng. 'laugh'	– laugh, laugh at
lai	AVM	<Eng. 'lie'	– lie, lying
lait	AVTM	<Eng. 'light'	– light, lighten
lɔng	AV	<Eng. 'long'	– long, tall, deep
kres	AV	<Eng. 'craze'	– mad, be mad
mari(t)	AVTM	<Eng. 'marry'	– marry, marriage

mεmba	VT	< Eng. 'remember'	— think over, remember
miamia	AVM	< ?Mende 'miamia'	— 'lightning'
		< ?onomatopoeia	— nag, grumble, nagging
mumu	AVM	< Fante 'mumu'	— 'deafness and dumbness', mute, be mute, foolish
nak	VTM	< Eng. 'knock'	— hit, beat, knock
nia	AV	< Eng. 'near'	— near, be near
nyu	AV	< Eng. 'new'	— brand new
ol	AVM	< Eng. 'old'	— old, old age, get old
ɔl	AVM	< Eng. 'all'	— all, every, very many
opεn	AVT	< Eng. 'open'	— open, tear open
pul	VTM	< Eng. 'pull'	— pull. (This word is ousting *hib* meaning both pull and push.)
pus	VTM	< Eng. 'push'	— push, heave
rait	AVT	< Eng. 'write/ right'	— write, right, fix
raun	AVTM	< Eng. 'round'	— round, make round, roundness
rεd	AVTM	< Eng. 'redden/ red'	— red, redden, white (as of a European's colour)
rεs	VTM	< Eng. 'rest'	— rest, relax
rid	VT	< Eng. 'read'	— read
rɔn	VTM	< Eng. 'run'	— run, chase
sabi/vi	VTM	< Port. 'saber'	— 'know, be able to', know, be able to, knowledge
sεl	VTM	< Eng. 'sell'	— sell, sale
shap	AVT	< Eng. 'sharpen/ sharp'	— sharpen, sharp, pointed
shidong	V	< Eng. 'sit+ down'	— sit, stay, live
sho	AVTM	< Eng. 'show'	— show, reveal, showy
shɔt	AV	< Eng. 'short'	— short, shallow, low
shut	VT	< Eng. 'shoot'	— shoot at, hit (one can 'shut' a stone)
si	VT	< Eng. 'see'	— see, look

sik	AVM	< Eng. 'sick'	– sick, be sick, sickness
sin	VM	< Eng. 'sin'	– sin (this is replacing 'du bad')
sing	VTM	< Eng. 'sing'	– sing
slip	VTM	< Eng. 'sleep'	– sleep, rest
smɛl	VTM	< Eng. 'smell'	– smell (less common than *hia sɔm smɛl*))
smɔl	AVM	< Eng. 'small'	– little, thin, young
snis	VM	< Eng. 'sneeze'	– sneeze
sɔf	AV	< Eng. 'soft'	– soft (less common than 'no had')
sɔfa	VM	< Eng. 'suffer'	– suffer (less common than *si trɔbu bad*)
swit	AVTM	< Eng. 'sweet'	– sweet, please, sweetness, deliciousness
swɔlɔ	VTM	< Eng. 'swallow'	– swallow
tai	VTM	< Eng. 'tie'	– build, tie
taia	VTM	< Eng. 'tire'	– tire, be tired, fatigue
tanap	VT	< Eng. 'stand+ up'	– stand
tek	VT	< Eng. 'take'	– take, seize
tia	VTM	< Eng. 'tear'	– tear, tear up
tif	AVTM	< Eng. 'thief'	– steal, stealing, theft
tik	AVM	< Eng. 'thick'	– thick, be thick, thickness
tink	VTM	< Eng. 'think'	– think, thought
tis	VTM	< Eng. 'taste'	– taste, sample
tish/lɛn	VT	< Eng. 'teach/ learn'	– teach/learn. (As in dialectal English, *lɛn* can be used for both 'teach' and 'learn'.)
tɔk	VTM	< Eng. 'talk'	– talk, speech
tɔs	VTM	< Eng. 'touch'	– touch
tot	VT	< Eng. 'tote'	– carry
trowei	VT	< Eng. 'throw+ away'	– throw out, spill
trɔng	AVM	< Eng. 'strong'	– strong, strength
wait	AVTM	< Eng. 'white'	– white, whiten
waka	AVTM	< Eng. 'walk'	– walk, walking
wikɔp	VT	< Eng. 'wake+ up'	– get up, rise
wɔk	AVTM	< Eng. 'work'	– work

| *wowo* | AV | < Fante 'wowow' | – 'cold, ugly', ugly |
| *yɛlo* | AVTM | < Eng. 'yellow' | – yellow, light-complex-ioned. |

3.4.12 *Function Words*

In addition to the 343 semantically full words cited above and the eight pronouns, *a, mi, yu, i, -am, wi, wuna, dɛm* (see p. 7), there are several closed set function words in CP. These can be described as determiners, interrogatives, auxiliary verbs, conjunctions, prepositions and adverbials. For the moment, we shall simply list them but their roles will be more fully described in 3.5 and 3.6.

Determiners

di	< Eng. 'the'	– the, that
sɔm	< Eng. 'some'	– a, some, a certain
dis	< Eng. 'this'	– this, these
dat	< Eng. 'that'	– that, yon, those
ɛni	< Eng. 'any'	– every
no	< Eng. 'no'	– no
ɔl	< Eng. 'all'	– all

Interrogatives

fɔ seka wɛti?	< Eng. 'for sake of what'	– why?
hau?	< Eng. 'how'	– how?
hu?	< Eng. 'who'	– who?
wɛti?	< Eng. 'what'	– what?
wich/wish?	< Eng. 'which'	– which?
wusai/usai?	< Eng. 'which side'	– where?

Auxiliary Verbs

bin	< Eng. 'been'	– remote past marker
di	< Eng. 'do'	– continuous aspect marker
dɔn	< Eng. 'done'	– perfect aspect marker – positive
nɛva	< Eng. 'never'	– perfect aspect marker – negative

fɔ	< Eng. 'for'	– future conditional marker
go	< Eng. 'go'	– future marker
wan	< Eng. 'want'	– inceptive aspect marker
fit	< Eng. 'fit'	– ability, permission
gɛtfɔ	< Eng. 'get for'	– obligation
mɔs	< Eng. 'must'	– necessity
savi/sabi	< Port. 'saber'	– habitual aspect marker.

Conjunctions

an/na	< Eng. 'and'	– and
bɔt	< Eng. 'but'	– but
ɔ	< Eng. 'or'	– or
if/ifi	< Eng. 'if'	– if
sei	< { Eng. 'say' Twi 'se' (that)	– that
wei	< Eng. 'where'	– who, which, that, whom.

Prepositions

Although many prepositions like *abaut, afta, bifoa, bihain* are entering CP, the following are still the most widely used in the language:

| *fɔ* | < Eng. 'for' | – for, to, in, on, etc. |
| *wit/witi* | < Eng. 'with' | – with, and. |

Adverbs

As we have seen, words are less rigidly confined to word classes in CP and so the same item can, depending on context, function as a noun, verb, adjective or adverb. The following four items, however, most frequently occur as adverbs:

jɔsnau	< Eng. 'just now'	– very soon
nau	< Eng. 'now'	– soon, now
naunau	< Eng. 'now now'	– immediately
sɔfrisɔfri	< Eng. 'softly softly'	– slowly, easily.

3.4.13 *Comments on CP's Core Vocabulary*

CP's core vocabulary is extensive. Not only is every English word a potential part of CP's lexicon but so are frequently heard French and African ones. In such circumstances, it is relatively hard to know exactly where one should draw the line regarding its core vocabulary. Our list could easily be expanded or reduced but it is certain that every speaker who uses CP regularly is familiar with all the items listed above, and it is equally certain that possession of such a vocabulary would allow a speaker to communicate fully with other CP speakers.

Taking the above items as basic, we can draw the following conclusions:

1. Excluding exclamations, we have listed 387 items (343 semantically full words, eight pronominal forms and thirty-six function words). Of these, 291 (75+%) come from English, four (1+%) are blends, involving English morphemes, fifteen (3+%) have dual or multiple origins, English being one of the possible source languages, twelve (3+%) come from English but have had their meanings influenced by the vernacular languages and the remaining sixty-five words (16+%) derive from languages other than English.

2. Of the sixty-five items not deriving from or being influenced by English, four are from Portuguese, two from Carib and the remaining fifty-nine are from African languages.

3. Of the items from African languages, only nineteen (5−%) are from local Cameroon languages. The remaining forty (10+%) plus the two Carib words probably entered CP from Krio.

Such statistics are interesting but, taken on their own, are gravely misleading because they tell us nothing about the frequency of occurrence of any item. The most frequently used word in CP is almost certainly *ashia* which can be an exclamation, a sympathy formula or a sentence filler. In addition, although Portuguese words are not numerically significant in CP, Portuguese has supplied the language with four essential items:

> *dash* – give something for nothing, tip, something extra
> *palava* – trouble, dispute, quarrel
> *pikin* – child
> *sabi/savi* – know, be able to, habitual aspect marker.

The core vocabulary of CP reveals not so much a borrowing as an adoption and adaptation. CP's lexical items overlap the meanings of their cognates although they rarely match them exactly. They have abandoned morphological change and inflection and they have acquired a multifunctionality greater than that of English or of any of the African languages referred to. The above vocabulary, together with a knowledge of word order, would permit full communication in CP and, since word order is easily specified, CP's simplicity, if measured in terms of ease of acquisition, is clearly apparent.

3.4.14 *Word Formation*

CP has no productive affixes and all semantically full items are multifunctional. The language is, however, capable of producing new meanings by the use of compounding, reduplication, calques (loan translations from African languages) and by idiomatic usage.

Compounding – Related sets of words can be created by the use of *man, wuman* and *pikin* thus:

> *man pikin got* – male kid
> *wuman got* – nanny goat
> *wuman palava* – all the troubles associated with being a woman
> *man brik* – brick with one hole
> *pikin pia* – an immature pear.

Mami and *masa* are also found fairly frequently in compounds:

> *mami wata* – a female water spirit
> *mami palava* – an inveterate trouble maker
> *mami kɔn* – the woman who sells corn
> *masa chakala* – the male destroyer, a destructive man
> *masa tɔk tɔk* – the man who talks too much.

The verbs *gɛt, gif* and *mek* are highly productive in compounding:

> *gɛt bɛlɛ* – become pregnant
> *gɛt flaua* – menstruate for the first time, germinate
> *gif bɛlɛ* – impregnate
> *gif palava* – invariably cause trouble
> *mek nyangga* – act grown up, put on airs and graces
> *mek kɔni* – trick, cheat.

Reduplication – This device is systematically exploited for emphasis:

fain – lovely	*fain fain* – really lovely
big – big	*big big* – very big

for stressing continuous or prolonged activity:

bos – boast	*bos bos* – to be continually boasting
tɔk – talk	*tɔk tɔk* – prolonged talk, talk all the time

for nicknaming:

> *Mami tɔk tɔk* – Mrs Loquacious
> *Masa tif tif* – Mr Can't-Keep-His-Hands-To-Himself

for indicating plurality:

> *so so ston ston* – stones everywhere
> *so so kapɛt kapɛt* – carpets everywhere

for creating abstract nouns:

> *mɛmba mɛmba* – recollections (remember remember)
> *savi savi* – omniscience (know know)

and for suggesting duplicity:

> *holi holi* – sanctimonious (holy holy)
> *tɔn tɔn* – make excuses (turn turn).

Calques – Many CP compounds are direct translations from African languages. Among them are:

> *fɔlɔ bak* – next child (follow back/behind)
> *krai dai* – wake (cry die) often for a young person
> *chɔp dai* – wake (eat die) often for an old person and so not a sad affair.

Idiomatic Usage – In CP, idiomatic expressions are often based on body parts, *ai, bɛlɛ, hat, han, hɛd, fut* and on a limited number of adjectives such as *smɔl, big* and *trɔng*:

> *trɔng ai* – brave (of a man), shameless (of a woman) (strong eye)

    bɛlɛ wuman – pregnant woman (belly woman)
    kul hat – console (cool heart)
was man i hɛd – humiliate (wash a man's head)
    tai han – mean, meanness (tie hand)
    smɔl wata – bribe (small water)
    big man – head of department, boss
    moto fut – tyre (motor foot).

3.5. SYNTAX

While it is true that emergent pidgins only permit rudimentary communication (largely because they are lexically and syntactically impoverished), with an expanded pidgin like CP we find stability, vitality and the flexibility of a structured syntax. As we have seen from the quoted utterances, inflection is absent from CP as it is absent from many other contact lingua francas. Berry expresses the position thus:

> That inflection is the commonest casualty in the contact situation seems true of both European and African pidgins. The massive reduction of the Bantu nominal prefix system in Fanagalo and other indigenous African pidgins parallels the less striking losses of gender, case and number distinctions in European pidgins.
>
> (Berry, 1971: 527)

and this 'massive reduction' of redundancies includes also in CP the virtual loss of tonal distinctions, of freedom of word order, of passive constructions and of prepositional variation.

3.5.1 *The Basic Sentence Structure*

As in other varieties of English, CP's basic sentence pattern is (Subject) Predicate (Object) (Complement) where bracketed elements are optional:

    Chɔp! – Eat!
    Chɔp di fufu – Eat the fufu
    Pita di chɔp di fufu – Peter is eating the fufu
Pita di chɔp di fufu fɔ han – Peter is eating the fufu with his
                       fingers.

Adjectives precede nouns:

> *sɔm fain pikin* – a beautiful child

and possession is indicated as follows:

> *sɔm man i haus* – a man's house
> *sɔm man dɛm haus* – some men's house
> *sɔm man dɛm haus dɛm* – some men's houses
> *Pita i haus* – Peter's house
> *Pita i wuman i haus* – Peter's wife's house
> *Pita i wuman dɛm haus* – Peter's wives' house
> *i haus* – his house
> *dɛm haus* – their house
> *Pita i on* – Peter's.

An examination of sentences in CP reveals that they can be comprehended by such rules as the following:

S→	NP VP
NP→	(det) (num) (adj) (gender) (dim) N (pl) (poss. marker) S
	pronoun
VP→	(aux) V (NP)
determiner→	(ɔl) (dis/dat) (ma/yu/i/wi/wuna/dɛm)
	(ɔl) (di)
	(sɔm) (ma/yu/i/wi/wuna/dɛm)
num→	numeral = *wan*, *tu*, etc.
adj→	e.g. *fain*, *big*, etc.
	reduplicated forms e.g. *fain fain*, *big big*, etc.
gender→	*man/wuman*
dim.→	*pikin*
N→	nominal e.g. *masa*, *trɔki*, *stik*
pronoun→	*a/yu* etc. *Hu? wɛti?*
poss→	*i/dɛm on*
aux→	*di/bin*, etc.
V→	verbal
verbal→	verb e.g. *kam*, *tek*, *trai*
	adj. e.g. *gud*, *big*, *fain*

modifier→ {
adj. e.g. *gud, big, fain*
reduplicated form, e.g. *gud gud, big big*
temporal, e.g. *tude, yestadei, las yia*, etc.
prepositional NP
}

prep→ *fɔ, witi*, etc.

The maximum NP might thus be:

ɔl dis ma tu fainfain man pikin – both my really fine male kids
got dɛm on

and a VP can range from *chɔp* to:

go chɔp di bif wei a bin shutam – will eat the animal that I have
naunau just this minute shot.

Such word order is basic to the language, but CP permits two types of foregrounding (i.e. the movement of one or more elements to the beginning of a sentence for emphasis). First, any semantically full word can be foregrounded by the use of *na*. Thus, if we take the sentence:

i bin kil di bif – he killed the animal

it is possible to highlight '*i*', '*kil*' and '*bif*', thus:

Na i bin kil di bif – *He* killed the animal/It was he who killed the animal

Na di bif i bin kil – He killed the *animal*/It was the animal he killed

Na kil i bin kil di bif – He *killed* the animal/*It was kill he killed the animal.

Second, temporal modifiers normally follow the verb, but they can also occur initially in the sentence:

I go kam tumɔrɔ – He'll come tomorrow
Tomɔrɔ i go kam – He'll come *tomorrow*
Na tumɔrɔ i go kam – It's tomorrow that he'll be coming.

3.5.2 *Negation*

In CP, negation is marked by putting *no* before the VP:

> *Kam!* – Come!
> *No kam!* – Don't come!
> *Pita bin di chɔp* – Peter was eating
> *Pita no bin di chɔp* – Peter wasn't eating
> *Pita go kam fɔ haus* – Peter will come to the house
> *Pita no go kam fɔ haus* – Peter won't come to the house.

For emphasis, *no* can also precede semantically full words:

> *No man no bin chɔp no* – Nobody ate anything
>   *smɔl*

but the one negative marker that is essential is the *no* that precedes *bin chɔp*.

There are two structures in CP which are not negated in the usual way. The first relates to the use of *dɔn*, the marker of perfective aspect:

> *I dɔn go* – he has gone

cannot be negated by using *no*:

> **I no dɔn go.*

Rather, there is a negative auxiliary *nɛva* which must be used:

> *i nɛva go* – he has not gone yet.

The second exception occurs when the polite imperative is used:

> *wikɔp* – get up
> *no wikɔp* – don't get up
> *mek yu wikɔp* – (won't you) get up
> *mek yu no wikɔp* – (please) don't get up.

3.5.3 *Interrogation*
In CP a change in intonation is often the only signal that a statement has become a question:

Yu di go hause	‾ ‾ ‾ _	You are going home
Yu di go haus?	– – _ ⟋	Are you going home?
I dei dei	‾ – _	He's there
I dei dei?	– – ⟋	Is he there?

When question words are used, the intonation contour is similar to that used for statements:

Hu di go haus?   ‾   ‾   –   _   Who is going home?
Hu dei dei?   ‾   –   _   Who is there?

There are six frequently-used interrogation words in CP, *hu,*
hau:

          Hau yu bin sabiam? – How did you know how to do it?
fɔ seka wɛti:

     Fɔ seka wɛti yu bin kam? – Why did you come?
wɛti:

            Wɛti yu di tɔk? – What are you talking about?
wich:

      Wich taim i go kam? – When will he come?
and *(w)usai:*

     Wusai yu bin kɔmɔt? – Where did you come from?

Question words usually occur at the beginning of a sentence but
hu, wɛti and *wusai* can for emphasis occur in final position:

Yu bi hu?   implying And who do you think you are?
Yu bin si wɛti?   implying *What* did you say you saw?
Yu bin go fɔ wusai?   implying *Where* did you say you went?

3.5.4 *Reported Speech*
In CP, reported speech and thought do not require any transformation in the verb phrase:

               I bin go – He went
              I go kam – He will come
       I tɔk sei i bin go – He says he went
    I bin tɔk sei i go kam – He said he would come
A no bin tink sei i go kam – I didn't think he would come.

Nor is there any modification of temporal or spatial markers:

       I go kam hia tumɔrɔ – He will come here tomorrow
I bin tɔk sei i go kam hia tumɔrɔ – He said he would go there the
                                following day.

First and second person pronouns may be changed if the context
demands it:

    Pita bin tɔk sei: 'A go kam' – Peter said: 'I'll come'
      Pita bin tɔk sei i go kam – Peter said he would come

Pita bin tɔk sei: 'Mek yu go' – Peter said: 'Go, please'
Pita bin tɔk sei mek i go – Peter said that he should go.

All verbs of saying, thinking, knowing, remembering and sensing are followed by *sei*:

> *A bin tɔk sei a go kam* – I said I would go
> *A bin dinai sei a go kam* – I denied that I would go
> *A tink sei a go kam* – I think that I'll come
> *A sabi sei a go kam* – I know I'll come
> *A shua sei a go kam* – I'm sure that I'll come
> *A bin mɛmba sei a gɛt fɔ go* – I remembered that I had to go
> *A hia sei a gɛt fɔ go* – I hear that I have to go.

The form *sei* functions like the relative pronoun 'that' in SE but it can also function as a verb:

> *A sei. Yu no di hia?* – I say. Can't you hear?

It may derive from the English verb 'say' and have been influenced by such Biblical expressions as: 'And Jesus spoke to the multitude saying . . .' but it may also owe its origin to African languages. Twi, for example, has a verb *se* meaning 'say' and Yoruba has constructions which closely parallel CP usage:

CP	Yoruba	Literal	English
i gud	ó dáa	it good	it's good
a sabi sei i gud	mo mọ pé ó dáa	I know say it good	I know it's good
a tink sei i gud	mo ro pé ó dáa	I think say it good	I think it's good

3.5.5 The Noun Phrase

The CP noun phrase can be a substantive phrase:

> *dat tu man pikin* – those two boys

a pronoun:

> *a, mi, i, -am, wi, wuna, dɛm*

and proper names like *Pita* 'Peter' and *Pita dɛm*, 'Peter and his friends'. As in SE, it is the substantive phrase which permits most modification and expansion and again, as in SE, when adjectives precede the noun, they do so in a fixed order:

> *di tu fain wait fawul* – the two nice white chickens
> *di tu fain fain wait fawul* – the two very nice white chickens
> *di tu fain big wait fawul* – the two nice big white chickens.

Thus descriptive adjectives precede adjectives of size and colour, and if nominals occur in a modifying capacity, they precede the head noun directly:

> *di tu wuman fawul* – the two hens
> *di tu fain wuman fawul* – the two nice hens.

Plurality tends to be implicit in the context, but can be made overt by the affixing of *dɛm*, the third person plural pronoun:

> *di tu wuman fawul dɛm* – the two hens
> *ɔl ma pikin dɛm* – all my children.

The two commonest forms of post-noun modification are preposition + noun:

> *wi brɔda fɔ haus* – our brother(s) at home
> *di man fɔ hɔspital* – the man in the hospital
> *wi papa fɔ wi bifoa* – our ancestors (we father for we before)

and embedded sentences introduced by *wei* (?English 'where'):

> *I gɛt tu pikin wei i nɛva siam* – He has two children whom he hasn't seen yet
> *Di buk wei a laikam fain dɔn lɔs* – The book that I really like has been lost/is lost
> *Man wei i gɛt bak gɛt i on bɛd* – A man who has a back has a bed.

3.5.6 *The Verb Phrase*

In CP, the verb is unmarked for person or number:

> *a/i/wuna/dɛm dei* – I/she/he/it/you pl./they BE there.

It does not change to indicate temporal or aspectual distinctions, though such distinctions can be made overt by the use of pre-verbal auxiliaries:

        Maria dei – Mary is there
     Maria bin dei – Mary was there
    Maria go dei – Mary will be there
  Maria fɔ dei if . . . – Mary would be there if . . .

The form of the verb which is used in CP is usually the form equivalent to the imperative in English:

Maria di sing – Mary is singing	*sing*	< 'sing'
Maria bin go – Mary went	*go*	< 'go'
Maria dɔn tek . . . – Mary has taken . . .	*tek*	< 'take'
Maria go trai – Mary will try	*trai*	< 'try'

but, occasionally, a marked form of the verb has been adopted:

Maria di brokam – Mary is breaking it	*brok*	< 'broke'
Maria dɔn lɔsam – Mary has lost it	*lɔs*	< 'loss/lost'

and, frequently, CP verbals, though deriving from English, do not derive from English verbs:

Maria dei – Mary is there	*dei*	< 'there'
Maria go fain – Mary will be lovely	*fain*	< 'fine'
Maria shua sei – Mary is sure that . . .	*shua*	< 'sure'.

In CP temporal and aspectual distinctions are carried not by modifications of the verb form but by auxiliaries which precede the verb in a fixed order:

    Di man di fait – The man is fighting
    Di man bin fait – The man fought
  Di man bin di fait – The man was fighting.

There are two temporal markers, *bin* and *go*:

    I no bin dei fɔ haus – He wasn't in the house
                 (*bin* = past/remote past)
    I no go dei fɔ haus – He won't be in the house
                 (*go* = future)

five aspectual markers, *di*, *dɔn*, *nɛva*, *sabi* and *wan*:

  I di (soso) hambag mi – He is always annoying me (*di* =
                   continuous/regularity marker)
    I dɔn tekam go – He has just taken it away (*dɔn* =
                   positive perfective marker)

I nɛva tekam go – He hasn't just taken it away
(*nɛva* = negative perfective marker)

I sabi chɔp fish – He's always eating fish
(*sabi* = habitual marker)

A bin wan fɔl brok ma fut – I almost fell and broke my leg
(*wan* = inceptive aspect marker)

and one marker of conditionality, *fɔ*:

A fɔ go if a gɛt chans – I will go if I get the chance (but it is most unlikely) (*fɔ* = conditionality)

A fɔ dɔn go if a bin gɛt chans – I would have gone if I had got the chance.

There are certain restrictions on the use of these primary auxiliaries:

1) *no* cannot directly precede *dɔn*:

I dɔn kam? No, i nɛva kam – Has he come yet? No, he hasn't come yet

but, when *dɔn* co-occurs with other auxiliaries, then *no* can precede them:

I no bin dɔn go – He hadn't already gone
I no go dɔn go – He won't have already gone
I no fɔ dɔn go if . . . – He wouldn't have gone if . . .

2) *nɛva* cannot co-occur with other auxiliaries
3) *bin*, *go* and *fɔ* are mutually exclusive:

I bin di hala – He was shouting
I go di hala – He will be shouting
I fɔ di hala . . . – He would be shouting . . .

5) *di* is frequently accompanied by *soso*:

I di soso giv palava – He is always causing trouble.

Di cannot co-occur with *dɔn/nɛva* but it can occur with *bin dɔn*, *go dɔn* and *fɔ dɔn*:

I bin dɔn di hala – He had been shouting
I no go dɔn di hala – He won't have been shouting

although such phrases have a low frequency in CP.

6) *wan* usually only co-occurs with *bin*:

A bin wan fɔl bɔt sɔm mami – I almost fell but a woman
              hol mi   caught me.

Some speakers, however, use and will accept *go wan* and *fɔ wan*:

A go wan dei dis taim tumɔrɔ – I'll be almost there this time
                         tomorrow
A fɔ wan dai if dat kain ting fɔ – I'd almost die if that sort of
              hapɛn   thing could happen

although I have never recorded either usage in colloquial or narrative styles. There is a further use of *wan* which is found in utterances like:

A wan go, a si sɔm man – As I went along, I saw a man.

This *wan* is almost a marker of narrative style and does not collocate with any other auxiliary. It indicates the contemporaneity of the actions in the two verb phrases.

Summarizing the above information, we can say that a rule for auxiliary could take the form:

$$\text{Aux} \rightarrow (bin/go/fɔ) \begin{cases} wan \\ (dɔn)\ (di) \end{cases}$$

and these auxiliaries have certain characteristics.

1. They cannot occur alone in an independent sentence. One can distinguish between *go* as an auxiliary and *go* as a full verb in that the former is not normally stressed.

2. They can be omitted in consecutive clauses:

A di wikɔp fɔ mɔningtam, was ma skin, mek chɔp . . . – I invariably get up in the morning, wash, prepare food . . .

This technique is particularly apparent in story-telling, where the raconteur sets the time at the beginning of the story, often by the use of such formula as : *Sɔm dei bin dei* – There was once a day, occasionally recapitulates the time setting in the course of the narration and then uses unmarked verb forms:

Sɔm dei bin dei, trɔki bin di waka tek smɔl bris. I wan waka i si sɔm hama hama ɛlɛfan . . . So trɔki bin go fain sɔm ɔda ɛlɛfan. I go i . . .	—Once upon a time Tortoise was out for a stroll. As he was walking he saw an enormous elephant . . . So tortoise went to look for another elephant. He went off . . .

3. When they occur in groups the order is fixed. This marks them out from co-occurring full verbs where we can have:

I bin kam tekam go — He came, took it and went off
I bin go tekam kam — He went, got it and came back
I bin tekam go kam — He took it, went off with it and came here
I bin tekam kam go — He took it, came here and went off

and:

I bin kam go tekam — He came so that he could go and get it.

4. Auxiliaries cannot take the bound morpheme -*am*:

A bin tekam

but not:

**A binam.*

5. Auxiliaries do not occur in tags. The universal CP tag question is *no bi so?*:

I di go, no bi so? – He's going, isn't he?
Wuna bin go, no bi so? – You went, didn't you?
Dɛm go go, no bi so? – They'll go, won't they?
I nɛva go, no bi so? – He hasn't gone yet, has he?

Apart from the above auxiliaries, there are three verbs in CP which function as full verbs but which have also certain characteristics of auxiliaries. These are *fit*, *mek* and *mɔs*. *Fit* can imply ability:

A di go skul, so a fit tɔk grama – I go to school and so I'm able to speak good English (i.e. grammar).

Mek is used to turn a command into a polite imperative:

Mek a go, a bɛg – Please, let me go
Mek yu go, a bɛg – Please, go
Mek wuna no go, a bɛg – Please, don't go
Mek dɛm no go, a bɛg – Please, don't let them go.

and *mɔs* indicates necessity:

Yu mɔs go naunau – You must go immediately.

Although these verbs act like auxiliaries in that they precede the head verb, they can all occur as finite verbs:

I fit ɔ i no fit? – Can he or can't he?
A go trai mekam kam – I'll try to persuade him to come
I tɔk sei a no mɔs, bɔt a mɔs – He says that I shouldn't but I should.

One of the ways in which CP differs from SE is in its extensive use of serial verbs:

No bigin kam hala man so – Don't start coming (here) to shout at people
I kam tekam go putam fɔ hol – He came to get it, took it away and put it in a hole.

Serial verbs frequently carry the same type of meaning that would be carried by verbs and prepositions or adverbs in SE:

Tekam go – Take it away (from me)
Bringam kam – Bring it over (i.e. to me/here)
I rɔn go rich di haus – He ran until he reached the house.

There is only one irregular verb in CP and, as one might expect, that verb is *BE*. The semantic area covered by *BE* in SE is covered by three CP forms *bi*, *dei* and *na*. *Bi* seems to be a relatively recently adopted form in that it is not used by many older speakers, but it is gradually taking over many of the usages of *dei* and *na*:

          Gɔd dei – God exists
    I go dei fɔ haus – He'll be in the house
    I go bi fɔ haus – He'll be in the house
    I fain, no bi so? – She's lovely, isn't she?
  Diswan na trenja – He/she is a stranger/visitor
  Diswan bi trenja – He/she is a stranger/visitor
Na dans a bin dans – I really danced.

Dei alone can have existential reference:

        Mɔni dei – There's money there

and it can be preceded by all the auxiliaries except *di*, *dɔn* and *nɛva*:

        A dei – I'm here
    A no bin dei – I wasn't there
    A go dei – I'll be there.

Bi is the only form of the BE verb that can occur in tags:

    I laikam, no bi so? – He likes it, doesn't he?

It normally takes a complement, either a noun phrase:

        I bin bi treda – He was a trader

or a locative phrase:

    I bin bi fɔ haus – He was at home/in the house.

Bi is less likely than *dei* to occur in simple locative sentences but more likely than *dei* to occur in verb phrases which require auxiliary modification. *Bi* can be preceded by all CP's auxiliaries and, although the combination *di bi* is rare, it occurs in such sentences as:

Wishkain nɔiz di bi fɔ hia? – What kind of noise do you get here? (i.e. What's the noise that regularly comes from here?)

Na can never replace or be replaced by *dei*. It has neither existential nor locative features. It can be used as an identifying verb:

    Datwan na ma sista – That one is my sister

and as a means of foregrounding and thus highlighting conten-
tives (see p. 137). *Na* is one of the most frequently used verbs
in CP[11] and it is unique in that it cannot take any auxiliary
modification. Indeed it cannot even be negated in urban CP,
although I recorded:

I no na soja – He's not a soldier

from an old, rural speaker.

Bi, dei and *na* are still clearly distinguished in CP:

dei can imply both existential and locative reference, *bi* can be
used for locative reference, in equative sentences and in tags and
na occurs in equative sentences and as a foregrounder, but
already *bi* is becoming more widely used and it is possible that it
will gradually replace *dei* and *na*.

3.6 CONCLUSION

There is very much more that one could examine in CP, its
idiomatic language, its narrative techniques, its wealth of prover-
bial wisdom, its speech styles. What I have tried to do, however, is
to indicate its uniqueness while at the same time taking into
account its relationship to English. In many ways it is a different
language, but this is partly because it reflects a different way of
life. As a language it gained a foothold in Cameroon because of
the contact between English and non-English speakers, but it
developed into the useful language it is today because it was,
albeit unconsciously, sanctioned by the Cameroon people.

NOTES

1. The country has been called 'Camerões' by the Portuguese,
   'Kamerun' by the Germans, 'Cameroun' by the French and 'The
   Cameroons' by the British. The country's official policy is to use
   'Cameroun' when writing in French and 'Cameroon' when writing
   in English.
2. References to Douala, then known as 'Cameroon', occur in
   Anterra Duke's diary. The entry for 3 October 1785, for example,
   reads:

148

. . . so I mak goods for Callabar antera to go in Commrown . . .
(i.e. so I got together goods for Calabar Anterra to go to
Cameroon)

(Forde, 1956: 90)

and when King Akwa of Douala wrote to Queen Victoria in
August 1879 he specifically referred to Calabar:

Dearest Madam,

We your servants have join together and thoughts it better to
write you a nice loving letter which will tell you all about our
wishes. We wish to have your laws in our towns. We wish to
have every fashioned altered, also we will do according to your
consul's word. Plenty wars here in our country. Plenty murder
and idol worshippers. Perhaps these lines of our writing will
look to you as an idle tale.

We have spoken to the English consul plenty times about an
English government here. We never have answer from you, so
we wish to write you ourselves.

When we heard about Calabar river, how they have all
English laws in their towns, and how they have put away all their
superstitions, oh, we shall be very glad to be like Calabar now.

(LeVine, 1964: 20)

3. See, for example, King Akwa's letter quoted above.
4. To refer to the population as 'francophone' does not imply that all
    or even most of the community can speak French. It simply means
    that the people in the region were governed by the French after the
    First World War and that education in early primary school is
    through the medium of French.
5. Swadesh's list is contained in Hymes (1960) and Swadesh (1972).
    To have followed either list precisely would have meant duplicat-
    ing or even triplicating many items because CP's vocabulary tends
    to be multifunctional and polysemous.
6. In these lists I have referred to only one language from which the
    item may have been borrowed although, in each case, several
    African languages could have been cited.
7. As one might expect, the greatest density of African-derived words
    occur in the vocabularies associated with culture, food and
    clothing.
8. Ideophones, where the sound of a word bears some resemblance to
    its meaning, are also important in CP and are particularly common
    in narratives. Often, they are onomatopoeic but they can also be
    used to imply colour, taste, smell, touch and intensity of feeling.
    The following are frequently-used ideophones:

    Kwakwa! A sei, kɔmbi, yu dei? – Knock-knock! I say, friend, are
    you in?

    Dat wowo dɔg di soso nwanwa – That ugly dog is always bark-
    ing

149

I bin fɔl pum! – He fell thump!
Wi bin go luk di tumtum wata – We went to look at the water-
fall.

9. *Dɔn* can occur as *dɔ̃*, *dɔn* and *dɔng*, depending on the initial
consonant in the following word:
A dɔ̃ bi fɔ haus – I have just been home
A dɔn tekam go – I have just taken it away
Yu dɔng kam! – Welcome!
I have regularised the spelling to *dɔn*.

10. Although *sɔfri sɔfri* derives from 'softly softly', the second syllable
is a suffix in English only. Indeed, this reduplication often
functions as a noun:
Sɔfri sɔfri kach monki – Easy does it
and in Liberian English *sɔfli sɔfli* is the name given to a lemur
believed to be so strong that it can choke monkeys to death.

11. *Na*'s origin is a mystery although it may have been reinforced by
'now', often pronounced *na*.

REFERENCES AND SUGGESTIONS FOR FURTHER READING

ARDENER. E. W., *Coastal Bantu of the Cameroons*, London: International African Institute, 1956.

ARDENER, S. G., *Eye-witnesses to the Annexation of Cameroon*, Buea:
Government Printer, 1968.

AUBRY, P., *Pidjin: Petite Grammaire et Vocabulaire*, Yaoundé:
Imprimerie St-Paul, n.d.

BERRY, J. AND GREENBERG, J. H., *Current Trends in Linguistics 7:
Linguistics in Sub-Saharan Africa*, The Hague: Mouton, 1971.

BRIDGEMAN, J. AND CLARKE, D. E., *German Africa*, Palo Alto: Stanford
University Press, 1965.

COURADE, C. AND G., *Education in Anglophone Cameroon*, Yaounde:
National Geographic Centre, 1977.

DALBY, DAVID, *Black through White: Patterns of Communication*,
Bloomington: Indiana University African Studies Publication, 1970.

DAVIDSON, BASIL, *Africa in Modern History*, London: Penguin Books,
1978.

DEBEL, ANNE, *Cameroon Today*, Tours: Editions, JA, 1977.

DE FÉRAL, CAROLE, *Le Pidgin-English Camerounais: essai de définition
linguistique et sociolinguistique*, Nice: Publications de l'Institut
d'Etudes et de Recherches Interethniques et Interculturelles, 1980.

FONLON, BERNARD, 'A Case for Early Bilingualism', *Abbia 4*, Yaoundé,
1963.

FONLON, BERNARD, 'The Language Problem in Cameroon', *Abbia* 22, Yaoundé, 1969.

FORDE, C. DARYLL, *Efik Traders of Old Calabar*, London: International African Institute, 1956.

GREGERSON, EDGAR A., *Language in Africa*, New York: Gordon and Breach, 1977.

GWEI, SOLOMON N., *History of the British Baptist Mission in Cameroon with Beginnings in Fernando Po*, unpublished BD thesis, Baptist Theological College, Rüschlikon-Zurich, 1966.

KING FO TOLY, Pidgin English column in the *Courrier Sportif du Bénin*, 28 January, 1974.

KOENIG, EDNA L. AND THE SOCIOLINGUISTIC SURVEY TEAM, *A Sociolinguistic Profile of Urban Centres in Cameroon*, mimeographed Working Paper of the University of Cameroon, Yaoundé, 1977–8.

HYMES, DELL, 'Lexicostatistics So Far', *Current Anthropology 1*, pp. 3–44, 1960.

JOHNSON, W. R., *The Cameroon Federation*, New Jersey: Princetown University Press, 1970.

LABARTHE, P., *Voyage à la Côte du Guinée*, Paris: Debray, 1803.

LEWIS, THOMAS, *These Seventy Years: An autiobiography by Thomas Lewis, Missionary in Cameroon and Congo, 1883–1923*, London: The Carey Press, n.d.

LEVINE, VICTOR, *Cameroon: Mandate to Independence*, Berkeley: University of California Press, 1964.

KERKVLIET, A., *The Sunday Gospels and Epistles with short explanations in Pidgin-English*, Buea: Catholic Mission Press, n.d.

MBASSI-MANGA, F., 'Cameroon: a marriage of three cultures', *Abbia 5*, Yaoundé, 1964.

MOORE, F., *Travels into the Inland Parts of Africa*, London: E. Cave, 1738.

MVENG, E., *Histoire du Cameroun*, Paris: Présence Africaine, 1963.

MVENG, E. AND NKOUMBA, D. BELING, *Manuel d'Histoire du Cameroun*, Yaoundé: Centre d'Edition et du Production pour l'Enseignement et la Recherche, 1978.

PALMER, F. R., *A Linguistic Study of the English Verb*, London: Longman, 1965.

ROWLANDS, E. C., *Teach Yourself Yoruba*, London: The English Universities Press Ltd, 1969.

RUDIN, HARRY, *Germans in the Cameroons*, New Haven: Yale University Press, 1938.

SCHNEIDER, G. D., *West-African Pidgin-English*, Athens, Ohio: G. D. Schneider, 1969.

SOCIÉTÉ BIBLIQUE, *Di Gud Nyus Hawe St Mark Bi Ratam*, Cameroun-Gabon: Société Biblique, 1966.

SPENCER, JOHN (ed.), *The English Language in West Africa*, London: Longman, 1971.

SWADESH, MORRIS, *The Origin and Diversifiction of Language*, Chicago: Aldine, 1971.

TODD, LORETO, *Some Day Been Dey: West African Pidgin Folktales*, London: Routledge and Kegan Paul, 1979.

TODD, LORETO, *Varieties of English around the World: Cameroon*, Heidelberg: Julius Groos Verlag, 1982.

CHAPTER 4

Case Study Two:
Papua New Guinea Tok Pisin

𝕊𝕊𝕊𝕊𝕊𝕊

4.1 HISTORICAL BACKGROUND

The large island which now constitutes Irian Jaya and Papua New Guinea (see Maps 6 and 8) was first visited by Europeans in the early sixteenth century. In 1512 a Portuguese navigator, Antonio d'Abreu, sighted the island and fourteen years later, in 1526, Jorge de Meneses, the Portuguese governor of the Moluccas, named it 'Ilhas dos Papuas' - Island of Curly-Haired People.[1] Spanish explorers also showed an interest in the island, referring to it in 1528 as 'Isla del Oro', Island of Gold, but it was in 1545 that the Spanish navigator Ynigo Ortiz de Retes, gave it the name by which it was to become best known - 'Nueva Guinea' — New Guinea,[2] and this was the name used by Mercator on his map of the world in 1569.

By the early seventeenth century the Dutch had begun to oust the Spanish from the East Indies, and by 1643 they had surveyed large stretches of the New Guinea mainland and many of the adjacent islands. At this time too the British began to show an interest in the Pacific but, although William Dampier sailed along the north-east coast of New Guinea in 1670, it was not until nearly a hundred years later, 1764–7, that John Byron and Philip Carteret named and annexed some of the islands in the area, principally New Ireland and New Britain.

In 1768 a French expedition to the area was led by Louis-Antoine de Bougainville. He surveyed the island which now bears his name, but apart from this venture the French showed very little interest in New Guinea.

The British were the first Europeans to try to settle on the New Guinea coast but their attempt in 1793 to colonise Bird's Head peninsula in modern Irian Jaya proved unsuccessful, and so they

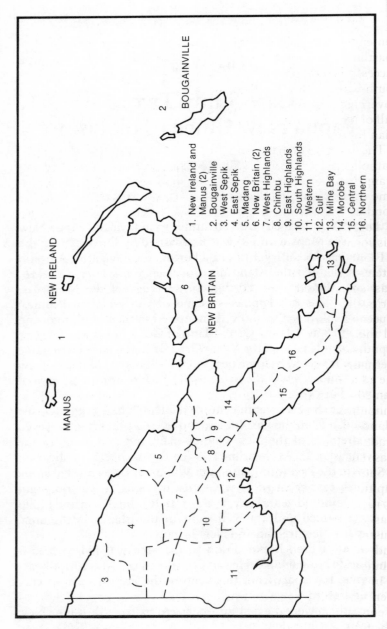

MANUS

NEW IRELAND

BOUGAINVILLE

NEW BRITAIN

1. New Ireland and
   Manus (2)
2. Bouganville
3. West Sepik
4. East Sepik
5. Madang
6. New Britain (2)
7. West Highlands
8. Chimbu
9. East Highlands
10. South Highlands
11. Western
12. Gulf
13. Milne Bay
14. Morobe
15. Central
16. Northern

MAP 6: DISTRICTS OF PNG

contented themselves with making an accurate map of the coastline, a task they completed in 1873. The Dutch were more successful colonisers. In 1828 they established a settlement in the south-west of New Guinea and twenty years later, in 1848, the government of the Netherlands laid claim to the entire western half of New Guinea, an area approximately equivalent to modern Irian Jaya.

The first Christian missionaries to New Guinea were a group of Catholic Marist Brothers who arrived in 1847 but this attempt to evangelise the country was soon abandoned. In 1874, by which time traders had opened up several routes into the interior, the London Mission Society established a permanent mission station in Port Moresby (see Map 7) and a year later a Methodist missionary centre was opened in New Britain.

From the 1870s the Germans began to show a greatly increased interest in the Pacific, and from 1880 their desire for New Guinea was so marked that the Queensland government became seriously alarmed. To pre-empt German designs on New Guinea, Queensland in 1883 annexed the eastern half of New Guinea and all the offshore islands on behalf of Britain. Britain, however, repudiated the action and, instead, came to an agreement with Germany. On 3 November 1884 north-eastern New Guinea and the adjacent islands were proclaimed a German Protectorate and named 'Kaiser Wilhelmsland'. On 6 November Britain announced that south-east New Guinea and its neighbouring islands were to become a British Protectorate. The British area gradually became the responsibility of Australia and the region was renamed 'The Australian Territory of Papua' in 1904.

Shortly after the outbreak of the First World War, the Germans capitulated to an Australian military force and, on 17 September 1914, German New Guinea came under Australian rule. This rule was ratified in 1920 when the League of Nations granted Australia the mandate to govern the 'Territory of New Guinea', and so Australia became responsible for both Papua and New Guinea although the territories were administered separately.

In 1942 the Japanese invaded and conquered New Guinea but were not able to gain complete control of Papua and they were eventually driven from the island by the Allied Forces in 1945. The following year the United Nations gave Australia the right to administer the two territories and in 1949 these were officially

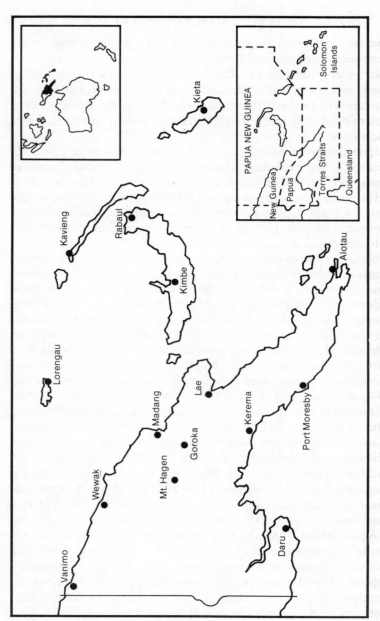

MAP 7: CHIEF TOWNS

amalgamated, with Port Moresby being designated capital of the Territories of Papua and New Guinea.

In 1962 Holland agreed to the independence of what is now Irian Jaya and this stimulated the desire for similar autonomy in the two territories, a desire that was fully encouraged by Australia. By 1971 the House of Assembly in Port Moresby adopted a national flag and decided to name the united territories 'Papua New Guinea'. On 1 December 1973 Papua New Guinea became self-governing and, less than two years later, on 16 September 1975, it achieved the status of an independent nation.

It is not possible to offer precise details of how and when Tok Pisin[3] arose. English may well have been heard on the New Guinea mainland as early as 1793 when the first attempt at colonisation was made, and a rudimentary Pidgin English was probably in widespread use in the Pacific in the nineteenth century (see 2.5). The creolising of Pacific Pidgin English was almost certainly a direct result of 'Blackbirding', the system of indentured labour which began in the middle of the nineteenth century and which involved the transportation of Pacific islanders to large, European-run plantations. Blackbirding did not affect Papua New Guinea markedly before 1879 but, after this date, considerable numbers of Papua New Guineans found themselves working in Samoa or Queensland. Because of the 1884 division of the country, the New Guineans tended to be employed in Samoa whereas the Papuans were taken to Queensland. In all, about six thousand New Guineans worked in Samoa as indentured labourers or *kanakas* between 1879 and 1912 and when they returned home, they found that their Plantation Pidgin had both status and value; status because it was the mark of a man who had travelled and value because of the multilingual nature of Papua New Guinea. The speech of these returned *kanakas* formed the nucleus of the modern TP.

As far as the Papuans are concerned, precise figures are not available but Parnaby (1964: 203ff) claims that 752 labourers from the Torres Straits area (some of whom may have been Papuans) worked in Queensland and would, undoubtedly, have acquired Queensland Plantation Pidgin English. Of these, 452 were eventually repatriated to the Torres Straits and if some of these men settled in Papua, they would have found their Pidgin English less valuable than their countrymen did in New Guinea, partly because of their numerical insignificance and partly because Papua already had a viable lingua franca in Hiri Motu.

4.2 SOCIOLINGUISTIC BACKGROUND

Papua New Guinea is, without doubt, one of the most multi-lingual countries on earth. Its three million inhabitants use approximately seven hundred different mother tongues which belong to two different language families – Austronesian (A) and Non-Austronesian (NA) (see Map 8). In addition, the country possesses two widely-used lingua francas, Hiri Motu and Tok Pisin. The former developed between speakers of A and NA languages and was used as a trade language in Papua. It spread quite rapidly in the twentieth century because trade was stimu-lated by the Australians and also because, under the name of *Police Motu*, it became the language of the multilingual police force. Today it is spoken by about 150,000 speakers and because of its widespread use on radio and its official status,[4] it seems in little danger of dying out.

TP, as we have seen, was at first mainly confined to the northern part of Papua New Guinea but it is now found throughout the country. It is spoken by more than 750,000 people, for many of whom, especially the children of inter-tribal marriages and those in urban communities, it is a mother tongue.

Papua New Guinea's constitution does not specify any lan-guage as the official language of the country, but as in other ex-British colonies, there is an acknowledgement of the value of English. English is the language of almost all education,[5] of much commerce and of most high-level diplomacy,[6] but the Papua New Guinea government is also keenly aware of the value of its two lingua francas in complementing the roles of English. Indeed, it requires citizenship applicants to be proficient in either TP or Hiri Motu as well as English.

Since much of Papua New Guinea's population lives in mountainous terrain with no access roads and few facilities, universal primary education is, as yet, only a dream although so-called 'community schools' are to be found in all towns and in a growing number of villages. After the Second World War, many parents were eager to send their children, especially their sons, to

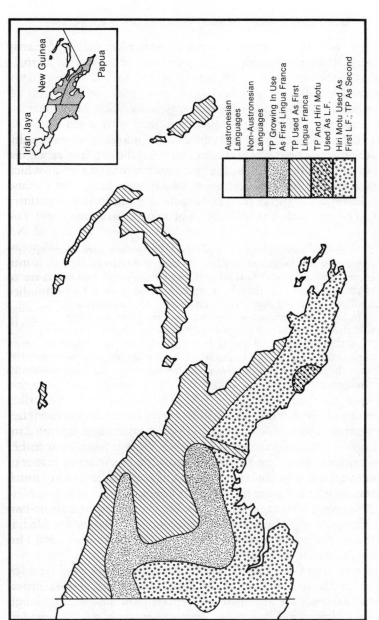

MAP 8: LANGUAGES OF PAPUA NEW GUINEA

Austronesian
Languages

Non-Austronesian
Languages

TP Growing In Use
As First Lingua Franca

TP Used As First
Lingua Franca

TP And Hiri Motu
Used As L.F.

Hiri Motu Used As
First L.F.; TP As Second

Irian Jaya

New Guinea

Papua

school, because after a few years of education they had learnt enough English to be able to get a job in one of the towns. There is today, however, some unwillingness on the part of many parents to send children who could otherwise work on the land to community schools for six years, especially since this education does not guarantee employment and may only open doors to expensive secondary school education. There is also increasing concern among parents and educators that the children emerging from community schools are not really proficient in any language. Percy Chatterton, in his autobiography *Day That I Have Loved* (Sydney, 1974: 50–51), summarises this feeling of malaise when he writes that an all-English primary education:

> . . . has produced a generation of school leavers who are not effectively literate in any language at all. . . . Their ability to read English with understanding is too limited and too tenuous to be of much use to them; . . . [and] . . . they have never learned to read and write their own language and they have been conditioned to despise it.
>
> In fairness to educational planners of the post-war years it must be said that they gave the customers, that is, the pupils and their parents, what they wanted or thought they wanted. For English had become a cargo cult. Somewhere in the white man's language, it was thought, were the secret words of power, the 'open sesame' to the white man's affluence.

It seems likely that the above claim would be less applicable if the estimated 250,000 children at present attending community schools were instructed initially in their mother tongues or in TP. And since it would be virtually impossible to use seven hundred languages for educational purposes, TP could be a very useful bridge between the vernaculars and English.

All spoken languages, including TP, show variation according to region, age, education and use but as TP has an official orthography and was standardised (and perhaps regularised[7]) by Hall in papers written between 1942 and 1955, it has fewer variants than CP. In addition, TP is the language employed for approximately one-third of all radio broadcasts and so Papua New Guineans are provided with a prestigious and standardising norm. Although TP is more homogeneous than CP, it is still possible to distinguish a Papuan from a New Guinean speaker, a mainland from an island speaker, or an Australian from a Papua

New Guinean, mainly because TP speakers tend to use the phonologies of their mother tongues. It is also comparatively easy to differentiate between an urban speaker and a rural one. The former is likely to use anglicised pronunciations and more English items, *rikrut* rather than *krut* (recruit), *stesin* rather than *tesin*(station), *spika* rather than *man bilong toktok* (speaker), and *maus bilong wara* rather than *lek bilong wara* for 'mouth of a river'. The lack of large-scale morphological or syntactic variation in TP does not, however, preclude a fluent speaker from using the language to indicate respect, amusement, wit, insult, appreciation of beauty or delight in verbal repartee.

4.3 THE PHONOLOGY OF TOK PISIN

As we have seen in 4.2, TP has been standardised and although idiolectal preferences and mother-tongue influences are still apparent, they are less obvious in radio TP than in the speech of older Papua New Guineans. Since the former TP has more prestige, that is the variety we will describe.

4.3.1 *Phonemes*
TP has eight vowel phonemes, five monophthongs and three diphthongs:

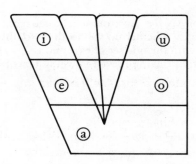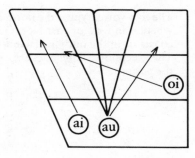

and it has eighteen consonantal phonemes although 'h', 'j' and 'y' have a light phonemic load:

	Bilabial	Dental	Palato-Alveolar	Palatal	Velar	Glottal
PLOSIVE	p b	t d			k g	
NASAL	m	n			ng	
AFFRICATE			j			
LATERAL		l r				
FRICATIVE	f v	s				h
SEMI VOWEL	w			y		

4.3.2. *General Comments on TP's Phonology – Vowels*

In TP all syllables are approximately the same length because, for most fluent speakers,[8] it is a syllable-timed language. Lengthened vowels do occur but only for emphasis:

Em i bi : : :kpela moa – He is extremely big.

The five-vowel system is almost certainly a carry-over from the Austronesian mother tongues. As Capell puts it:

> The five-vowel type is the norm for AN [i.e. Austronesian] languages, whether in west or east New Guinea, whether on the north or south coasts or in the outlying islands, with the one set of exceptions . . . . The exceptional languages are a group having a seven-vowel system of the pattern:

$$
\begin{array}{ccc}
i & & u \\
e & & o \\
\varepsilon & & \mathfrak{o} \\
& a &
\end{array}
$$

(1969: 27)

Diphthongs are relatively uncommon in TP, except in idiolects which have been influenced by SE. Frequently, /ai/ is realised as /e/

so that for many speakers *wel* can mean 'wild' as well as 'oil' and some speakers either monophthongise /au/ and /oi/ or realise them both as /ɔ/. As more and more speakers become literate, however, spelling will reinforce and possibly extend the use of the three diphthongs.

4.3.3 *Consonants*

We have listed eighteen consonant phonemes because this is the system favoured by young, educated speakers. Older, less well-educated users of TP frequently use only a fourteen-consonant system, omitting 'h', 'j' and 'y' and not differentiating between 'p' and 'f'. For many speakers too, 'l' and 'r' are not differentiated but are both realised as /ɹ/. Once again, however, education and spelling conventions are contributing to their differentiation.

In TP 'p', 't' and 'k' are usually without aspiration, even when they occur in word initial position. Their voiced counterparts, 'b', 'd', and 'g' are devoiced in word final position and are transcribed as 'p', 't' and 'k':

rap < 'rub'
bat < 'bad'
bik < 'big'.

The devoicing of consonants in word final position may have become regularised when TP was being used as a lingua franca between New Guineans and Germans. In TP 'f' and 'v' are bilabial plosives and so are often heard as 'p' and 'b' by mother-tongue English speakers. It was the acoustic similarity between /ø/ and /p/ which almost certainly led to the now accepted spelling of 'fellow' as *pela*.

Consonant clusters are often split by the insertion of an intrusive vowel, especially by Papuans. The intrusive vowel may be 'i', 'a' or 'u', largely depending on the vowel in the syllable beginning with the cluster:

$s^a tap$ – 'stop', 'stay'
$g^i rin$ – 'green'
$k^u ru$ – 'sprout', 'shoot'.

In TP, it is possible for 'ng' to occur in word initial position:

ngong – mute

but many Papuans tend to substitute 'n' for 'ng' in all positions, and there is a tendency for all speakers to nasalise 'b', 'd', and 'g', especially when they occur medially:

$ta^{m}bu$ – taboo
em i ^{n}dai – he fainted.

This tendency is much less obvious in the speech of young speakers, particularly in English-derived words, and so it is not indicated in the orthography.

4.4 TP'S LEXICON

4.4.1 *Tok Pisin's Core Vocabulary – Numbers*
The numbers in TP all derive from English although their forms may have received some reinforcing from German and their patterning from the vernaculars. The first ten numbers have two forms depending on whether or not they precede a noun:

wan –	1	*wanpela man* –	1 man
tu –	2	*tupela man* –	2 men
tri –	3	*tripela man* –	3 men
foa –	4	*fopela man* –	4 men
faiv –	5	*faipela man* –	5 men
sikis –	6	*sikispela man* –	6 men
seven –	7	*sevenpela man* –	7 men
et –	8	*etpela man* –	8 men
nain –	9	*nainpela man* –	9 men
ten –	10	*tenpela man* –	10 men.

The remaining numbers have only one form, thus:

wanpela ten wan – 11   *wanpela ten wan man* – 11 men
wanpela ten tu – 12
wanpela ten tri – 13
tupela ten – 20
tupela ten tu – 22
tripela ten – 30
tripela ten tri – 33
faipela ten faiv – 55
wan handet – 100

wan handet wan – 101
wan handet wanpela
ten wan – 111
wan tausen – 1000
faiv tausen faiv
handet faipela
ten faiv – 5555.

4.4.2 *Body Parts and Functions*

ai – eye, opening, lid (<Eng. 'eye')
1. *Bipo tru, diwai i gat tupela ai na wanpela ia* – A long time ago, trees had two eyes and one ear.
ai occurs in many compounds including:
    ai bilong botol – bottle lid/opening
    ai bilong sua – the mouth of a wound
    aipas – blind (<Eng. eye + fast).

as – anus, buttocks, foundation, cause (<Eng. 'ass/arse')
2. *Bai em i paitim as bilong pikinini* – Soon she will spank the child (lit. By-and-by she fight + T-marker buttocks belong child).

baksait – back, rear (<Eng. 'backside')
3. *Em i givim baksait long pikinini meri* – He turned his back on the little girl.

banis – ribs, chest, enclosure, fence (<Eng. 'fence')
4. *Banis bilong mi i pen. Mi laik i go long haus sik* – My chest hurts. I want to go to the hospital.
Occasionally *bros* (<Ger. 'Brust') is used instead of *banis*:
5. *Narapela man i gat bikpela pen long bros bilongen* – Another man has a terrible pain in his chest.

bel – belly, stomach, womb, heart, seat of the emotions (<Eng. 'belly', reinforced by vernacular usage)
6. *Ol i bel hevi long liklik pikinini em i sik nogut tru* – They were all very sad because the little child was very ill.
Bel occurs in many calques and idiomatic expressions, among them:
    belgut – happy, good humoured (<belly + good)
    belklin – sincere (<belly + clean)

beltru – faithful (< belly + true).
givim bel – impregnate (< give + belly)
kisim bel – become pregnant (< catch + belly)
rausim bel – miscarry (< Ger. raus + belly).

blut – blood (< Ger. 'Blut' reinforced by Eng. 'blood')
7. *Wanpela pikinini man i katim em long busnaip na blut i kamap* – A young boy cut himself with a bushknife and the blood gushed out.

bokis (occasionally *kan*) – female genitals (< Eng. 'box'/'can')
8. *Yu no ken lukim bokis bilong meri* – You must not look at a woman's genitals.

bun – bone, skeleton (< Eng. 'bone')
9. *Em i bun nating, olsem stik masis* – She's just skin and bone, just like a matchstick.

fut – foot, leg (< Eng. 'foot' reinforced by Ger. 'Fuss')
10. *Em i lukim mak bilong fut long wesan* – He saw footprints in the sand.

gras – grass, hair, fur, feathers (< Eng. 'grass')
11. *Bai yu mas sevim gras bilong het bilong yu* – You'll have to shave the hair off your head.
The compound *mausgras* (< mouth + grass) can refer to a moustache, a beard or a catfish.

han – hand, arm, sleeve, branch (< Eng. 'hand' reinforced by Ger. 'Hand')
12. *Mi no gat lek na han. Mi save wokabaut long bel tasol. Ol man i lukim ol i save pret. Kaikai bilong mi em i rokrok na natnat na rat. Wanem nem bilong mi? Moran.* – I have no legs nor arms. I go around on my belly. Everyone who sees me is afraid. My food is frogs, mosquitoes and rats. What's my name? A python.

hat (occasionally *pam, klok*) – heart (< Eng. 'heart', 'pump/clock')
This refers only to the organ, never in the TP of Papua New Guineans to the seat of the emotions.
13. *Hat i meknois* – The heart is beating (making noise).

het – head, skull, top (<Eng. 'head')
14. *Het bilong yu diwai!* – You're stupid! (lit. Head bilong you wood/tree).

ia (occasionally *yau*) – ear (<Eng. 'ear' reinforced by Ger. 'Ohr')
15. *Yupela pikinini, putim ia* – You children, listen attentively.

kok – penis (<Eng. 'cock')
16. *I no longtaim, em i katim laplap bilong kok bilong dispela pikinini man* – Soon, he will circumcise this child.

kokeru – clitoris (<Eng. 'cock')
17. *Sapos yu katim kokeru bilong pikinini meri, yu mekim samting nogut* – Female circumcision is wrong (lit. Suppose you cut a little girl's clitoris, you are doing something bad).

lek – leg, foot, footprint (<Eng. 'leg'). See 12.

maus – mouth, opening, beak, snout (<Eng. 'mouth')
18. *Em i brukim maus bilong nil* – She broke the eye of the needle.

nek – neck, throat, melody (<Eng. 'neck' reinforced by vernacular usage)
19. *Papa i pasim liklik rop long nek bilong hos na em i holim rop* – Papa is putting a little rope round the horse's neck and he is holding the rope.

nus – nose, prow of a boat (<Eng. 'nose' reinforced by Ger. 'Nase')
20. *Nus bilong pikinini i gat kus* – The child's nose is running (*kus* – mucus).
Nus occurs in a number of combinations and calques:
    hul bilong nus – nostril (hole belong nose)
      kukim nus – rub (i.e. cook) noses, kiss,
                make love
     sutim nus – punch/make a fool of someone
              (shoot nose).

pekpek – excrement, manure, scum (<Gaz. 'pekpek' – 'excrement')
21. *Yu pekpek blut?* – Have you got dysentery?

pes – face, front (< Eng. 'face')
22. *Pes bilong haus i bruk pinis* – The front of the house has fallen down.

pinga – finger (< Eng. 'finger')
23. *Em wanem? Em wanpela pinga bilong lek?* – What is it? It's a toe.
Pinga occurs in such compounds as:
> *bikpela pinga bilong lek* – big toe
>> *bikpela pinga* – thumb
>> *skru bilong pinga* – knuckle.

pispis – urine, urinate (< Eng. 'piss')
24. *Ol i pispis blut* – They have blackwater fever.

skin – skin, hide, body, corpse (< Eng. 'skin' reinforced by vernacular usage)
25. *Skin bilongen slek* – He is tired (lit. Skin belong + him slack).

skru – joint, screw (< Eng. 'screw')
26. *Pikinini i sindaun long skru bilong mama bilongen* – The child is sitting on his mother's knee.
Skru combines with *bilong* plus other body parts to indicate specific joints:
> *skru bilong fut* – ankle
> *skru bilong han* – elbow
> *skru bilong lek* – knee
>> *tanim skru* – twist a joint
>> *mama skru* – nut
>> *papa skru* – bolt.

susu – milk, breast (< Mal. 'susu' – 'breast', 'milk')
27. *Dispela pikinini meri em i no gat susu* – This girl has not reached puberty.

tang – tongue (< Eng. 'tongue')
28. *Bai em i givim tang long em* – They will become intimate (lit. Fut. she give + T marker tongue long he).

tit – tooth, teeth (< Eng. 'teeth')
29. *Tit bilong lapun papa i pen* – The old man's tooth is aching.

wanpilai – playmate (one play)
wantok – speaker of the same language (one talk).

4.4.4 People/Professions

boskru – deckhand, sailor (<Eng. 'boat's crew')
  42. *Ol boskru i subim bot i go* – The sailors pushed out the boat.
  boskru bilong balus is the term for 'air steward/ess'.

dewel/tewel – soul, shadow, ghost (<Mel. 'tewel' reinforced by Eng. 'devil')
  43. *Mi pilim sik olsem dewel bilong mi i no stret* – I feel ill as if my spirit is not at ease.

didiman – farmer (<Ger. name 'Bredeman')
  44. *Em i nius bilong ol didiman* – Here is the news for farmers.

dokta – doctor (<Eng. 'doctor' reinforced by Ger. 'Doktor')
  45. *Pikinini bilong mi bai i kamap dokta* – My child will be a doctor.
  Dokta boi is the term used for a male nurse or orderly, whereas *nes/sista* are the terms normally applied to women.

draiva/draivaboi – local driver (<Eng. 'driver + boy')
  46. *Draivaboi bin bagarap ka bilong misis* – The driver ruined/wrote off the European woman's car.

kalabusman – prisoner, convict (<Port. 'calabouço' + Eng. 'man')
  47. *Dispela kalabusman bin stilim wilwil* – This prisoner stole a bicycle (i.e. wheel + wheel).

kamda – carpenter (<Eng. 'carpenter')
  48. *Bai em i go lainim wok kamda* – He will learn to be a carpenter.

kanaka – man, native, indentured labourer (< ? Malay 'kanak' – 'child' ? Eng. 'cane + hacker')
  49. *Dispela kanaka em i gat meri o nogat?* – Has this man got a wife or not?

kiap – official of the government, District Officer (<Eng. 'captain')

50. *Kiap i tokim long ol luluai* – The official is talking to the local chiefs.

kuskus – clerk, secretary, office (<? Malay 'kuras' – 'quire of paper')
51. *Dispela hap bilong kuskus bilong inkam takis i raitim tasol* – For office use only (Part of the income tax form).

lapun – old person, old (< Sol. I. 'lapun' – 'old')
52. *Lapun mama i save dispela stilman i mekim planti pasin nogut* – The old lady knows that this thief does lots of bad things (i.e. make + T marker plenty fashion no + good).

luluai – leader, chief (< Gaz. 'luluai' – 'chief'). See 50.

man – man, husband, person, male (< Eng. 'man' reinforced by Ger. 'Mann')
53. *Em i man bilong pait* – He is a warrior (i.e. man belong fight).

masalai – water spirit that can take the shape of a snake (< Manus 'masalai' – 'water spirit')
54. *Bai em i tanim long masalai* – He's going to turn into a spirit.

masta – master, ruler, European (< Eng. 'master')
55. *Ol masta i save kaikai bulmakau* – Europeans like to eat beef.

misis – European woman, single or married (< Eng. 'Mrs')
56. *Oltaim oltaim dispela misis i save go long bung* – This European woman is always going to the market.

ngong – deaf mute, ignorant person (< New I. 'ngong' – 'mute')
57. *Dispela ngong i no inap i go lang taun* – This deaf person is not able to go to town.

plismasta – police officer (< Eng. 'police + master')
58. *Long wanem taim plismasta bai i kam?* – When will the police officer come?

pris – priest (< Eng. 'priest' reinforced by *pris* meaning 'preach')
59. *Em i pris bilong popi* – He is a Catholic priest.
Popi is rarely used by Catholics to describe Catholics.

stilman – thief (< Eng. 'steal + man'). See 52.

sutboi – hunter (< Eng. 'shoot + boy')
60. *Sutboi i gat kainkain abus long bilum* – The hunter has all sorts of game in his bag.

tisa – teacher (< Eng. 'teacher')
61. *Tisa i kirap nogut long tokbek bilong ol pikinini* – The teacher is furious at the children's cheek.

tultul – chief's assistant, luluai's assistant/interpreter (< Gaz. 'tultul' – 'chief's assistant')
62. *Sapos tultul i wok gut, orait bai i kisim bikpela pe* – If the tultul works hard, he'll earn a good salary.

waitman – European, Caucasian (< Eng. 'white + man')
63. *Em haus bilong waitman* – That's a European's house.

4.4.5 Animals

anis – ant, ants (< Eng. 'ants' reinforced by Ger. 'Ameise')
64. *Mi save kaikai anis wantaim natnat* – I usually eat ants and mosquitoes.

binatang – bug, insect, grub (< Malay 'binatang' – 'animal, creature')
65. *Binatang bilong saksak i switpela* – The sago grub is delicious.

binen – bee, bees (< Ger. 'Beinen' reinforced by Eng. 'bee')
66. *I gat binen long bus* – There are bees in the woods.

blakbokis – flying fox (< Eng. 'black + fox')
67. *Blakbokis save painim kaikai long nait tasol* – Flying foxes can only hunt for food at night.

bulmakau – cow, cattle, beef (< Eng. 'bull and cow'). See 55.

dok – dog (< Eng. 'dog')
68. *Em i kisim wanpela weldok tru* – He caught a really wild dog.

donki – donkey (< Eng. 'donkey')
69. *Donki i no inap goapim dispela maunten* – A donkey won't be able to climb this mountain.

hos – horse (<Eng. 'horse'). See 19.

kakaruk – rooster, chicken, fowl (<Gaz. 'kakaruk' – 'rooster')
70. *Bai em i wokim wanpela haus kakaruk* – He is going to build a chicken coop.

kapul – tree kangaroo (<Gaz. 'kapul' – 'tree kangaroo')
71. *Kapul i go long wanpela diwai na em i lukim wanpela kumul* – The tree kangaroo went up a tree and saw a bird of paradise.

kavivi – hawk (<Gaz. 'kavavi' – 'hawk')
72. *Kavivi ting: Sapos mi no kisim sampela pisin kwiktaim, mi laik i dai* – The hawk thought: If I don't catch some birds quickly, I'm going to die.

kumul – bird of paradise (<Gaz. 'kumul' – 'bird of paradise')
73. *Nau em i tambu long sutim kumul* – It's now illegal to shoot birds of paradise.

meme – goat (<Gaz. 'meme' – 'goat' reinforced by onomatopoeia)
74. *Planti manmeri ol i laik i kaikai meme* – Lots of people like to eat goat.

muruk – cassowary (<Gaz. 'muruk' – 'cassowary')
75. *Man bilong pait i sutim muruk long supsup bilong banara* – The warrior killed a cassowary with an arrow from his bow.

natnat – mosquito, gnat (<Eng. 'gnat'). See 12.

pato – duck (<Port. 'pato' – 'duck')
76. *Bai yumi baim pato. Mama i mas kukim na bai mipela amamas* – You and I will buy a duck. Mama will cook it and we'll celebrate.

paul – fowl (<Eng. 'fowl')
77. *Ol i kisim tupela paul na wanpela sipsip* – They caught two chickens and one sheep.

pik – pig (<Eng. 'pig')
78. *Tripela liklik pik ol i stap long bus* – The three little pigs lived in the woods.

pis – fish (< Eng. 'fish' reinforced by Ger. 'Fisch')
79. *Papa i tromoim umben long wara bilong kisim pis* – Papa casts a net into the water to catch fish.

pisin – bird, tribe, Pidgin (< Eng. 'pigeon'/'pidgin')
80. *Ol pisin i laik i sindaun long dispela diwai* – The birds like sitting in this tree.

pislama – seaslug (< Port. 'bicho da mar' – 'sea slug')
81. *Ol man bilong Saina i save kaikai pislama tumas* – The Chinese really love eating seaslugs.

pukpuk – crocodile (< Mel. 'pukpuk' – 'crocodile')
82. *Pukpuk i no planti tumas. Ol i stap long tais long Sepik* – There are not many crocodiles. They stay in the swamps near Sepik.

pusi – cat (< Eng. 'pussy')
83. *Mi gat wanpela pusi. Em i no laikim rat* – I have a cat. She does not like rats.

rat – rat, mouse, rodent (< Eng. 'rat' reinforced by Ger. 'Ratte'). See 83.

rokrok – frog, toad (< Gaz. 'rokrok' – 'frog/toad' reinforced by onomatopoeia). See 12.

sipsip – sheep (< Eng. 'sheep'). See 77.

trausel – tortoise, turtle (< Eng. 'tortoise + shell')
84. *Wanpela liklik trausel em i lukim bikpela hos* – A little tortoise looked up at a big horse.

4.4.6 *Objects/Natural Phenomena*

akis (occasionally *tomiok*) – axe (< Eng. 'axe, and 'tomahawk')
85. *Em i tekim akis bilong daunim diwai* – He is taking the axe to fell a tree.

ain – iron, metal, steel, weapon tipped with metal (< Eng. 'iron')
86. *Ol i ken sutim pik long ain* – They can kill a pig with a metal-tipped weapon.

balus – dove, bird, aeroplane (< Gaz. 'balus' – 'dove')
87. *Balus bai i pundaun long Lae* – The plane will land at Lae.

banara – bow, bow and arrow (< Eng. 'bow and arrow'). See 75.

baret – ditch, groove, trench (< Malay 'parit' – 'trench')
   88. *Yu save wokim baret?* – Can you build a ditch?

brus – local tobacco (< ? Eng. 'brush')
   89. *Mi dai long brus* – I'm dying for a smoke.

bung – market, meeting (< Gaz. 'kivung' – 'meeting' reinforced by Eng. 'bung together' and Ger. 'Bund' – 'association')
   90. *Mi go long bung bilong baim kiau* – I am going to the market to buy eggs.

bunim – the north wind (< ? Solomon Is. 'bumburu' – 'north wind')
   91. *Bunim i kirap* – The north wind is rising.

bus – woods, jungle, outback (< Eng. 'bush')
   92. *Wailpik i stap long bus* – Wild pigs live in the woods.
Bus occurs in a number of compounds:
   bus kanaka – an uncivilised man
      bus man – a man who does not live in a city
      bus paul – wild fowl.

daiman – a dead/dying man (< Eng. 'die + man')
   93. *Ol i planim ol daiman long ples tambu* –They bury the dead in a sacred place.
   94. *Yu save wokim hul bilong planim daiman?* – Can you dig a grave?

de –day (< Eng. 'day')
   95. *Asde, i de namba faip bilong Februeri* – Yesterday was the fifth of February.
The days of the week are:
Mande, Tunde, Trinde, Fonde, Fraide, Sarere and *Sande*
and the day is divided into:
   sankamap – day break (sun come + up)
      tulait – day time (too + light)
   belo kaikai – noon (bell/signal eat)
   sangodaun – dusk, evening (sun go + down)
      tudak – night time (too + dark).

diwai – tree, wooden (< Gaz. 'diwai' – 'wood, tree'). See 80.

glasman – seer, prophet, fortune-teller (<Eng. 'glass (i.e. spy-glass) + man')
96. *Bai ol i go lukim glasman* – Eventually they'll go to visit a soothsayer.

graun – ground, earth (<Eng. 'ground')
97. *Bilong wanem mi kamap long dispela graun?* – Why am I on earth?

gris – fat, lard (<Eng. 'grease')
98. *Em i gat gris tumas* – He is too fat.

hama – hammer (<Eng. 'hammer' reinforced by Ger. 'Hammer')
99. *Bilong paitim liklik nil yu ken holim han bilong hama klostu long het bilong hama na paitim isi* – Before striking a little nail you should hold the shaft of the hammer close to the head and hit it gently. (From a manual *Buk bilong ol Kamda* – Book for Carpenters.)

haus – house (<Eng. 'house')
100. *Tupela i go bek long haus bilong kandere* – The two went back to their relatives' house.
Haus occurs in many compounds including:
    haus balus – hangar (house plane)
    haus blut – menstrual hut (house blood)
    haus dring – hotel (house drink)
    haus karim – birth hut (house bear + T-marker)
    haus kot – court (house court)
    haus lotu – church (house worship)
    haus pepa – office (house paper)
    haus sik – hospital (house sick)
    haus tambaran – ceremonial temple (house spirits of ancestors).

kiau – egg, pill (<Manus 'kiau' – 'egg'). See 90.

klaut – cloud, sky (<Eng. 'cloud')
101. *Mi lukim klaut bilong ren* – I see rain clouds.
Klaut occurs in the phrases:
    klaut i bruk/pairap – thunder (cloud break/fire + up)
    lait bilong klaut – lightning.

kopra – copra (< Malay 'kopra')

102. *Gavman bai i holim dispela mani bikos em i laik strongim prais bilong ol kopra sapos bai i go daun* – The government will hold this money because it wants to strengthen/support the price of copra if it goes down.

kunai – sword grass, brush (< Gaz. 'kunai')

103. *Bai ol i kukim kunai* – They will burn the brush.

malolo – rest, holiday, break from work (< Samoan 'malolo' – 'rest')

104. *Yu laik go long malolo?* – Do you want to go on a holiday?

mani – money (< Eng. 'money'). See 102.

maunten – mountain, hill (< Eng. 'mountain')

105. *Ol man bilong maunten i mekim singsing* – The Highlanders are celebrating.(The man bilong mountain [i.e. from the New Guinea Highlands] make song + and + dance.)

mumu – earth oven, local method of cooking (< Mel. 'mumu' – 'earth oven')

106. *Em i kukim kaukau long mumu* – She is cooking a type of yam in an earth oven.

mun – moon, month (< Eng. 'moon')

107. *Mun i lukim meri* – The woman is menstruating.

nambis – beach, shore (< ? Eng. 'on a beach/on the beach')

108. *Skul i pinis na mi go long nambis* – When school is over I go to the beach.

nil – needle, thorn, nail, injection (< Eng. 'nail'). See 99.

paia – fire (< Eng. 'fire')

109. *Bai yu mekim dai paia?* – Will you put out the fire? The term for 'ashes' is *sit bilong paia* (shit belong fire).

pipia – dirt, rubbish, refuse (< Mel. 'pipia' – 'dirt')

110. *Pikinini bilong diwai i olsem pipia nating long dispela ples* – Fruit (i.e. children of tree) is as plentiful as dirt in this place/village.

ples – village, region, town, place (<Eng. 'place' and 'village').
See 110.
   Ples occurs in a number of compounds including:
     longwe ples – distant land
     ples balus – airport
     ples bung – market place
     ples malolo – pleasure resort.

ren – rain (<Eng. 'rain'). See 101.

rot – road, path, way (<Eng. 'road')
   111. *Mi bin go long rot nogut* – I went the wrong way.

sip – ship (<Eng. 'ship')
   112. *Ol bikpela sip i kam long Wewak* – The big ships come to
Wewak.

smok – smoke, a smoke, steam, mist (<Eng. 'smoke')
   113. *Mi no dringim smok* – I don't inhale (i.e. drink smoke).

spia – spear, arrow (<Eng. 'spear')
   114. *Em i kilim pik long spia i gat huk* – He killed a pig with a
spear that had a hook on it.

sta – star, stars (<Eng. 'star')
   115. *Sta i lait nau tasol* – The stars are shining now.

supsup – spear, arrow with several prongs (<? N. I. 'supsup' –
'spear' reinforced by *supia* a pronunciation of 'spear'). See 88.

tais – swamp (<Ger. 'Teich' – 'pond, swamp')
   116. *Tais i wel tumas* – A swamp is slippery.

wara/wata – water, liquid (<Eng. 'water')
   117. *Yu rausim doti wata* – Throw out the dirty water.

yia – year, age, period of time (<Eng. 'year')
   118. *Bipo long wanpela yia em i sik nogut tru* – A year ago he
was very ill.

4.4.7 Food

abus – meat, game (<Gaz. 'abus' – 'animal'). See 60.
anian onion (<Eng. 'onion')

119. *Em i hangre nogut tru na em i kaikai anian pinis* – He was so hungry he ate an onion.

banana – banana (< Eng. 'banana')
120. *Dispela pikinini em i kaikai wanpela banana wantain bret* – This child ate a banana with bread.

bin – beans (< Eng. 'bean')
121. *Meri bilong mi em i kukim kon wantaim bin na hebsen* – My wife cooks corn with beans and peas.

bret – bread (< Eng. 'bread' reinforced by Ger. 'Brot'). See 120.

buai – betel nut (< ? Malay 'buah' – 'fruit, round object')
122. *Mi dai long buai* – I am longing for some betel nut.
In Papua New Guinea *buai* is the equivalent of Cameroon's *kola*. It is shared as a mark of friendship and eaten extensively.

galip – nut, peanut (< Gaz. 'galip' – 'type of chestnut')
123. *Mama miksim liklik galip wantaim gris na i kukim* – Mama puts (i.e. mixes) some nuts with fat and cooks it.

hebsen – peas (< Ger. 'Erbsen'). See 121.

kaukau – sweet potato (< Manus 'kaukau' – 'sweet potato' reinforced by China Coast Pidgin English 'chow chow' – 'eat, food'). See 106.

kokonas – coconut (< Eng. 'coconut')
124. *Planti kokonas i gat kru* – Many of the coconuts have got shoots.

kon – corn, maize, millet (< Eng. 'corn'). See 121.

kurita – octopus (< Gaz. 'urita' – 'octopus')
125. *Wanpela kurita em i lukim umben na em i swim i go* – An octopus looked at the net and then swam away.

mami/yam – yams (< Eng. 'yam' reinforced by 'mami' – 'mother')
126. *Papamama wantaim ol pikinini ol i hangre na ol i kaikai mami* – The children and the parents were hungry and they ate yams.

muli – orange, lemon, citrus fruit (< Gaz. 'muli' – 'citrus')
127. *Bai mi go long bung bilong baim solmuli* (salt + muli),

switmuli (sweet + muli) *na muliwara* (muli + water) – I'll go to the market to buy lemons, oranges and soft drinks.

pitpit – wild sugar cane, type of grass (< Gaz. 'pitpit' – 'grass')
  128. *Dispela didiman i kukim pitpit pinis* – This farmer burnt off the wild sugar cane.

saksak – sago (< Eng. 'sago'). See 65.

sol – salt (< Eng. 'salt')
  129. *I gat sol tumas* – It's too salty.

sup – soup, stew, broth (< Eng. 'soup')
  130. *Papa bilong mi bai em i mekim sup long yu* – My daddy will make mincemeat (i.e. soup) out of you.

taro – taro (< Fiji 'taro')
  131. *Em i bringim taro i kam* – He came bringing taro (i.e. a root vegetable).

4.4.8 Dress

bilas – finery, ornaments, flashy clothes (< Eng. 'flash')
  132. *Mipela mas baim bilas inap long ol bratasusa long ples* – We have to buy nice things to wear for our relatives in the village.

bilum – net bag, net covering (< Mel. 'bilum' – 'net')
  133. *Em i pasim bilum* – She is wearing a net (as clothing).

dukduk – ceremonial headdress (< Eng. 'duck' – 'cotton material')
  134. *Yu kisim i kam dispela dukduk* – Bring this headdress with you.

hat – hat (< Eng. 'hat')
  135. *Bai mi baim hat long papa bilong mi na su bilong mama bilong mi* – I'll buy a hat for my father and shoes for my mother.

kalang – earring, tailfeather of a bird (< Gaz. 'kalang' – 'feather')
  136. *Em i putim klos meri na kalang, na em i smat moa i stap* – She put on a dress (i.e. clothes woman) and earrings, and she looks great.

klos – clothes, dress, European clothing (< Eng. 'clothes'). See 136.

kolsinglis – sweater, jersey (< Eng. 'cold + singlet')
   137. *Em i rausim kolsinglis bilongen* – He took off his sweater.

kot – coat, jacket (< Eng. 'coat')
   138. *Bai yu samapim kot i bruk?* – Will you sew the torn coat?
   Kotren is the term used for 'raincoat'.

laplap – loincloth, cloth draped from the waist (< Fiji 'laplap' – loincloth, reinforced by English 'lap' – 'wrap around')
   139. *Mami i pasim nupela laplap* – Mama is wearing a new loincloth.

makmak – brightly coloured, spotted (< Eng. 'mark + mark')
   140. *Em i baim makmak long stua* – He bought colourful clothes in the store.

mal – genital covering, gourd used to cover penis (< Gaz. 'mal' – 'cover for genitals')
   141. *Dispela lapun papa i gat planti yia na em i pasim mal* – This old man is very old and he wears a mal.

paspas – bangle, bracelet, armband, band (< Manus 'paspas' – armlet reinforced by English 'pass' – 'go round')
   142. *Bai yumi bilasim paspas long het* – We'll decorate our headbands.

purpur – grass skirt (< Gaz. 'purpur' – 'shrub')
   143. *Wanpela mama i wokim purpur na arapela mama i baim* – One woman makes grass skirts and another sells them.

singlis – T-shirt, vest (< Eng. 'singlet')
   144. *Em i laikim singlis i gat mak* – He likes T-shirts with motifs/drawings, monograms on them.

sket – skirt (< Eng. 'skirt')
   145. *Omo i mekim klos i lait tru – siot, sket, olgeta samting* – Omo makes clothes really bright – shirts, skirts, everything.

siot – shirt (< Eng. 'shirt'). See 145.

su – shoe, shoes (< Eng. 'shoe'). See 135.
   Su is found in compounds such as:

su diwai – clogs (shoe wood)
su gumi – rubber shoes (shoe rubber)
su let – leather shoes (shoe leather).

trausis – trousers, pants (<Eng. 'trousers')
146. *Yu lukim trausis bilong mi o nogat?* – Can you see my trousers or not?
The compound *sot trausis* from 'short trousers' is used for shorts.

4.4.9 *Exclamations*

It is virtually impossible to give the precise meaning of TP exclamations in that they can be used in widely-differing contexts. The following are, however, the most frequently occurring items and illustrative sentences are provided so as to help with their contextualisation:

a – This can be attached to almost any semantically full word and tends to be somewhat unfavourable:
    Yu no sem, a? – Aren't you ashamed of yourself?
    Em a! – Him!

kalapa – is an empathy formula and is used in very much the same way as CP *ashia*:
    Kalapa O, brata bilong mi! – I empathise with you, my brother/ sister!

nating – is like colloquial English 'No way!' 'Who knows?':
    Em i stap long Mosbi? – Does he live in Port Moresby?
    Nating! – No way!

o – is also a type of sympathy formula and it can precede or follow an item:
    O kalapa! Gris Got o! – O heavens! Good Lord!
    Jon o! – Hello John!
    Inap o! – That's really enough!

olaboi – is usually an exclamation of delighted surprise:
    Olaboi! Yu no lukim em? – Wow! Can you not see her?

sori – is a variant of *kalapa* and is possibly not quite so serious:
    O sori! Bifo tru em i no stap olsem! – Terrible! In the past it wasn't like this!

tarangu – is roughly the equivalent of 'What a pity!':
> *Tarangu! Ol i dai pinis!* – What a pity! They are dead!

4.4.10 *Verbals*

The lexical items in Sections 4.4.1 to 4.4.8 can, like the items in 3.4.1 to 3.4.8, all function as nominals and many of them are similarly multifunctional. Thus *gris* from 'grease' can function in all of the following contexts:

> *Em i grisman tru* – He is a very fat man/He is a flatterer
> *Em i gat planti gris* – He is very fat/He has the gift of the gab
> *Yu gris long mi tasol* – You are only buttering me up
> *Ol i grisim mi na mi kam* – They talked me into coming.

The most frequently used verbals in TP can be divided into two types:

a) verbals which can modify a noun as well as functioning predicatively:
> *wanpela bikpela pikinini* – a big child
> *Pikinini i bikpela* – The child is big

b) verbals which cannot modify an NP:

> **wanpela kam pikinini*
> *Pikinini i kam* – The child came.

The former are, as in CP, classified as AV (adjective verbs) and the latter as V, but the system is somewhat more complex in TP in that both AV and V can again be subdivided.

In TP, AVs differ in function depending on whether they are monosyllabic or polysyllabic. Monosyllabic AVs take the suffix *-pela* from 'fellow':

> *bikpela* – big
> *olpela* – old
> *smolpela* – small
> *yangpela* – young.

The suffix is obligatory when the AV precedes a nominal but optional when used predicatively:

> *bikpela haus* – a big house
> *Dispela haus i big tumas* – This house is very big
> *Dispela haus i bikpela tumas* – This house is very big

although there is a strong tendency for the *bikpela* form to be used consistently on the radio. In addition, a number of compounds occur using the adjective without the *-pela* suffix but these are like idioms in that their meanings are not immediately decipherable from the meanings of their parts:

> *bikpela ples* – a big village
> *bikples* – the mainland
> *smolpela papa* – a short man
> *smolpapa* – paternal uncle.

Polysyllabic adjectives do not need the *-pela* suffix:

> *arakain klos* – a different dress
> *nambawan kaikai* – the best food

although there is a tendency to regularise frequently occurring ones like *liklik*:

> *liklik pikinini* – a little child
> *liklikpela pikinini* – a little child (possible more emphatic).

The V items can be subdivided into those which take the suffix *-im* and are followed by a noun phrase:

> *Mi no inap lukim meri* – I can't find the woman
> *Ol i wokim haus* – They are building a house

and those which do not take the *-im*:

> *Bai ol i kam* – They'll come
> *Ol i dai pinis* – They died.

Many verbs can, depending on meaning and context, occur with and without the *-im*:

> *Bai mi goapim maunten* – I'll climb the hills
> *Bai mi goap long maunten* – I'll climb into the hills
> *Mi no ken draiv* – I can't drive
> *Bai mi draivim balus* – I'll be a pilot (i.e. drive a plane)

but *gat*, even when it is followed by an NP:

Mi no gat mani – I have no money

does not take the *-im* suffix.

A verbal will be given the marker T (transitive) if it can take the *-im* suffix. The following examples will illustate the system:

1. *nupela* <Eng. 'new+fellow' is AV:
     nupela trausis – new trousers
     Mi nupela long dispela – I'm new here/to this village
                    ples

2. *kam* <Eng. 'come' is V:
     Husat i kam? – Who's coming?

3. *baim* <Eng. 'buy+'em/'im' is VT:
     Mi baim kiau long stua – I bought eggs in the store
     Bai mi baim balus – I'll pay for my plane ticket

4. *hat(pela)(im)* <Eng. 'hot+(fellow)+('em/'im)' is AVT:
     hatpela wara – hot water
     Bel bilong mi i hat – I'm angry (belly belong me hot)
     Bai mi hatim wara – I'll heat the water.

Items which are multifunctional, that is which can occur in more than one grammatical category, will take an M marker. Thus *blak* will be AVM because, as well as:

blakpela man – a black man

we can have:

arapela blak – a different black/dark colour.

4.4.11 *Verbals in TP's Core Vocabulary*

abrus(im)	VTM	<Mel. 'abrus' – 'miss'	– avoid, elude, alongside
aipas	VM	<Eng. 'eye + fast'	– blind, blind person
amamas(im)	VTM	<Mal. 'kemamoran' – 'peace + plenty'	– delight, be happy
askim	VT	<Eng. 'ask + 'em/'im'	– ask, request
bagarap(im)	VT	<Eng. 'bugger + up + 'em/'im'	– spoiled, ruined, damage, wreck
baim	VT	<Eng. 'buy + 'em'	– buy, pay for, hire
bek(im)	VTM	<Eng. 'back + 'em'	– give back, answer, repay, avenge

beten	VM	< Ger. 'beten' – pray	– pray
bihain(im)	VTM	< Eng. 'behind + 'em'	– follow, imitate, obey, late, after
bik(pela)	AV	< Eng. 'big + fellow'	– big
bilas(im)	VTM	< Eng. 'flash'	– decorate, adorn, finery
bilip(im)	VTM	< Eng. 'belief/ve'	– believe, have faith, faith
blak(pela)	AVM	< Eng. 'black + fellow'	– black, dark (including green and blue)
blu(pela)	AVM	< Eng. 'blue + fellow'	– blue
boil(im)	VT	< Eng. 'boil + 'em'	– boil, swirl
boin(im)	VT	< Eng. 'burn + 'em'	– burn, singe, beat severely
bosim	VT	< Eng. 'boss + 'em'	– boss, order, be in charge of
bringim	VT	< Eng. 'bring + 'em'	– bring, take
bruk(im)	VT	< Eng. 'broke + 'em'	– break, tear, split, broken, torn
brukbrukim	VT	< Eng. 'broke + broke + 'em'	– pulverise
buka	AVM	< PNG place-name 'Buka'	– jetblack
bulsitim	VT	< Eng. 'bullshit + 'em'	– deceive, cheat
dai	AV	< Eng. 'die'	– die, dead, faint, long for
daunim	VT	< Eng. 'down + 'em'	– defeat, overcome, humiliate
dia	AV	< Eng. 'dear'	– expensive, dear, precious
dinau	VTM	< Fiji 'dina' – 'debt'	– borrow, debt
doti	VM	< Eng. 'dirty'	– be filthy
drai(pela)	AV	< Eng. 'dry + fellow'	– dry, dried up, strong
driman	VTM	< Eng. 'dream + man/ in'	– dream, dreamer
dring(im)	VT	< Eng. 'drink + 'em'	– drink, suck, smoke, inhale
du(im)	VTM	< Eng. 'do + 'em'	– incite, force, tempt, provocation
gat	V	< Eng. 'got/get'	– have, own, be
giaman(im)	VTM	< Eng. 'gammon' – 'cheat'	– deceive, cheat, lie, trick
givim	VT	< Eng. 'give + 'em'	– give, entrust to

glas(im)	AVTM	< Eng. 'glass + 'em'	– peep, use a spyglass, spy
go	V	< Eng. 'go'	– go
goap(im)	VT	< Eng. 'go + up + 'em'	– climb, ascend, run over, copulate
grin(pela)	AVM	< Eng. 'green + fellow'	– green
gumi	AVM	< Ger. 'Gummi'	– rubber
guria	VM	< Gaz. 'guria' – 'quake'	– shake, tremble, quake, tremor
gut(pela)	AVM	< Eng. 'good + fellow'	– good, kind, attractive
hait(im)	VT	< Eng. 'hide + 'em'	– hide, protect, secret
hambak	AVM	< Eng. 'humbug'	– brag, be boastful, vain
hap(im)	AVTM	< Eng. 'half + 'em'	– halve, half, side
hariap (im)	VT	< Eng. 'hurry + up + 'em'	– hurry, leave in a hurry, make X hurry
harim	VT	< Eng. 'hear + 'em' reinforced by Ger. 'hören'	– hear, listen, smell, perceive, understand
hat(pela)(im)	AVTM	< Eng. 'hot + fellow + 'em'	– tough, warm, heat
help(im)	VTM	< Eng. 'help + 'em'	– help, assist, aid
hevi	VM	< Eng. 'heavy'	– heavy, be heavy, weight
hip(im)	VTM	< Eng. 'heap + 'em'	– pile, heap
hol(im)	VTM	< Eng. 'hold + 'em'	– hold, keep, be faithful to
kais(im)	AVTM	< N.I. 'kais' – 'left'	– left, left side, aim to left
kalabus(im)	VTM	< Eng. 'calaboose + 'em'	– imprison, detain, gaol, safety pin
kamap(im)	VT	< Eng. 'come + up + 'em'	– come up, appear, rise
kapsait(im)	VT	< Eng. 'capsize + 'em'	– turn over, spill, pour out
karamap(im)	VT	< Eng. 'cover + up + 'em'	– conceal, cover, parcel
kat(im)	AVTM	< Eng. 'cut + 'em'	– cut, delete, crossed out, cutting
kela	AV	< Ger. 'kahl' – 'bald'	– hairless, bald
kirap (im)	VT	< Eng. 'get + up + 'em'	– get up, start, awaken
kisim	VT	< Eng. 'catch + 'em'	– get, catch, obtain
klin(pela) (im)	AVT	< Eng. 'clean + fellow + 'em'	– clean, clear, polish
kol(pela)(im)	AVTM	< Eng. 'cold + fellow + 'em'	– cold, make cold, freeze

kolim	VT	< Eng. 'call + 'em'	– call, announce
krai	VM	< Eng. 'cry'	– cry, weep, mourn for
kranki	AVM	< Eng. 'cranky'	– clumsy, wrong, stupid
kros(im)	AVTM	< Eng. 'cross + 'em'	– angry, cross, scold, be angry with
krunkut(im)	VT	< Eng. 'crooked + 'em'	– crooked, bent, bend, squeeze
kus	VM	< Eng. 'cough' reinforced by Ger. 'husten'	– cough, mucus
kwik	AV	< Eng. 'quick'	– quick, fast
laik(im)	VTM	< Eng. 'like + 'em'	– want, desire, like, love
lap	VM	< Eng. 'laugh'	– laugh, smile, ridicule
larim	VT	< Eng. 'let + 'em'	– let, allow, leave
les	AV	< Eng. 'laze/lazy'	– to be lazy, tired, exhausted
liklik	AVM	< Gaz. 'ikilik' – 'little' reinforced by Eng. dial. 'likkle'	– little, small, trifle
limlimbur	VM	< Gaz. 'lilimbur' – 'amuse oneself'	– walk, stroll
longlong	VM	< Gaz. 'longlong' – 'mad'	– mad, stupid, drunk, madness
long(pela)	AVM	< Eng. 'long + fellow'	– long, tall, length
(luk)luk(im)	VTM	< Eng. 'look + look + 'em'	– look, see, visit, watch, look at
lus(im)	VT	< Eng. 'lose + 'em'	– detach, forget, to be lost
mangal (im)	VTM	< Manus 'mangal' – 'desire'	– covet, envy, long for
marit(im)	AVTM	< Eng. 'married'	– marry, married
mau	AV	< Gaz. 'mau' – 'ripe'	– ripe, soft, rotten
mauspas	AVM	< Eng. 'mouth + fast'	– dumb
mekim	VT	< Eng. 'make + 'em'	– cause, do
mekim dai	VT	< Eng. 'make + 'em + die'	– kill
nambawan	AV	< Eng. 'number + one'	– first class, excellent
nogut(im)	VTM	< Eng. 'no + good + 'em'	– bad, evil, spoil
nu(pela)	AV	< Eng. 'new + fellow'	– fresh, new, raw
olgeta	AV	< Eng. 'altogether'	– all, every, entire

orait(im)	VTM	< Eng. 'all right + 'em'	– all right, fix
painim	VT	< Eng. 'find + 'em'	– discover, look for, seek, find
pairap	VM	< Eng. 'fire + up'	– explode, crash, chatter (of teeth)
pait	VM	< Eng. 'fight'	– fight, war, bitter
pas(im)	VTM	< Eng. 'fast + 'em'	– close, fasten, delay, firm, fast
pat(pela)	AV	< Eng. 'fat + fellow'	– fat
pei (m)	VTM	< Eng. 'pay + 'em'	– pay, reward, wages
planim	VT	< Eng. 'plant + 'em'	– bury, plant
planti	AVM	< Eng. 'plenty'	– many, plenty, much
pinis(im)	VTM	< Eng. 'finish + 'em'	– over, finish, end, destroy
pret(im)	VTM	< Eng. 'afraid + 'em'	– afraid, fear, frighten
pulap (im)	VT	< Eng. 'full + up + 'em'	– to be full, fill
pul(im)	VTM	< Eng. 'pull + 'em'	– compel, pull, drag, beg, coax, oar, paddle
pundaun	V	< Eng. 'put/fall + down'	– fall, land
puspusim	VT	< Eng. 'push + push + 'em'	– have intercourse with
rabis(im)	AVT	< Eng. 'rubbish + 'em'	– worthless, poor, be poor, ridicule
rait(im)	AVTM	< Eng. 'right/write + 'em'	– right, write, hand-writing
ran(im)	VTM	< Eng. 'run/ran + 'em'	– run, flow, chase
raun(im) (pela)	AVTM	< Eng. 'round + 'em + fellow'	– round, encircle
raus(im)	VT	< Ger. colloquial 'raus' – out!'	– get out, be kicked out, dismiss, erase
ret(pela)	AVM	< Eng. 'red + fellow'	– red
salim	VT	< Eng. 'sell/send + 'em'	– sell, send
sanap(im)	VT	< Eng. 'stand + up + 'em'	– be erect, stand up
save	AVTM	< Port. 'saber' – 'know'	– know, understand, be able to, do habitually
sem(im)	VTM	< Eng. 'shame + 'em'	– shame, embarrass, be embarrassed
senis(im)	VTM	< Eng. 'change + 'em'	– change, alter
sindaun	V	< Eng. 'sit + down'	– sit down, live, stay

singaut(im)	VTM	< Eng. 'sing + out + 'em'	– call, shout, invite
skirap (im)	VTM	< Eng. 'scrape + 'em'	– itch, scrape, scale fish
slip(im)	VTM	< Eng. 'sleep + 'em'	– sleep, lean, fell
smol(pela)	AV	< Eng. 'small + fellow'	– little
sori	VM	< Eng. 'sorry.'	– regret, mourn for, long for
spak	AV	< Eng. 'spark'	– drunk, get drunk
stap	V	< Eng. 'stop'	– stay, live, reside
stret(im) (pela)	AVTM	< Eng. 'straight + 'em + fellow'	– calm, correct, straighten, smooth
strong(im) (pela)	AVTM	< Eng. 'strong + 'em + fellow'	– hard, tough, powerful, toughen
surik	V	< Ger. 'zurück' – 'back'	– move, flinch, cower
sut(im)	VTM	< Eng. 'shoot + 'em'	– shoot, hit, inject, right (hand)
swit(pela)	AV	< Eng. 'sweet + fellow'	– delicious, attractive, agreeable
tait(im) (pela)	AVTM	< Eng. 'tight + 'em + fellow'	– stiff, tight, taut, tighten
tan(tan)(im)	VT	< Eng. 'turn + turn + 'em'	– turn, become, revolve
tarangu	VM	< Gaz. 'tarangu' – 'alas'	– miserable, exile
tekimautim	VT	< Eng. 'take + 'em + out + 'em'	– remove, dig out, harvest
ting(ting) (im)	VTM	< Eng. 'think + think + 'em'	– remember, think, thought
tok(tok)(im)	VTM	< Eng. 'talk + talk + 'em'	– talk, tell, say, converse
toknogutim	VT	< Eng. 'talk + no + good + 'em'	– curse, insult
traim	VTM	< Eng. 'try + 'em'	– try, test, taste, attempt, fail
trik(im)	AVTM	< Eng. 'trick + 'em'	– fool, cheat, deceive, deceptive
tru(pela)	AV	< Eng. 'true + fellow'	– trustworthy, true, real, very
wail(pela)	AV	< Eng. 'wild + fellow'	– wild
wel(im) (pela)	AVTM	< Eng. 'oil + 'em + fellow'	– oil, oily

wet(im)	AVT	< Eng. 'wet/wait + 'em'	– wet, wait, hesitate, expect
win(im)	VTM	< Eng. 'win + 'em'	– beat, win, wind, blow, breath
wokabaut	VM	< Eng. 'walk + about'	– walk, walk about, way of life
wok(im)	AVTM	< Eng. 'work + 'em'	– build, work, be busy
yang(pela)	AVM	< Eng. 'young + fellow'	– young, youth
yelo(pela)	AV	< Eng. 'yellow + fellow'	– yellow.

4.4.12 *Function Words*

In addition to the 316 semantically full words listed above, there are several closed set function words in TP's vocabulary. These can be categorised as pronouns, determiners, interrogatives, a verb phrase marker, negators, auxiliary verbs, conjunctions, prepositions and adverbs.

Pronouns – TP's personal pronouns are:

mi	< Eng. 'me'	– I, me
yu	< Eng. 'you'	– you
em[10]	< Eng. 'him/'em'	– he, she, it, him, her
yumi	< Eng. 'you + me'	– we, us (inclusive, i.e. you and me)
mipela[11]	< Eng. 'me + fellow'	– we, us (exclusive, i.e. not inc. you)
ol	< Eng. 'all'	– they, them.

This set of pronouns can be expanded to indicate the number of people thus:

> *mitupela* – the two of us (but not you)
> *mitripela* – the three of us (but not you)
> *yumitripela* – the three of us (including you)
> *yutupela* – the two of you
> *emtripela* – the three of them.

It is possible to indicate other numbers:

> *yumifoapela* – the four of us (you included)

but this type of compounding is most frequently used when speaking or referring to two or three people.

All the above pronouns with the exception of *mi* and *yu* are followed by the predicate marker *i* (see p. 194 and note 12):

> *Mi kam pinis* – I have come
> *em i kam pinis* – he has come
> *ol i kam pinis* – they have come.

TP's pronouns can be made emphatic by the use of *yet*, *tasol* and *wanpela/olgeta*. *Yet* from English 'yet' is similar in force to SE 'self':

> *Em yet i wokim haus* – He himself built the house
> *Ol i paitim mi yet* – They hit me myself
> *Bai ol i no helpim ol yet* – They won't help themselves.

Tasol from English 'that's all' implies 'only':

> *Em i paitim mi tasol* – He hit only me
> *Ol tasol i mekim* – Only they did it.

The singular pronouns can be emphasised by the use of *wanpela*:

> *Mi wanpela i save wokim haus* – I can build a house
> *Em i paitim em wanpela* – He hit *him*

and the plural ones can be emphasised by using *olgeta* from 'altogether':

> *Em i paitim yumi olgeta* – He hit *us*
> *Yupela olgeta bai yupela kisim pe* – *You* will get your pay.

Determiners

arapela	< Eng. 'other + fellow'	– other, any other
dispela	< Eng. 'this + fellow'	– this, these
narapela	< Eng. 'another + fellow'	– another, a specific one
olgeta	< Eng. 'altogether'	– all, every
sampela	< Eng. 'some + fellow'	– some, several
wanpela	< Eng. 'one + fellow'	– a, one.

Interrogatives

Interrogatives – The following are the commonest interrogatives in TP:

bilong wanem?	< Eng. 'belong what + name'	– why?
husat?	< Eng. 'who's + that'	– who?

193

haumas?	< Eng. 'how + much'	– how much? how many
olsem wanem?	< Eng. 'all + the + same what + name'	– how?
we?	< Eng. 'where'	– where?

Verb Phrase Marker[12] – There is only one verb phrase marker 'i' and although its form may have been reinforced by the recapitulation of 'he' in such sentences as:

That big man, he's a fool

its function seems to derive from New Guinea languages. Capell (1969: 49) claims

> In general, [in A languages] the verb is preceded by a subject-marking particle. . . . Every verb, even if it has a noun subject expressed, must be preceded by such a marker. The pattern is reproduced in Pidgin where one says, e.g. *man i kam*, 'a/the man comes/came', not just *man kam*. . . . In this, as in so many regards, Pidgin reproduces with largely English lexemes, Austronesian form and modes of expression.

Indeed, in Kuanua, a Gazelle, New Britain language which has contributed considerably to TP's vocabulary, *i* can actually occur in a very similar role to its TP counterpart:

A pal dia ga gire i ikilik muka – The house they saw was very small (lit. the house they past see VP-marker small much).

(Capell, 1969: 38)

Negators
maski – Don't/Be unwilling to/It doesn't matter. This may well be from Malay 'melepaskan' – 'allow to escape' reinforced by Ger. 'macht nichts'.

no	< Eng. 'no'	– no, not
nogat	< Eng. 'no + get'	– no emphatic.

Auxiliary Verbs

bai	< Eng. 'by and by'	– future time marker
bin	< Eng. 'been'	– past time marker
inap	< Eng. 'enough'	– ability
ken	< Eng. 'can'	– permission, willingness
klosap	< Eng. 'close-up'	– inceptive aspect marker

laik	< Eng. 'like'	– proximate future
mas	< Eng. 'must'	– necessity, obligation
pinis	< Eng. 'finish'	– perfect aspect marker
save	< Port. 'saber'	– habitual aspect marker
stap	< Eng. 'stop'	– continuous aspect marker.

Conjunctions

na	< Eng. 'and'	– and
o/no	< Eng. 'or/nor'	– or
sapos	< Eng. 'suppose'	– if
taim	< Eng. 'time'	– when
tasol	< Eng. 'that's + all'	– but, however.

Prepositions – Quite a number of SE prepositions are making their way into SE-influenced TP as can be seen from an examination of Text 7a in Appendix B. The only two prepositions which are essential in TP, however, are:

long < Eng. 'along' – indicates location, in, at, on, to, from, with, etc.

bilong < Eng. 'belong' – indicates possession, of.

Adverbials – As in CP, many TP words are multifunctional and so many of the items already listed can function adverbially:

> *Ol i go wanpela wanpela* – They went singly (one one)
> *belo kaikai* – noon, at noon
> *Pulim strong dispela rop* – Pull the rope hard/strongly.

The following items, however, occur most frequently as adverbials:

arere	< ? Mal. 'arah'	– 'direction, course' influenced by Eng. 'other' – alongside
bipo	< Eng. 'before'	– formerly
gen	< Eng. 'again'	– again
klostu	< Eng. 'close to'	– almost, nearly
isi isi	< Eng. 'easy easy'	– slowly, gradually
(n)ating	< Eng. 'I think'	– perhaps
nau	< Eng. 'now'	– now
wantaim	< Eng. 'one + time'	– immediately.

4.4.13 *Comment on TP's Core Vocabulary*

As with CP, TP's vocabulary is large and increasing, and our list offers the minimum number of items which would permit fluent conversation. Taking the above vocabulary as basic, we can draw the following conclusions:

1. Excluding exclamations, we have listed 373 items (327 semantically full words, six pronominal forms and forty function words). Of these, 274 (73 +%) come from English; nineteen (5 +%) have dual or multiple etymologies, English being one of the possible source languages; nine (2 +%) come from English but have had their meanings modified by the vernacular languages; and the remaining seventy-one words (19 +%) of the core vocabulary derive from languages other than English. A point worth stressing is that some parts of the vocabulary are more strongly English-derived than others. Almost 88% of TP's verbals are from English and close on 94% of its function words. When we realise that in CP almost 92% of the verbals and over 97% of the function words derive from English, we are in a position to hypothesise that an English-related pidgin or creole is a variety of English, rather than a new though related language, if we use word order, function words and a shared vocabulary as our criteria for establishing relationships.
2. Of the seventy-one items not deriving from or being influenced by English, seven are from German, five from Portuguese and the other fifty-nine are from Pacific languages.
3. Of the items from Pacific languages, forty (10 +%) are from local languages and the remaining nineteen (5 +%) are from non-local languages including Malay, Fijian and Samoan.

These statistics are remarkably similar to those provided for CP but, as with CP, they say nothing of the frequency of occurrence of items. Nor do the words adopted from English retain their English meanings. In most cases the TP meanings overlap those of their English cognates but the TP items are more polysemous. TP speakers have abandoned the morphological and inflectional changes found in British/Australian English but they have evolved new methods of indicating syntactic relations. The morpheme *i* is a predicate marker:

Ol i go pinis – They have gone

-im indicates that the verb is transitive

Em i orait – He is all right
Em i oraitim em – He is fixing it

and *-pela* indicates that the item is adjectival[11]:

Em i lukim bikpela moran – He saw a big snake.

4.4.14 *Word Formation*
TP, as we have seen, has two affixes, *-pela* and *-im* but it is the latter which is most productive in the language. In addition, TP is capable of producing new meanings by the use of compounding, calques, reduplication and idiomatic usage.

Compounding – Related sets of words can be created by the use of *man*, *meri* and *pikinini*:

hos man – stallion
hos meri – mare
hos pikinini man – colt
hos pikinini meri – filly.

Structures involving *man bilong X* are also extremely common:

man bilong giaman – cheat
man bilong pait – warrior
man bilong trabel – trouble-maker.

It is theoretically possible to have *meri bilong trabel* but such a structure is rare, possibly because *man* has generic reference.

Wan from 'one' is perhaps the most productive compounding element in the language, normally suggesting unity and friendship:

wanblut – a close kinsman (one blood)
wanmak – a person of the same size (one mark)
wansmok – a person who shares one's cigarettes/pipe (one smoke).

Pasin from 'fashion' is often used to create an abstract noun:

daunpasin – humility (down fashion)

spakpasin – drunkenness, a tendency to drunkenness (spark fashion)
stilpasin – thieving, tendency to steal (steal fashion).

Save occurs in many compounds including:

savemanmeri – educated people (know man woman)
tokplessaveman – linguist (talk place know man)[13]
woksaveman – specialist.

The verbs *gat*, *givim*, *tanim* and *wokim* are productive in compounding:

gat bel – become pregnant
gat gras ananit long han – reach puberty
givim bel – make pregnant (usually outside marriage)
givim tang – put out one's tongue, invite intimacies
tanim bel – change someone's mind
tanim tok – translate, translator
wokim kago – shift a cargo
wokim saksak – prepare sago.

Reduplication – This device is systematically exploited for emphasis:

bikpela – big   *bikpela bikpela* – very big
oltaim – always   *oltaim oltaim* – absolutely all the time

to express 'each other', 'one another':

Tupela man i pait. Ol i paitim – Two men fought. They hit each
      wanpela wanpela   other
Ol i kisim tripela tripela – They got three each

to stress continuous or prolonged activity:

luk – look   *lukluk* – stare
tok – talk   *toktok* – talk a great deal, chatter

to indicate the intensity of an action:

brukim – break   *brukbrukim* – break into little pieces
tanim – turn   *tantanim* – revolve

and to disambiguate homophones:

sip – ship   *sipsip* – sheep
was – watch, guard   *waswas* – wash, bathe.

Calques – Many TP compounds are direct translations of vernacular languages. Among them are:

> *mauswara* – saliva, idle talk (mouth water)
> *nek bilong singsing* – the melody of a song (neck belong sing-sing)
> *pinga bilong lek* – toe (finger belong leg)
> *putim skin* – brag (put skin/body).

Idiomatic Usage – As in CP, idiomatic expressions in TP are often calqued from the vernaculars and are often based on body parts, such as *as*, *bel*, *han*, *het* and *nus* and on a number of verbals such as *gut*, *hevi*, *pas*:

> *as bilong mun* – beginning of the month (ass/source belong moon)
> *bel hevi* – sad (belly heavy)
> *gat tupela bel* – be in doubt (get two belly)
> *gut het* – clear thinker, very bright
> *maus pekpek* – verbal diarrhoea (mouth faeces)
> *nus bilong kanu* – prow (nose belong canoe)
> *plantihan* – centipede.

4.5 SYNTAX

TP has been used as a plantation lingua franca, as a medium for military propaganda,[14] and as one of the key languages in court, parliament and in urban communities. It has had a standard grammar for forty years and an official orthography for thirty, and although it is still referred to as a 'pidgin', it has a considerable number of native speakers[15] and the largest body of literature, translated and original, of any pidginised language in the world. Certain structures, like passives, are absent from TP but such absences, like the failure of SE to differentiate between

you (singular) and you (plural), in no way detract from the
flexibility, vitality and productivity of the language.

4.5.1 *The Basic Sentence Structure*

As in other varieties of English, the basic sentence pattern is S P
(O)(C):

> *Yumi kaikai* – Let's eat
> *Yumi kaikai kaukau* – Let's eat sweet potatoes
> *Yumi kaikai kaukau wantaim* – Let's eat sweet potatoes and
> *pato* duck.

Adjectives precede nouns:[16]

> *wanpela bikpela man* – a big man

and possession is indicated as follows:

> *haus bilong man* – a man's house
> *haus bilong sampela man* – some men's house
> *ol haus bilong sampela man* – some men's houses
> *haus bilong Pita* – Peter's house
> *haus bilong meri bilong Pita* – Peter's wife's house
> *haus bilong ol meri bilong Pita* – Peter's wives' house
> *haus bilong em* – his/her house
> *haus bilong ol* – their house.

An examination of TP utterances suggests that the sentence
structure of TP utterances can be comprehended by such rules as
the following:

S→ NP   VP
NP→ (det) (num) (adj) (dim) N (gender) (poss + N) (S) (pro)
VP→ i (aux) V (NP) (PNP) (S) (mod)
det→ determiner e.g. *olgeta*
num→ numeral e.g. *wanpela*
adj→ adjectival e.g. *bikpela*
gen→ gender i.e. *man/meri*
dim→ diminutive i.e. *pikinini*
pro→ pronoun e.g. *mi*
poss→ possessive i.e. *bilong*
aux→ auxiliary e.g. *bin*

$$V \rightarrow \text{verbal} \begin{cases} V_t \text{ e.g. } wokim \\ V_i \text{ e.g. } go \\ \text{Adj} \end{cases}$$

$$\text{mod} \rightarrow \text{modifier} \begin{cases} \text{adverbial e.g. } tude \\ \text{prep} + \text{NP} \end{cases}$$

prep → preposition e.g. *long*

The maximum (albeit unlikely) NP might thus be:

dispela tripela liklik pikinini pik man bilong Pita – these three little male piglets of Peter's

and a VP can range from:

i kaikai – eat

to:

i bin kaikai wanpela pato em i switpela tru – ate a duck that was very tasty.

Generally, temporal modifiers follow the verb:

Bai em i kam tumora – he'll come tomorrow

but they can occur initially in the sentence if we wish to stress the time:

Tumora bai em i kam – It's tomorrow that he'll come

or if the VP is long:

Tumora bai em i wokim simen long baret – Tomorrow he'll be putting cement into the trenches.

4.5.2 *Negation*

In TP the most usual type of negation occurs when *no* precedes the VP:

Em i no kam – He didn't come
Ol i no go – They didn't go
Yu no kam! – Don't come!

Nogat is the term used in answering questions:

Em i kam? Nogat, em i no kam – Did he come? No, he didn't come

or as an emphatic in yes/no questions:

> *Em i kam o nogat?* – Did he come or not?

Nogut can occur as an adjectival:

> *Em i nogut* – It's not right/good

or as an emphatic negative imperative:

> *Nogut yu kam!* – Don't come!

Maski is used to mean 'no matter/it doesn't matter':

> *Bilong em, maski* – As far as he is concerned, it doesn't matter
>
> *Maski mi sik, mi save go long stua* – It doesn't matter that I'm ill, I can still go to the store.

4.5.3 *Interrogation*

In TP a change in intonation is often the only signal that differentiates statements, questions or orders:

Yu go long haus ⁻ ⁻ – _ You are going home/to the house
Yu go long haus? – – _ ╱ Are you going home?
Yu go long haus ⌐ _ _ _ Go home

When question words are used, the intonation pattern is similar to that used for statements:

Husat i go long haus? ⁻ ⁻ – _ Who is going home?
Husat i stap? ⁻ ⁻ – _ Who's there/that?

There are five frequently used interrogation words in TP:

bilong wanem:
Bilong wanem yu stap long Mosbi? – Why do you live in Port Moresby?
husat: *Husat i kam?* – Who's coming?
haumas: *Haumas klok nau?* – What time is it now?
         Haumas taim ol i mekim? – How many times did they do it?
olsem wanem:
  Olsem wanem pik i dai pinis? – How did the pig die?

and *we*:   *Yu stap we?* – Where do you live?

We can occur initially in the sentence:

  We stap brata bilong yu?

but it can have impatient overtones so that the above sentence is interpreted as: 'Where the hell is your brother?'

There are two other question words which imply impatience or discourtesy, *wasmara?* and *watpo?*:

Wasmara yu bagarapim ka – What the hell do you mean by
bilong mi? wrecking my car?
Watpo kopi i kolpela? – Why the hell is the coffee cold?

but such question words tend to be limited to urban areas or to situations where a speaker intends to stress his superiority in rank to the listener.

4.5.4 *Reported Speech*

In TP structures involving reported speech or thought do not trigger off any transformations in the verb phrase:

Mipela bai go – We'll go
Mipela bin go – We went
Em i tok mipela bai go – He says/said we'll go
Em i tok mipela bin go – He says/said we went.

As we can see, a connective like 'that' is not required and there is no modification for spatial or temporal markers:

Yu stap hia – Stay here
Em i tok yu stap hia – He said you should stay there
Yu kam tumora – Come tomorrow
Em i tok yu kam tumora – He said you should come the next
day.

Sometimes, in mission-influenced speech, verb forms are used in a connective capacity:

Em i bekim tok i spik: Yupela – He answered saying: Come . . .
kam . . .
Em i tokim ol i spik: Yupela – He spoke to them saying:
kam . . . Come . . .
Em i tok se: Yupela kam . . . – He spoke saying: Come . . .

The *tok se* construction is identical in form and meaning to CP's method of dealing with reported speech (see 3.5.4) and although

MODERN ENGLISHES: PIDGINS AND CREOLES

it is not the only method used in TP, it is quite widely used by
older speakers and may in the past have been in more widespread
use.

4.5.5 *The Noun Phrase*
The TP noun phrase can be a substantive phrase:

> *tripela liklik pik* – the three little pigs

a pronoun

> *mi, yu, ol . . .* – I, you, they . . .

and proper names like *Pita* and *Wanipe*. As in SE and CP, it is the
substantive phrase that permits most modification and expansion. Again, as in SE and CP, when adjectives precede the noun
they do so in a fixed order:

> *dispela tupela liklik pik* – these two little pigs
> *dispela tupela naispela liklik pik* – these two nice little pigs.

If nominals occur in a modifying capacity, they tend to follow the
headnoun:

> *bikpela sospen ain* – a big iron saucepan
> *wanpela haus diwai* – a wooden house
> *liklik hos man* – a little male horse

whereas the diminutive marker *pikinini* precedes its headnoun:

> *wanpela pikinini man* – a boy
> *wanpela pikinini pik man* – a young male boar.

Certain intensifiers such as *nogut* and *tru* tend to follow the
headnoun they modify:

> *tok nogut* – bad language
> *mama tru* – real mother
> *man nogut tru* – a very bad man

and modifying sentences also follow the headnoun:

> *mi lukim wanpela meri i gat bel* – I saw a woman who was
> pregnant.

Plurality tends to be implicit in the context but can be made
overt by the prefixing of *ol*, the third person plural pronoun:

204

pikinini bilong mi – my child/children
ol pikinini bilong mi – my children
olgeta pikinini bilong mi – all my children.

4.5.6 *The Verb Phrase*

In TP the verb is unmarked for person or number:

Mi stap – I stay
Em i stap – He stays
Ol i stap – They stay.

Its form does not change to indicate temporal or aspectual distinctions, although such distinctions can be made overt by the use of auxiliaries:

Em i kam – He is coming
Bai em i kam – He will come
Em i kam pinis – He came/has come.

The form of the verb which is used in TP is usually the form equivalent to the imperative in English:

kam < Eng. 'come'
go < Eng. 'go'
bring < Eng. 'bring'

but, occasionally, a marked form of the English verb has been adopted:

bruk < Eng. 'broke'

and, frequently, TP verbals although deriving from English do not derive from English verbs:

Em i kranki – He is wrong *kranki* < 'cranky'
Ol i ken krungutim ain – They can bend iron *krungut* <
'crooked'
Bai mi oraitim em – I'll fix it *orait* < 'all right'.

In TP temporal and aspectual distinctions are carried, not by morphological change in the verbal, but by a set of auxiliaries or by sentence modifiers:

Mi bin lukim em – I saw him
Mi lukim em asde – I saw him yesterday

Bai paia i lait – The fire will light/burn
Paia i lait nau – The fire will light/burn very soon
Em i save kaikai – He's always eating
Em i man bilong kaikai – He loves eating
Em i lus pinis – It has been lost
Em i lus olgeta – It's completely lost.

In TP there are three temporal markers, *bai*, *bin* and *laik*:

Bai em i no lukim mi } – He won't see me
Em bai i no lukim mi }   (*bai* = indef. future)
Em i no bin lukim mi – He didn't see me
                         (*bin* = past time marker)
Em i no laik kaikai – He won't soon eat
                         (*laik* = proximate future)

four aspectual markers, *klosap*, *pinis*, *save* and *stap*:

Klosap mi pundaun – I almost fell (*klosap* = inceptive aspect
                      marker)
Em i kaikai pinis – He has eaten (*pinis* = perfect aspect
                      marker)
Em i stap kaikai }
Em i kaikai i stap } – He is eating (*stap*=continuous marker)
Em i save kaikai – He is always eating (*save* = habitual
                     aspect marker)

and three markers of modality, *inap*, *ken* and *mas*:

Yu no inap goapim – You aren't able to climb (*inap* = ability)
hil
Yu no ken kilim – You shouldn't kill birds of paradise
kumul   (*ken* = permission)
Ol i mas mekim – They must behave well (*mas*=
gutpela pasin   necessity).

The above are the most widely-used auxiliaries in TP, especially on the radio, but other items in the language perform similar roles and allow speakers to express subtle shades of meaning. The use of *gen*, *nau*, *tasol* and *yet*, for example, in post verbal position can imply repeated actions, actions just begun, actions habitually engaged in and actions still in progress:

Em i kaikai gen – He is eating again!
Em i kaikai nau – He has just started eating
Em i kaikai tasol – He does nothing but eat
Em i kaikai yet – He is still eating.

Repeated or prolonged actions can be implied by the repetition of the verb:

Em i painim, painim, painim, – He looked for it everywhere,
               nating   but to no avail
Em i katim, katim, katim . . . – He went on cutting . . .

and the structure *mekim + verbal* is causative:

Em i mekim dai man – He killed a man (i.e. caused a man to die)
Yumi mekim dai kros – We'll settle the problem (cause the anger to die).

TP auxiliaries have certain characteristics:

1. *bin, bai* and *laik* are mutually exclusive
2. *bai* and *stap* can occur in two positions:

     Bai em i kam – He'll come
     Em bai i kam
     Em i stap kam – He is coming
     Em i kam i stap

3. *no* negates all auxiliaries. It follows the first *i* in the sentence or, if *i* does not occur, the subject NP:

        Bai em i no kam – He won't come
        Em bai i no kam
        Mi no stap kam – I'm not coming
     Wanipe i no ken kam – Wanipe cannot come
   Em i no save kaikai i stap – He is not always eating

4. *bai, bin, inap* and *klosap* cannot occur alone as independent verbs. When *ken, laik, mas, pinis, save* and *stap* occur as independent verbs they have more stress than when they occur as auxiliaries:

        Ating i ken – Perhaps it's possible
      Mi laikim dok – I like dogs
        Em i mas – It's essential

   Bai mi pinisim em – I'll finish it
   Mi save dispela man – I know this man
   Mi stap long Mosbi – I live in Port Moresby

5. auxiliaries can be omitted and understood in consecutive clauses:

   Klosap mi pundaun na mi dai – I almost fell and (almost) died
           pinis
   Em i kam i stap na em i karim – He is coming and he is carry-
           kunai   ing sword grass.

TP, like CP though to a lesser degree, makes use of serial verbs:

   Em i luk save dispela man – He recognises this man (look +
                    know)
   Ol i wokim traim haus – They are trying to build a house
   Em i holim pasim wanpela – He arrested a man
           man   (hold + fasten)
   Em i kam lukim em – She came to see him
   Em i go kisim em – He went to get it.

Again, as in CP, serial verbs can indicate direction towards or away from the speaker:

   Bringim i go – Take it away (i.e. from me)
   Bringim i kam – Bring it here (i.e. to me)
   Kisim i kam – Pick it up and bring it here
   Ol i go kamap long haus – They reached the house (not mine)
   Ol i kam kamap long haus – They reached the house (mine)

and it is one way of making comparisons:

   Em i bikpela i win long – He is taller than I (he big surpass
           mi[17]   prep. me).

4.6 CONCLUSION

To write a grammar of a language in one chapter is like attempting to carry away the sea in a bucket. It is an impossible task. Yet one can tell a lot about sea-water by examining the contents of the bucket. We have not been able to explore TP in all its richness but our description has shown it to be a vital, flexible language, a language well suited to expressing the unique way of life of the people of Papua New Guinea.

NOTES

1. The name 'Papua' probably comes from the Malay term 'orang papuwah' – 'man curly-haired'.

2. It isn't certain why the name 'New Guinea' was chosen. It may have been because the inhabitants looked African and 'Guinea' was widely used as a descriptive term for West Africa. It may also have been because New Guinea was almost diametrically opposite parts of West Africa.

3. The pidginised English of Papua New Guinea has been referred to by many names including 'Beachlamar', 'New Guinea Pidgin' and 'Neo-Melanesian'. In July 1981 the government of Papua New Guinea declared 'Tok Pisin' (< Talk Pidgin) to be its official name.

4. The government of PNG is very anxious not to give preference to New Guineans by overvaluing TP and undervaluing Hiri Motu. There are enough potential causes for splits between the communities, racial, historical and linguistic, without exacerbating the situation by preferring one lingua franca to the other.

5. Some missionaries, especially members of the Summer Institute of Linguistics, urgently stress the value of vernacular education and are successfully using vernacular languages, especially with mature Papua New Guineans in adult literacy centres.

6. An interesting counter example to this point was reported in Port Moresby's *Post-Courier* for 14 December 1977. The newspaper article on a meeting between the Japanese and Papua New Guinean prime ministers includes the following comment:

> Shortly before he met the Japanese Prime Minister, Mr Fukuda, a few days ago Mr Somare [premier of Papua New Guinea] surprised Japanese officials by requesting a three-way interpretation. When the talks got underway Mr Somare, whose English is excellent, spoke in pidgin. The Secretary for Foreign Relations, Mr Tony Siaguru, translated the pidgin into English and this in turn was translated for Mr Fukuda by the Japanese interpreter. A PNG official said later Mr Somare believed he should use pidgin because he could express his thoughts better. The nonplussed Japanese seemed to think Mr Somare wanted to use the time required for the interpretation to think ahead in the negotiations. . . .

7. It is not being suggested that Hall misrepresented TP but merely that his 1943 grammar which emphasised the use of *-im* as a marker of transitivity, for example, may have encouraged its use in

others and in particular in those who wished to use TP in the written medium.

8. Many English-speaking settlers still use the stress-timed system of SE.

9. When we claim that certain words derive from English, we mean that they were in widespread use among native speakers of English by the 1850s, the period just before TP came into being. Thus, although 'banana' ultimately derives from Kikongo, it seems reasonable to claim that mother-tongue speakers of English of the mid-nineteenth century would not have been aware that it was a 'foreign' word.

10. *Em* is often realised as 'en' when it is unstressed and follows *long* or *bilong*.

11. The morpheme *-pela* is an adjectival marker except when it occurs in *mipela* which probably derives from 'me and this/these fellow(s)'. The nearest SE analogy I can give is the use of 'some'. It can occur as an adjectival marker in such words as: fulsome, gladsome, handsome, irksome, lonesome, and tiresome and as a plural pronoun in:

    Some like it hot.

12. There is some variability in the use of 'i'. It occurs most consistently in written texts and in scripted radio broadcasts but it seems to be optional in the speech of some mother-tongue speakers of TP. It may therefore be dying out. A good account of this variability can be found in Woolford's article.

    A point in favour of the suggestion that 'i' may derive from 'he' is the fact that 'I gat' and 'I ken' can be used to mean 'There is/are' and 'It's possible'. Otherwise these must be interpreted as subjectless sentences.

13. The value of linguists and translators in Papua New Guinea can hardly be overestimated. It is not unusual in a law case to have as many as six translators if the person under examination comes from a remote highland community whose language is not well known. Brown (1969: 90–91) gives the following hypothetical cameo of the sort of difficulties that can occur when translations do not go smoothly:

Counsel:	Was the witness's wife present at the sing-sing?
Pidgin interpreter:	Long taim dispela sing sing i kamap, meri bilong im stop wantaim long ol, or nogat?
'Dialect' interpreter to witness:	Was your wife present at the sing-sing?
Witness:	My wife has always been disobedient and uncooperative.

'Dialect' interpreter:	Yes but the judge wants to know whether or not she was at the sing-sing?
Witness:	She frequently even insults me.
'Dialect' interpreter:	Yes but was she at the sing-sing?
Witness:	She is lazy. I often have to cook my own meals.
'Dialect' interpreter:	You can tell the court about that later. Was she at the sing-sing?
Witness:	In fact women generally are unpredictable, volatile, capricious.
'Dialect' interpreter:	Look, do me a favour and answer the question.
Witness:	She wasn't worth the bride-price.
'Dialect' interpreter:	Look, I'll get into trouble in a minute. Was she at the sing-sing?
Witness:	One enters marriage with high hopes but very often it is a saddening experience.
'Dialect' interpreter:	If I lose my status as an interpreter over this I'll fix you when the court has gone. Was she at the sing-sing?
Witness:	What sing-sing?
'Dialect' interpreter:	You know the one when Sam over there got fresh with her.
Witness:	Of course she was there, how else would the trouble have started?
'Dialect' interpreter to Pidgin interpreter:	Yes.
Pidgin interpreter to Court:	Yes.

14. The following is an example of the use of TP to tell Papua New Guineans that the war was over. Thousands of such leaflets were dropped by plane in September 1945:

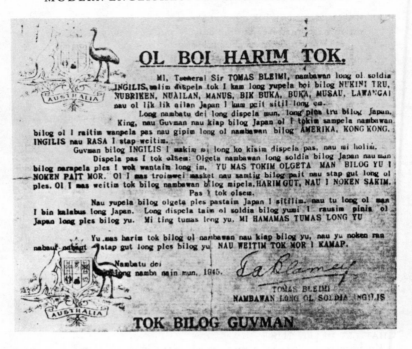

15. Most native speakers of TP learn it in conjunction with one or more vernacular languages so that TP rarely becomes the only language of a speaker or of a community.

16. There are some extremely interesting differences between CP and TP with regard to:

    a. the positioning of noun + noun compounds. The languages often choose a different order:

CP	TP	
biabia mɔt	mausgras	hair mouth – beard/moustache
man hɔs	hos man	stallion
man pikin	pikinini man	child

    b. the indication of plurality. Both pidgins use the third person plural pronoun to mark plurality overtly, but in CP the marker follows and in TP the marker precedes:

man dɛm	ol man	men

    c. the indication of possession:

man i han	han bilong man	the man's hand.

    The correspondences seem so regular that there must be an underlying rule. It seems clear that SE could offer two models for possession i.e. (i) 'the man's foot' where the possessor precedes the possessed and (ii) 'a friend of the family' where the possessor follows the possessed. CP chose (i) and TP (ii) and perhaps this choice conditions the ordering of other combinations in the language.

17. TP can imply precise degrees of comparison by the use of:
   a. *liklik : Em i bikpela liklik long mi* – He is a little bigger than me
   b. *moa : Em i moa bikpela long mi* – He is bigger than me
   c. *olgeta : Em i bikpela olgeta* – He is the biggest
   d. *wantaim : Ol i bikpela wantaim* – They are equally big.

REFERENCES AND SUGGESTIONS FOR FURTHER READING

BRAMMALL, J. AND MAY, R. J., *Education in Melanesia*, Canberra: ANU, 1975.

BRASH, E., 'Tok Pilai, Tok Piksa na Tok Bokis', *Kivung* 4.1, pp. 12–21, 1971.

BROWN, B. J. (ed.), *Fashion of Law in New Guinea*, Sydney: Butterworths, 1969.

CAPELL, A. C., *A Survey of New Guinea Languages*, Sydney: University Press, 1969.

CHATTERTON, P., 'The Origins and Development of *Police Motu*', *Kivung* 3.2, pp. 95–8, 1970.

CHATTERTON, P., *Day That I Have Loved*, Sydney: Pacific Publications, 1974.

DUTTON, T. E., *Conversational New Guinea Pidgin*, Canberra: Pacific Linguistic Series D.12, 1973.

DUTTON, T. E., *Language and National Development: Long Wanem Rot?* Inaugural Lecture, University of Papua New Guinea, 1976.

DUTTON, T. E. AND KAKARE, J., *The Hiri Trading Language of Central Papua: A First Survey*, Port Moresby: UPNG Occasional Paper No. 5, 1977.

GWYTHER-JONES, R., 'Vernacular Literacy: Bridge to a National Language', *Kivung* 4.3, pp. 161–70, 1971.

HALL, ROBERT A. JR., 'Two Melanesian Pidgin Texts', *Studies in Linguistics*, 1.6, pp. 1–4, 1942.

HALL, ROBERT A. JR., *Melanesian Pidgin English: Grammar, Texts, Vocabulary*, Baltimore: Linguistic Society of America, 1943.

HALL, ROBERT A. JR., *A Standard Orthography and a List of Suggested Spellings for Neo-Melanesian*, Port Moresby: Department of Education, 1955.

HALL, ROBERT A. JR., 'Innovations in Melanesian Pidgin (Neo-Melanesian)', *Oceania* 26, pp. 91–109, 1956.

HALL, ROBERT A. JR., 'The Life Cycle of Pidgin Languages', *Lingua 11*, pp. 151–6, 1962.
HOWELLS, WILLIAM, *The Pacific Islanders*, London: Weidenfeld and Nicolson, 1973.
HANCOCK, IAN F., 'Recovering Pidgin Genesis: Approaches and Problems', in Valdman (ed.), pp. 277–94, 1977.
LAYCOCK, D., *Materials in New Guinea Pidgin (Coastal and Lowlands)*, Canberra: Pacific Linguistics Series D, No. 5, 1970.
LIEFRINK, F. AND TODD, LORETO, 'Pidginisation and the Multilingual', *Kivung 8.1*, pp. 23–38, 1975.
LYNCH, J. (ed.), *Pidgins and Tok Pisin*, University of Papua New Guinea: Occasional Papers 1, 1975.
MCELHANON, K. (ed.), *Tok Pisin I Go We?* Special Publication of *Kivung*, Port Moresby: Linguistic Society of PNG, 1975.
MEAD, MARGARET, 'Talk Boy', *Asia 31*, pp. 144–51, 1931.
MIHALIC, F. *The Jacaranda Dictionary and Grammar of Melanesian Pidgin*, Brisbane: Jacaranda Press, 1971.
MÜHLHÄUSLER, P., 'Samoan Plantation Pidgin English and the Origin of New Guinea Pidgin', Paper presented at the 1975 Annual Conference on the Linguistic Society of Australia, 1975.
MÜHLHÄUSLER, P., 'Creolization of New Guinea Pidgin', Wurm (ed.), pp. 567–76, 1977.
MÜHLHÄUSLER, P., 'Papuan Pidgin English Rediscovered', Wurm and Carrington (eds), pp. 1377–1446, 1978.
MÜHLHÄUSLER, P., *Growth and Structure of the Lexicon of New Guinea Pidgin*, Canberra: Pacific Linguistics C, No, 52, 1979.
MÜHLHÄUSLER, P., 'Continuity and Discontinuity in the Development of Pidgins and Creoles', unpublished paper, mimeographed, 1982.
MURPHY, JOHN, *The Book of Pidgin English*, Brisbane: Smith and Patterson, 1943.
NELSON, HANK, *Papua New Guinea*, Harmondsworth: Penguin, 1972.
ORKEN, M., 'Pidgin English', *South Pacific*, 7, p. 863, 1954.
PARNABY, O. W., *Britain and the Labor Trade in the Southwest Pacific*, Durham, N.C.: Duke University Press, 1964.
PECK, CHARLES, 'The Status of Verbal Suffixes in Papua New Guinea Languages', *Kivung, 5.3*, pp. 192–205, 1973.
REINECKE, J. E., *Marginal Languages: a sociological study of creole languages and trade jargons*, unpublished PhD thesis, University of Yale, 1937.
SANKOFF, G., 'The Genesis of a language', in K.C. Hill (ed.) *The Genesis of Language*, Ann Arbor: Karoma Publishers Inc., 1979.
SANKOFF, G. AND LABERGE, S., 'On the Acquisition of Native Speakers by a Language', *Kivung, 6.1*, pp. 32–47, 1973.
SAYER, E. S., *Pidgin English*, Toronto: mimeographed, 1943.
SCHUCHARDT, H., 'On Melanesian English', in T. L. Markey (ed.), *The*

Ethnography of Variation: Selected Writings on Pidgins and Creoles, Ann Arbor: Karoma Publishers Inc., 1979.

TODD, LORETO, 'Pidginisation and Creolisation: A Worldwide Phenomenon', in Lynch (ed.), pp. 1–20, 1975.

TODD, LORETO AND MÜHLHÄUSLER, P., 'Idiomatic Expressions in Cameroon Pidgin English and Tok Pisin', in *Papers in Pidgin and Creole Linguistics no. 1*, S. A. Wurm et al. (eds), Canberra: Pacific Linguistics A, No. 54, pp. 1–35, 1978.

TRAUGOTT, E., 'Pidginization, Creolization and Language Change', in Valdman (ed.), pp. 70–98, 1977.

VALDMAN, A. (ed.) *Pidgin and Creole Linguistics*, London and Bloomington: Indiana University Press, 1977.

WOOLFORD, E., 'The Developing Complementizer System of Tok Pisin', in K. C. Hill (ed.) *The Genesis of Language*, Ann Arbor: Karoma Publishers Inc., pp. 108–24, 1979.

WURM, S. A., *Phonological Diversification in Australian New Guinea Languages*, Canberra: Pacific Linguistics Monograph, 1964.

WURM, S. A. (ed.), *New Guinea Area Languages and Language Study*, Canberra: Pacific Linguistics C, No. 40, 1977.

WURM, S. A. AND CARRINGTON, L., (eds), *Second International Conference on Austronesian Linguistics: Proceedings*, Canberra: Pacific Linguistics C, No. 61, 1978.

WURM, S. A. (ed.), *New Guinea and Neighbouring Areas: A Sociolinguistic Laboratory*, The Hague: Mouton, 1979.

CHAPTER 5

Creoles and the Classroom in Britain

꧁꧁꧁꧁꧁꧁

5.1 INTRODUCTION

As we have seen in earlier chapters, pidgin- and creole-speaking communities exist in many parts of the world. At least two creoles, Anglo-Romani and Shelta, have arisen in the British Isles, but most varieties are to be found along trade routes and in ports, often thousands of miles from England. Since the 1950s, however, Britain has received large numbers of immigrants from the Caribbean, many of whom speak a creole as a mother tongue and who transmit their creolised English to their children born here. Precise figures for creole-speaking Britons are not available because questions on ethnic origins no longer appear on census forms. In 1971, however, an estimated 543,000 people of Caribbean origin lived in Britain and, assuming that most of these spoke either a creole or a creole-influenced English, then over 1% of today's population can be assumed to speak a form of English differing in many respects from other varieties in Britain. In addition, since this 1 + % is not evenly distributed throughout Britain but is concentrated in a number of urban centres, children of Caribbean parents can form up to 50% of the population of certain inner-city schools.[1]

The first non-white Caribbean settlers came to Britain after the Second World War. Some soldiers who had enlisted in the British West Indies[2] remained in Britain after the war, but large-scale immigration only began in the 1950s when London Transport and the National Health Service advertised for West Indian workers. These workers were needed to take the poorly-paid jobs that British workers refused to fill.

The majority of the immigrants were from Jamaica where there was a large population and severe unemployment, but people from many parts of the Caribbean were attracted by the idea of settling in the 'mother country' and sharing in its post-war prosperity. Thus, within Britain, we have a microcosm of the British West Indies, with considerable numbers of people from Barbados, Trinidad and Guyana, as well as Jamaica, and smaller numbers of people from the Leeward and Windward Islands. It is perhaps worth stressing that many of the inhabitants of the Caribbean and many Caribbean settlers in Britain speak and write SE but the majority of immigrants, like the majority of working-class British people, have had limited education and so speak a non-standard variety of the language.

5.2 CARIBBEAN CREOLE ENGLISHES

Varieties of creolised English stretch from the Southern United States, through the islands of the Caribbean, along the east coast of Central America to the South American countries of Guyana and Suriname (see Map 9). All the varieties have a good deal in

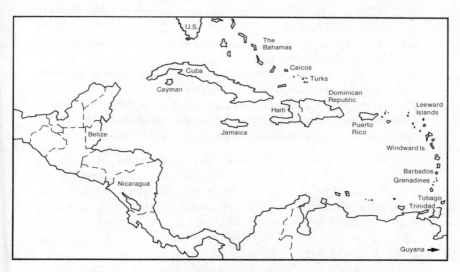

MAP 9: THE CARIBBEAN

common because the English language has provided most of their vocabulary and much of their grammar. In addition, the creoles also share many non-English structural similarities because of their indebtedness to West African languages. This indebtedness is most apparent at the level of idiom and folk culture.[3] New World idioms such as:

> *cut eye at* X – look contemptuously at X
> *get hard ears* – be stubborn
> *like* X *bad* – like X very much
> *suck teeth at* X – show disparagement for X

have parallels in several West African languages, and many tales and traditional beliefs have their origins in Africa.

All the creoles of the area under discussion developed as a direct result of the Slave Trade (see 2.4) and, because of differences in the patterns of settlement, individualised creoles evolved in each area. This individuality can be indicated by juxtaposing sentences from Jamaican Creole (JC) with counter-parts from Guyana (GC):

JC: *Him go a school every day last year, now sometime him go, sometime him no go*

GC: *Him a go a school every day last year, now sometime him a go, sometime him naa go*

SE: He used to go to school every day last year, now sometimes he goes and sometimes he doesn't go

JC: *George did a play wid mi wife when mi neba dei*
GC: *George did a play wid mi wife when mi no bin dei*
SE: George played with my wife when I wasn't there

and such structural differences are augmented by regional pronunciation. It would be wrong, however, to overemphasise the individuality of each creole. They are, like Yorkshire and Lancashire dialectal Englishes, mutually intelligible and, in each region of the Caribbean, we also find a post-creole continuum (see 1.4), so that a local standard English is part of the linguistic competence of many Caribbean speakers.

Thus, when Caribbean immigrants came to Britain, Trini-dadians would have used a variety of English that, to them, was clearly distinguishable from Jamaican or Guyanese, but all speakers from the Caribbean shared enough common-core features to permit us to consider them as a reasonably homogeneous linguistic group. In any case the homogeneity was increased in Britain by the numerical dominance of Jamaican speakers, by the tendency for Caribbean immigrants to settle in the same areas and for their shared experiences of racism and exclusion to reduce linguistic differences.

5.3 WEST INDIAN ENGLISH IN BRITAIN

A number of white linguists and educationists[4] have claimed that there are many West Indian children in Britain 'whose language differs in no way or very little' (Rosen and Burgess, 1980: 31) from that of their white contemporaries. This claim may be true of middle-class West Indian children and in parts of Liverpool, Cardiff and Bristol where there have been sizeable black and mixed communities for many years, but such findings have been challenged. Sutcliffe (1977) found that there was little difference in the knowledge of creole possessed by speakers born in the Caribbean and those born in Britain. Of the people tested, 88% of those born in the Caribbean and 79% of those born in Britain claimed to use a level of creolised English equivalent to such a sentence as:

Mi aks di man fi put mi money eena im pocket (I asked the man to put my money in his pocket).

The reason for such different findings may well be that if a child's pronunciation is not radically different from that of his peers 'many features of creole syntax [may] pass unnoticed' (V. Edwards, 1982: 158).

Obviously some people of Caribbean origin, especially those who have done well in Britain, speak the English of the British in their equivalent group, but large numbers can still be distinguished by their speech, the salient characteristics of which are as follows.

5.3.1 *Phonology*
British speakers of Caribbean origin tend to use twelve vowel sounds, five short monophthongs,[5] i, e, a, o and u, three long

monophthongs, ii, aa and uu and four diphthongs, ie, ai, ou and uo:

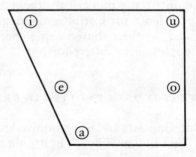

Short Monophthongs

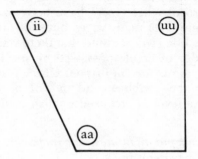

Long Monophthongs

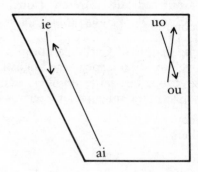

Diphthongs

These vowel sounds can be illustrated by the following words:

i	*kil* – kill	aa	*daag* – dog
e	*dem* – they, them	uu	*duu* – do
a	*mada* – mother	ie	*biesin* – basin
o	*op* – up	ai	*blain* – blind
u	*put* – put	ou	*roun* – round
ii	*trii* – three	uo	*uol* – old.

Twenty-one[6] consonantal sounds are used:

	Bilabial	Dental-Alveolar	Palatal	Velar
PLOSIVES	p b	t d		k g
NASALS	m	n	ny	ng
FRICATIVES	f v	s z	sh	
AFFRICATES			ch j	
LIQUIDS		r l		
SEMI-VOWELS	w		y	

Every speech community has its own inventory of sounds and sound combinations, but the distinctiveness of a group's speech only becomes fully apparent when we become aware of how the speech sounds pattern. Because speakers of West Indian English in Britain (WIEB) utilise thirty-three sounds as opposed to the forty-four in RP or the forty-five used in some rural communities in N. Ireland,[7] they make fewer vocalic and consonantal distinctions than speakers of some other varieties of British English. Thus in WIEB

rat can, depending on context, mean either 'rot' or 'rat'
den can, depending on context, mean either 'den' or 'then'

goli can, depending on context, mean either 'gully' or 'golly'
laad can, depending on context, mean either 'lord' or 'lard'
tai can, depending on context, mean either 'toy' or 'tie'
tin can, depending on context, mean either 'thin' or 'tin'.

Apart from the extra homophones that occur in WIEB, other systematic sound differences are found that help to mark WIEB out from other British dialects: *ie* is used in words like 'lady', 'mate' and 'same' thus giving

> *Den di liedi sii di siem skuulmiet* — Then the lady saw the same school friend;

uo is the vowel sound in words like 'don't', 'go' and 'know':

> *Di bwai duon nuo if dem guo huom* — The boy doesn't know if they've gone home;

ong tends to replace /aun/ giving *tong* and *dong* for 'town' and 'down'; *in* is widely used for '-ing'; palatalisation occurs frequently after 'g' and 'k', producing forms like *gyal* for 'girl, gal' and *kyaan*[8] for 'can't'; 'boy' and 'boil' are often realised as *bwai* and *bwail*; 'v' is frequently heard as 'b' in words like *beks* (vex) and *shob* (shove); and 't' and 'd' tend not to occur in word-final position after 'f', 'k', 'l', 'n' and 's':

laf – laughed	*san* – sand
bak – back, backed	*pas* – pass, past, passed
tuol – told	*yesidie* – yesterday.

Such realisations, taken in conjunction with non-English stress and intonation[9] patterns, contribute to the distinctiveness of WIEB.

5.3.2 *Lexicon*

The overlap between the lexicons of WIEB and other British varieties is large and increasing. The differences that exist can be classified under eight main headings:

1. Words deriving from English but no longer current in British English:
   atwin < atween – between
   limba < limber – slim
   tinin < tinnen – made of tin.

2. Words deriving from non-standard British dialects:

    fiesti < face + ty – cheeky, impertinent
    jag < jagged – prick, pierce
    lap < lap – wrap.

3. Words deriving from English but modified either in form:

    buzin < abusing – scold
    krach < scratch – scratch
  waswas < wasp wasp – wasps

or in function:

    bin < been – past time marker
    fi < for – of *A fi mi buk dat* – That's my book
    se < say[10] – that *Yu nuo nuo se . . .* - Don't you know that . . .?

4. Words deriving from other European languages:

bobo/bubu	< Sp. 'bobo'	– fool
boku	< Fr. 'beaucoup'	– many, plenty, a lot
palava	< Port. 'palavra'	– row, discussion, problem.

5. Words deriving from African languages:

fufu	< Yoruba 'fufu'	– mashed yams
kong-kosa	< Fante 'ngkɔngkɔnsa'	– gossip
okro	< Igbo 'ɔkurɔ'	– okra.

6. Words deriving from now extinct Carib languages:

    calalu – green vegetable
    caiman – crocodile
    jiga – sandfly.

7. Calques on African languages:

    ai wata – tears
    bak tai – piece of cloth for tying a baby to one's back, extended now to cover the Mothercare 'baby-sling' and 'kiddy carrier'
  beli wuman – pregnant woman.

8. Rastafarian elements:[11]

backative – strength		*dreadtalk* – Rasta talk	
burn (weed) – smoke		*I-and-I* – I, Rastafa-	
(ganja)		rian	
deaders – meat		*Idetate* – meditate	
downpression – depression		*morgue* – refrigerator	
dreadlocks – Rasta hair		*Reggae* – type of	
style		music.	

5.3.3 *Syntax*

Just as in the Caribbean, a post-creole continuum exists in Britain. The most creolised varieties are heard in the speech of the old who have not tried or have not been able to modify the speech patterns current in the Caribbean in their youth, and in the speech of the young who feel alienated from the white community and who adopt creolised speech[12] as a marker of their ethnic identity. In this description, we shall focus on the acrolectal end of the spectrum, emphasising those creole carry-overs which most speakers of WIEB are unaware of. It will be obvious to any reader that WIEB syntax is in no way linguistically *deficient*. Some of the patterns, however, evoke negative social judgements from many British users of English.

At the level of the sentence, there are eight main ways in which even acrolectal WIEB differs from SE. So as not to overemphasise differences, we will use normal English orthographic conventions.

1. Questions are distinguished from statements mainly by intonation:

You get money? – Have you any money?

This resembles such colloquial British questions as:

You're coming?
You're broke?

which differ from statements in that the pitch of the voice rises at the end of the sentence. Even when question words are used in WIEB, there is little tendency to use either inversion or auxiliaries:

When you hear that? – When did you hear that?
Where we going? – Where are we going?

2. Double and multiple negatives are common:

Don't eat no sweets, you hear?
She can't never go out
Nobody don't tell me nothing.

3. There are marked differences between equative sentences in
SE and WIEB. The *BE* verb is not required in the latter:

Mary a good girl
George one fine mechanic.

Nor is *BE* required before an adjective complement in such
sentences as:

We happy now
The story funny.

Similar sentence patterns for complements have been described
for US Black English but sometimes even sympathetic linguists
make the mistake of talking about Black English and WIEB as if
they were standard English with deletions. J. R. Edwards (1979:
63) for example, talks of 'copula deletion', 'the deletion of the "s"
in third person singular verbs and the omission of the possessive
"s"'. Caribbean Creole Englishes, like CP (see Chapter 3) never
possessed such features, and what we are seeing in WIEB is the
remains of a verbal system which owes at least as much to the
linguistic structures of West African languages as it does to
English.

4. Serial verbs are more common in WIEB than in other British
varieties:

Come bring the thing
Take it go.

And *se*, which probably derives from English 'say' and Twi *se*
meaning 'say' but used as a clause introducer after verbs of
talking, hearing and thinking (see 3.5.4), is still quite frequent
in WIEB:

He talk say you stupid, man
I hear say you going back to Georgetown.

5. Often, as in CP (see 3.5.6), there is no concordial agreement between subject and verb:

John stay here all the time
My mother sing in the church.

6. There is a marked tendency to use few or no transformations in the construction of complex sentences:

He told me say he coming – He told me that he would be
soon   coming soon
He seeing if the man coming – He's seeing whether or not
or he not coming   the man is coming.

7. Foregrounding of the verb occurs for emphasis:

A talk Mary talk make she – Mary talks too much and
trouble   that makes trouble for her.

This type of foregrounding is not found in non-creolised Englishes but it occurs in many West African languages. Yoruba, for example, has:

Mi mu ni won mu mi – They really took/arrested
 | | | | | | me

Me|take BE they take me
and Twi has:
Hwe na me hwe ase – I really fell.
 | | | | |
Fall BE I fall down   (Alleyne, 1980: 172)

8. WIEB avoids passive structures, although it can express passive meanings:

The grass cut – The grass has been cut
Di flower plant – The flower has been planted
One apple can't divide – One apple cannot be divided
This record play a lot – This record is played a lot.

As far as the Noun Phrase is concerned, there are, again, certain systematic differences between WIEB and SE.

1. There is a strong tendency in WIEB to overgeneralise the use of the unmarked noun:

> I get two brother
> I keep ten rabbit.

Occasionally *dem* is used to mark plurality overtly:

> The rabbit dem eat, eat, eat.

This *dem* can also follow a proper noun like George or Mary as in:

> George dem and Mary dem

to imply 'George and his gang', 'Mary and her close friends'. This usage also occurs in West African pidgins and creoles:

> *Pita dem kam* – Peter and his cronies came

and a similar structure is found in Hawaii where: 'We goin' meet Jane-guys at the movie' (Carr, 1972: 132) means 'We are going to meet Jane and her crowd/group at the cinema'.

2. WIEB uses two methods of indicating possession, both of them different from SE. The first method is simply to juxtapose nouns with the possessor preceding the possessed:

> Mary house – Mary's house
> the man coat – the man's coat.

The second involves the use of *fi*, probably deriving from 'for':

> fi Mary – Mary's
> The coat a fi mi – the coat is mine.

3. WIEB has a smaller set of pronouns than SE and, often, especially in colloquial speech, no distinction is made between subject, object and possessive pronouns:

> She see he come take he coat and go
> Carry that book to she mother.

The most frequently occurring WIEB pronouns are as follows:

Sing	Subject	Object	Possessive
1.	a	mi	mi
2.	yu	yu	yu
3.	hi	hi (him)	hi (his)
	shi	shi (her)	she (her)
	(it)	(it)	(it)

Plur			
1.	wi	wi (us)	wi (our)
2.	yu [unu]	yu [unu]	yu [unu]
3.	de [dem]	dem	de [dem] (their)

Pronouns in brackets have low functional loads: those in square brackets are the more markedly creole pronouns; those in round brackets are the standard variants.

The WIEB Verb Phrase differs in three main ways from its SE counterpart.

1. There is a tendency to use the unmarked verb form to express the past. This is particularly true of dynamic[13] verbs:

> Mary come last week
> We drive to school every day last year.

With common stative verbs like SEE, HEAR and KNOW, there is a preference for did + V rather than for a simple past tense:

> I did see her just now
> He did know she father in Georgetown.

2. Speakers of WIEB often use da/di/a to mark continuous actions:

> He da work now – He's working now/at the moment
> She di eat well – She's eating well
> David a try – David is trying.

There is a growing tendency to use *a* where 'is' would be used in SE:

The house a fi Mary – The house is Mary's

and since there is some lengthening of *a* in such utterances as:

She aa sweet girl

it is possible that the Creole verbal marker *a* has fused with the English article.

3. As in US colloquial English, adjective forms often occur in adverb slots:

I like it bad – I like it very much
She sing real soft
Everything I do, I do it good.

The above features are found in the idiolects of many speakers of WIEB who were born in this country, and although some of the individual features are shared by other non-standard English speakers, their co-occurrence marks WIEB speakers out as a distinctive linguistic group. And the impression of WIEB's distinctiveness is reinforced by three other speech characteristics. There is greater multifunctionality in WIEB than in SE:

I readying the tea – I'm getting the tea ready
All this murder and kill must – All this murdering and kill-
stop   ing should stop;

there is greater freedom in the creation of words so that formations like *feverous, fussify* and *jokify* are frequently heard; and finally, speakers of WIEB share with speakers of other non-standard English the tendency to hypercorrect. In N. Ireland, for example, hypercorrection is seen in the use of such structures as:

I have did
I have saw

for the more usual 'I seen' and 'I done', and among speakers of WIEB it appears mainly in the overuse of concordial agreement:

I sees you
I did boughted it.

5.4 LINGUISTIC HANDICAPS IN SCHOOL

The handicaps faced in the classroom by children of Caribbean origin merge into a bigger problem, one which Bernstein (1973: 278) summed up in the question:

> Why, for example, in a similar experimental setting, do middle-class children at five years of age score more highly on verbal tests than working-class children, and why, on non-verbal tests is the advantage very much reduced?

There is certainly no dearth of evidence that children from the lowest socio-economic groups do less well in our school system than their middle-class peers. And this under-achievement is likely to be even greater if, as well as coming from the working classes, they also belong to the West Indian community. Scarman (1981: 9) lists education as one of the causes contributing directly or indirectly to the Brixton riots and claims:

> . . . the under-achievement of West Indian children at school has been well chronicled recently in the Rampton report. Though the extent and the causes of the under-achievement remain a matter of controversy, I have received evidence from many organisations and individuals pointing to the failure of black youths to acquire sufficiently early the skills of language and literacy, and to the sense of disappointment and frustration which at least some black parents and children feel in the education system.

It is not part of our brief to criticise the British education system but it is worth our while, I think, to draw attention to two fundamental paradoxes. Firstly, education is seen by many working-class parents as the most viable means of social mobility, and yet our school system is perhaps the major device for reinforcing social, cultural and linguistic prejudices. Secondly, the majority of school children are from working-class backgrounds, whereas teachers are drawn mainly from middle socio-economic groups. In many inner city areas, therefore, there are often striking social, cultural and ethnic differences between the teachers and the taught. The 1977 Home Office report on *Urban Deprivation, Racial Inequality and Social Policy* acknowledged this gulf between teacher and pupil particularly in areas with large West Indian populations and yet the report found that:

The appointment of minority staff to meet the distinctive language or cultural needs of ethnic minority children and parents was not part of the educational policy (64).

Few linguists or educationists now hold the belief that working-class children employ 'restricted codes' while their middle-class playmates use 'elaborated codes' (Bernstein, 1962: 35–6) and yet Bernstein's oversimplification was a response to a very real problem. He was aware that in our school system it is often a child's use of language rather than his innate ability that may determine his performance at school. It is certainly true that working-class children do, in a school environment, use language differently from middle-class children, not because they are less intelligent or less linguistically creative, but because they are in an environment where a different *form* of the language is being used and they are being asked to play roles and linguistic games which are not part of their early experience. A working-class child learns his brand of English as he learns to fit in with his society. He learns attitudes and habits as he acquires speech. This is, of course, equally true of the middle-class child, although the variety of English and the uses to which it is put, differ. Working-class communities, both black and white, can certainly use their non-standard varieties to discuss with clarity and precision such abstractions as love, duty, emotional and spiritual needs, as well as the less abstract elements of their daily life. Their form of language is adequate to all the needs of their social group, but the middle-class roles which have been integrated into school life are not as central to the behaviour of a working-class child as they are to his middle-class peer. An example may clarify this point. A child from a poor, rural community in Tyrone, N. Ireland, was recently asked at school: 'What is the masculine form of duck?' and, after a pause, he answered: 'A hen'. The child lived on a farm and knew the difference between ducks and hens, males and females, but none of his everyday experience had taught him how to answer such a question. The role of answering questions which have, apparently, little relevance or value was not one which he had learnt to play.

In brief, schools are middle-class institutions, teaching middle-class values and stigmatising all but middle-class speech. Examinations are set and marked by middle-class examiners. It is not, therefore, surprising, that middle-class children succeed in the system whereas working-class children, of whatever colour, rarely do. This equation of 'getting on' with middle-class aspirations was made explicit by Lord Scarman in a speech to the Convocation of London University in May 1982. Referring to the need for universities to discriminate in favour of ethnic minorities, he added:

> If we may be critical of West Indian society, it is that they do not seem to have the will to help themselves. If we compare their efforts to get on in our middle-class society with the efforts of Asians and others, they will not show up well.
> (Quoted in the *Times Higher Education Supplement*, 14 May 1982: 2)

5.4.1 *Children Whose Mother Tongue Is Not English*
The handicaps experienced by children whose mother tongue is not English are considerable and yet they are probably the most easily dealt with. If a child comes to school speaking only Urdu or Bengali or Greek, then both teacher and child are aware of the linguistic problems. And, even when the child has mastered enough English to participate in classroom activities, both are still aware of the possibility of misunderstanding. It is this awareness on the part of the teacher that the child's errors may be due to language use rather than to intellectual inadequacy that helps to account for the fact that children with Indian parents do better at school than children whose parents came from the Caribbean.[14]

5.4.2 *Children Who Speak Non-Standard English*
Less obvious but more intractable problems are faced by children who speak a non-standard variety of English. And within this category, the most seriously disadvantaged are urban-dwelling children of Irish, Caribbean and Gypsy origin. All of these children grow up speaking a variety of English that has been markedly affected by another language or languages. Most Irish people speak English, but the language shift whereby the ancestral mother tongue, Gaelic, was replaced in the recent past

has left considerable marks on their variety of English. Caribbean English, as we have seen, still shows the influence of West African languages, and Anglo-Romani is a hybrid tongue, markedly different from all other varieties of British English. One cannot, of course, *prove* that Irish, West Indian or Gypsy children do badly at school mainly because their mother tongue differs from SE norms, but certain facts make such a suggestion likely. Firstly, many IQ tests depend on verbal skills where 'verbal' is to be equated with 'standard English'. Secondly, a child's speech is indivisible from his sense of identity. In the words of the 1953 UNESCO report on *The Use of Vernacular Languages in Education*, a child's mother tongue is the most suitable medium for education because:

> Psychologically, it is the system of meaningful signs that in his mind works automatically for expression and understanding. Sociologically, it is the means of identification among the members of the community to which he belongs. Educationally, he learns more quickly through it than through an unfamiliar linguistic medium.

A child whose mother tongue is not identical with the language of the school is thus at a double disadvantage. He has to learn a new variety of English before he can be integrated into the school system and, in the process, there is the danger that he will perceive any criticism levelled at his speech as a criticism of himself, his background, his people. And thirdly, Caribbean and Irish children do not show the same tendency to perform poorly in schools in the Caribbean or Ireland. Part of the explanation for this discrepancy is that Caribbean and Irish teachers share the cultural and linguistic heritage of their pupils and can thus judge the *content* as well as the *form* of the utterance. Where the teacher does not share this heritage, there is danger that linguistic differences will be equated with deficiency and that a child's entire educational performance may be conditioned by the teacher's response to his non-standard speech forms. Low expectations on the part of the teacher are almost invariably matched by poor performance on the part of the pupil. And if the child fails to master SE, he may be condemned to unemployment or to casual and unfulfilling labour. Moulton (1975: 4) was referring to the underprivileged in the United States when he wrote:

The lower-class speaker who, for whatever reason, is unable to learn middle-class English will generally be barred forever from holding a middle-class job.

But his claim is equally applicable to Britain as is clear from the Scarman report, in which the following claim is made (1981: 10):

Disadvantage in education and unemployment are the two most crucial facets of racial disadvantage. They are closely connected. Without a decent education and the qualifications which such education alone can provide, a school-leaver is unlikely to find the sort of job to which he aspires, or indeed any job.

5.4.3 The West Indian Child's Problem in British Schools

So far, we have concentrated mainly on the problems shared by all children who come from the lowest socio-economic strata of British society, but it would be foolish and unhelpful to under-value the particular educational problems faced by the child of Caribbean origin. Non-standard Englishes have traditionally been stigmatised. As early as the fourteenth century, Higden claimed:

Al the longage of the Northhumbres, and specialliche at York, is so scharp, slitting, and frotynge, and unschape, that we southerne men may that longage unnethe understonde.

(Quoted from Wakelin, 1972: 34)

and regional pronunciation has continued to be disparaged as the following sentence from *The Times* (24 March 1971) indicates:

Trial by combat ended centuries ago, but trial by mispronunciation still flourishes as a method of detecting outsiders who do not belong to some magic circle of proper pronouncers of English.

But no regional accent or dialect of English has been singled out for the scorn that is often attached to pidginised languages, even by their users. In a debate on a 1953 UNESCO report, Tok Pisin was described as 'inferiority made half articulate' (quoted in Hall, 1966: 106) and as recently as 9 December 1981, a Cameroonian intellectual writing in the *Cameroon Tribune* (a prestigious, and semi-official paper) described a pidgin as 'an expression of meanness and weak intellect', 'a tool of careless thinking' and referred to Cameroon Pidgin specifically as lacking 'a code of analysis', as being linguistic 'dirt' and the 'canker worm of anglophone society'.[15] Nor are some British teachers more enlightened. V. Edwards (1979: 42) refers to teachers who described the speech of West Indian children as being 'babyish', 'careless and slovenly', 'lacking proper grammar' and even 'very relaxed like the way they walk'.

The Caribbean child thus faces both linguistic and sociological problems at school. In his home community, as among Black Americans and Africans, verbal skills like ritualised insults, repartee, the use of an apt proverb, and dramatic recreations of events, are highly prized, but such skills may be discouraged in British schools as 'rudeness', 'talkativeness', 'lies'. In addition, his variety of English only partially overlaps the teacher's, with the result that there is failure to communicate on both sides, largely because both child and teacher assume that the child is speaking British English. And so communication problems tend to be attributed to lack of intelligence or prejudice. Even when the child makes considerable efforts to modify his speech and his written work, to produce the '-ed' and '-s' endings that the teacher seems to want, his efforts often result in hypercorrect forms like the following which occurred in the written work of seven-year-olds:

We wants to go
I tried to talked
He eated it all up.

When such sentences are criticised, the child is reinforced in his prejudice that, no matter what he does, he is picked on. And the teacher who repeatedly receives such work is often convinced that the child is educationally subnormal.

5.5 SOLUTIONS

Few teachers of West Indian children are as sanguine as J. Wright who wrote in the *Times Educational Supplement* (14 May 1976):

> Nearly all those West Indian children whose parents speak a broad West Indian dialect are bidialectal. They will speak one dialect with their family and other West Indians, another with their white peers (and perhaps a third with their teacher).

Children do not seem to be automatically capable of matching school activities with an appropriate use of the standard language, although they can certainly switch their language behaviour to indicate respect, disdain, affection, suspicion or insolence. Many progressive educators believe that bidialectalism or competence in both the standard language and a non-standard variety is the answer. Trudgill puts the case like this:

> This approach [i.e. bidialectalism] recognises that both the standard English dialect and the child's native dialect are valid and good linguistic varieties worthy of attention; and both are to be considered 'correct'. . . . The differences between the two dialects are pointed out and discussed as an interesting fact – children do appear to find this sort of thing interesting. And non-standard dialect users can then be taught how to convert their own dialect forms into the standard dialect when it is required. The important thing about this approach is that it respects the child's dialect and his feelings about it, and does not try to eradicate it or even alter it. It attempts to give the child competence in another dialect – standard English – in addition to the one he already has.
>
> (1975: 68–9)

Trudgill was not specifically referring to West Indian children but it would indeed seem desirable to produce bidialectals, individuals who are equally at home in both SE and WIEB. If this were possible, children would retain the English associated with their Caribbean cultural heritage and, in addition, master the linguistic repertoires useful in school and in examinations. But unfortunately this type of bidialectalism does not seem to be easily attained. Labov, who has worked extensively with speakers of Black English, claims (1972b: 187):

> We have not encountered any non-standard speakers who gained good control of a standard language, and still retained control of the non-standard language.

And my own study of Hiberno-English dialect speakers supports this finding. A speaker of WIEB who masters SE will continue to possess a good passive knowledge of his mother tongue and will almost certainly have a wider stylistic repertoire than an SE speaker who has never known and used a non-standard variety, but the knowledge acquired in SE will be reproduced in SE.[16] The acquisition of SE would thus involve some loss for the West Indian child, the loss of flexibility in the use of WIEB structures, but if the aim of the West Indian parents is that their children should pass examinations and obtain fulfilling employment, they might well echo Wordsworth's sentiment:

> . . . for such loss, I would believe,
> Abundant recompense.
>
> (*Tintern Abbey*, 87–88)

If bidialectalism among children is not easily attained, should WIEB be taught in the classroom?[17] Dillard (1972: 294), writing about the analogous use of Black English in American schools, envisages a time when white children in some schools may have to be taught the language variety of the majority group:

> It might even come about, in some areas, that white children would need to learn Black English – by ESOL techniques of course – in order to be able to integrate themselves into Black-dominated school systems. And this new minority might just as well be prepared to hear statements like: 'The white knows nothing and can learn nothing'.

One can sympathise with the passion underlying Dillard's views. It *is* unfair that minority speech patterns (i.e. Standard English) should be imposed on the majority (i.e. speakers of non-standard varieties) but it is also 'unfair' that some people should be strong and others weak, some handsome while others are ugly. The basic injustices in life and in society, however, cannot be remedied by shouting: 'It's unfair', by shifting the injustice from 'the beggar on horseback to the beggar on foot' or by taking delight in a teacher's use of non-standard forms:

> It is very encouraging to see sentences like *We never done that before* appearing boldly in the teacher's handwriting in a child's exercise book.
>
> (Trudgill, 1975: 83)

Attractive as the idea of teaching WIEB[18] in the classroom is, there are two main objections to it. Firstly, few teachers have the necessary skills to talk knowledgeably about WIEB and pupils might well resent an inaccurate representation, however well-meaning. But secondly, it is very unlikely that West Indian parents would approve of the appearance of non-standard English in the classroom. The London headmaster who said:

> Should I create a Black curriculum? Should I put Creole on the time-table? Over my dead body; and the majority of my parents would cheer me to the skies.

(Quoted in Stone, 1981: 112)

had a West Indian school population of almost 80% and he certainly knew the feelings of their parents.

Perhaps the solution is the creation of West Indian schools with West Indian teachers? This would indeed have many advantages for the West Indian child. He would no longer be moving between 'two separate and different cultures which have to be kept firmly apart' (Bullock Report, 1975: 286) but would be in a position analagous to that of a middle-class white child who goes to school and finds that the teacher's language, culture and aspirations match his own. Many West Indian communities have felt the need to help their children in this way and so they have started 'Supplementary Schools' on Saturdays. They have done so because they are dissatisfied with the lax discipline in state schools and because they refuse to accept that their children are intellectually inferior. And, as well as many supplementary schools, a private school was set up by the Seventh Day Adventist Church in Tottenham in 1980, with a West Indian headmaster, a majority of West Indian teachers and only a handful of white pupils, all of whom shared the religious views of the other children. Within five months of its opening in April 1980, and in spite of substantial fees, the enrolment had risen from forty-eight to three hundred (Mike Phillips, *Observer Colour Supplement*, 15 Feb., 1981: 39). Such schools, both supplementary and private, undoubtedly fulfil a need but they are not the whole answer. They underline the dissatisfaction West Indians feel with the British education system, but they cannot offer an alternative education to all children of Caribbean origin. And even if they could, even if West Indian-run education was available to every child of West Indian origin, colour-segregated education would only increase the problems of racism and lack of integration that have resulted in a West Indian feeling of alienation from and disenchantment with Britain.

The solution that seems to offer most hope for the British of all colours and classes is to educate the teacher. He must learn that although SE is the socially prestigious variety and the most useful over the widest social and geographic areas, it is in no way intrinsically superior to any other mother-tongue English. We can educate our students in the knowledge that the English language did not stop changing when a standard dialect emerged and that pidginised Englishes have at least as much right to be studied as Old and Middle English. No scientist would feel competent to deal with twentieth-century scientific problems if he had only studied alchemy, yet many students and teachers of English know little or nothing about what has happened to the English language since the time of Shakespeare. And, by a judicious use of the media, we could educate the public that difference does not equal deficiency, that changing one's mother-tongue form of English is not as simple or as praiseworthy as changing one's clothes. Because a variety of language is not just a device for naming different objects in the physical world but is also a means of expressing one's perceptions of reality, it is not a system that should be tampered with lightly.

The education that we are proposing will take time. A change in the attitude of the teacher towards WIEB will not automatically or immediately change the pattern of West Indian under-achievement and many teachers may echo the view expressed by an American teacher in Spolsky (1972: 39), a teacher who was prepared to acknowledge that prejudice could affect one's attitude to one's pupils:

> I think all of this is very interesting. I think you have succeeded in making me culturally aware. I am very sympathetic with the plight of the Mexican American and feel no prejudice against him. However, as a teacher, I want to know what to do *differently* for the Mexican American child from what I do for the Anglo child when I am teaching $2 + 2 = 4$.

If they do, however, the battle will already be won because they will have become aware of the significant inter-relationships between social class, language varieties and performance at school.

NOTES

1. The percentage can, of course, be even higher than 50%. Stone (1981: 112) refers to a London Comprehensive School 'with over 80% "immigrant", mostly West Indian, pupils'.
2. We shall use the terms 'Caribbean' and 'West Indian' virtually interchangeably, but 'Caribbean' will be used to refer to the area designated in Map 9, whereas 'West Indian' will refer mainly to the British West Indies and, in particular, to Jamaica, the Leeward Islands, the Windward Islands, Barbados, Guyana, Trinidad and Tobago.
3. Some account of these can be found in Rickford (1976) and Todd (1979).
4. Linguists like J. R. Edwards (1979) and Rosen and Burgess (1980) and dialectologists like Stanley Ellis in the BBC TV series *Word of Mouth* (1976).
5. We are using the Cassidy–LePage conventions from the *Dictionary of Jamaican English* (1980).
6. Cassidy and LePage distinguish twenty-three consonantal phonemes for Jamaican English because they distinguish between 'g' and 'gy' as in *Gaadn* (Gordon) and *gyaadn* (garden) and between 'k' and 'ky' as in *kata* (cotter) and *kyata* (scatter) but these are not distinctive phonemes in WIEB although 'k' and 'g' are markedly palatalised when followed by a front vowel.
7. The Catholic community in Coalisland, Co. Tyrone uses forty-four phonemes, fourteen vowels and thirty-one consonants.
8. The difference between WIEB 'can' and 'can't' is often only a difference of intonation:

$\qquad$ *Hīm kyāan hia* $\qquad$ *Hīm kyaan hīa*
$\qquad$ (He can understand) $\qquad$ (He can't understand).

And intonation also disambiguates
di mān daag (the man's dog) and *di man daag* (the male dog) and:

$\qquad$ *Mieri Blak* (Mary Black) from *Mieri blak* (Mary is black/dark).

9. It is impossible in the confines of this chapter to describe in detail the intonation, rhythm and stress patterns of WIEB. The reader can find some information on this in Wells (1973 and 1981). In brief, however, syllables tend to be equally stressed in WIEB with rising pitch corresponding to English strong stress. WIEB's 'singsong' intonation is almost certainly due to West Africans speaking English according to the patterns of their own tone languages.

10. Many words in WIEB have multiple etymologies, thus *se* may come from Twi *se* which means 'say' and which is used like a subordinating conjunction:

    Me pe se ɔkɔ – I want him to go

    | | | |

    I want say he + go

    and from English 'say'.

11. According to Pollard (1981)

    'Dread Talk, the speech of the Rastafarians of Jamaica, evolved as the language of a lower class socio-religious group emerging in the Jamaica of the nineteen thirties. It is, in fact, Jamaican Creole, the speech of the Jamaican poor, with significant lexical adjustments informed by the social and economic realities and by the religious and philosophical positions of the people involved in the movement. In the last decade [i.e. during the 1970s] Dread Talk has increasingly become the code not only of the Rastafarians but of Jamaican youth of all classes.'

    And, we might add, of many disillusioned young West Indians in Britain. Referring to their use of language, Pollard quotes Yawney (1972) as follows:

    'The Rastas have always represented English as the language of colonialism and have developed their own based on its bastardization.'

    A good, simple account of the growth and development of Rastafarianism can be found in Stone (1981: 80ff).

12. The creole adopted by the young and often referred to as 'Jamaican' is not identical with any Jamaican Creole of the past or present. It is a type of creolised English, deriving mainly from Jamaican Creole but influenced by London speech and by Rasta talk, and it is deliberately acquired by many black youths as a symbolic act to emphasise their alienation from white British society.

13. Verbs in English can be divided roughly into two main types, viz. dynamic or action verbs like *GO, RUN, SING* which frequently co-occur with the progressive, thus:

    I am going/he is running/we have been singing

    and stative verbs like BE, HAVE, SEE, HEAR, REMEMBER which rarely co-occur with the progressive:

    *I am being tired/he is having a house/she is seeing a dog, etc.

14. Asian children often perform better than either West Indian children or British children in school examinations, as the Rampton report reveals. With regard to CSE and 'O' levels, for example, Rampton's team found that 3% of West Indians obtained 5 or more higher grades compared with 18% for Asians and 16% for other leavers (1981: 7). Again, in the Rampton

sample, only 1% of West Indians went on to full-time degree courses in further education compared with 5% of Asians and 4% of other school leavers (9).

15. An examination of such descriptions applied mainly to US and Caribbean creoles is to be found in Turner (1949: 6ff).

16. A widely-held assumption that one can acquire knowledge in one language and easily reproduce this knowledge in another is questioned by Paul Kolers. In an article (1968: 86) Kolers offers the following insights into the acquisition, storage and retrieval of knowledge among bilinguals, i.e. among people who had a good to excellent control of two languages:

> Nearly all our bilingual subjects remarked during interviews that they did mathematical operations in the language in which they were taught the operations. They could always tell us the results of their operations in either language, and they could even describe what operations they had performed and how they had performed them, but the operations could be performed in only one way. Indeed, a bilingual colleague once told me that, having moved from France to the US at the age of twelve, he does his arithmetic in French and his calculus in English.

17. It is certainly true that many children use WIEB in the classroom. The following version of *Jack and the Beanstalk* was told in class by a seven-year-old child who was born in Leeds of Jamaican parents. There are a number of creole features in her narrative:

> Once upon a time Jack mother was very poor and he had a cow and Jack swop it for two bean and his mother was vex and he threw it through the window outside. In the morning when they wake up, the tree – the tree – the beantree turn a big tree and Jack climb it and went to another earth and a old man tell him how his father rich years ago. And he went to the king house and beg his wife to hide him and when he hide him the king say – and the king come: 'I smell fresh meat'. And the wife say it must be some one of the cook get it and throw it on the roof of the house. And the king call for his bag of money and he count and count and count till he drop asleep. Jack run out and steal the bag of money and run away.
>
> And the next time Jack come back again and beg his wife and the wife hide him again. And the king come in and say: 'I smell fresh meat.' The wife tell him it must be some one of the cook get it and throw it on the roof of the house. And he call for his golden hen – and on it – and he touch him and say: 'Lay, honey, lay gold' until he fall asleep. Jack pick the golden hen and run away. And the next now, Jack come back now and beg his wife to hide him again and he hide him. And the king come and said: 'I smell

fresh meat.' And he said it must be one of the cook get it and throw it on the roof of the house. And the king call for his bag of – for his harp and it play and play till he fall asleep. He – Jack run out and pick the harp and the harp begin to halla: 'Master! Master!' And Jack run down the beanstalk and the king run after him. And Jack halla for his mother and Jack call for the axe and Jack fall the tree and kill the king. And that is the end of the story.

(The dash signifies a slight pause in the narrative.)

18. There is no doubt that, given enough money and good will, WIEB could be used as a medium for education. Caribbean creoles have been used for centuries for the transmission of oral culture and traditions and been perfectly adequate to the task. Papua New Guinea, Vanuatu and the Solomons are all experimenting with the use of their pidginised Englishes in the classroom, and the difficulties encountered are related more to book and teacher availability rather than to any problem with the language. And South Africa has taken a creolised language, Afrikaans, and shown that it can be used to fulfil all the requirements of a technologically advanced society. There is thus little doubt as to the *linguistic* adequacy of pidgins and creoles, but to use WIEB as a medium of instruction in British schools would be to stress the racial and cultural differences.

REFERENCES AND SUGGESTIONS FOR FURTHER READING

ABRAHAMS, R. D., *Talking Black,* Rowley, Massachusetts: Newbury House, 1976.

ALATIS, J. E. (ed.), *International Dimensions of Bilingual Education*, Washington: Georgetown University Press, 1979.

ALLEYNE, MERVYN, *Comparative Afro-American*, Ann Arbor: Karoma Publishers, Inc., 1980.

APPLE, M. W., 'Deschooling Society', in *Society, State and Schooling*, eds M. Young and G. Whitty, Brighton: Falmer Press, 1977.

BERNSTEIN, BASIL, 'Social class, linguistic codes and grammatical elements', *Language and Speech 5*, pp. 31–46, 1962.

BERNSTEIN, BASIL, *Class, Codes and Control*, Vols 1–3, St Albans: Paladin, 1973.

BULLOCK, ALAN, *A Language for Life*. London: HMSO, 1975.

CASSIDY, F. G., *Jamaica Talk: Three Hundred Years of the English Language in Jamaica*, London: Macmillan, 1961.

CASSIDY, F. G. and LePAGE, R. B., *Dictionary of Jamaican English*, Cambridge: University Press, 1980.

CLAYDON, L., KNIGHT, T. and RADO, M., *Curriculum and Culture*, Sydney: Allen and Unwin, 1977.

CRE (Commission for Racial Equality), *Urban Deprivation, Racial Inequality and Social Policy: A Report*, London: HMSO, 1977.

CRAIG, D. R., 'Education and Creole English in the West Indies. Some Sociolinguistic Factors', in Dell Hymes (ed.) *Pidginization and Creolization of Languages*, Cambridge: University Press, 1971.

DALE, PHILIP S., *Language Development, Structure and Function*, 2nd edn. New York: Holt, Rinehart and Winston, 1976.

DAVISON, R. B., *Black British: Immigrants to England*, London: Oxford University Press, 1966.

DeCAMP, DAVID, 'Neutralizations, Iteratives and Ideophones: the Locus of Language in Jamaica', in DeCamp, D. and I. F. Hancock *Pidgins and Creoles: Current Trends and Prospects*, Washington: Georgetown University Press, 1974.

DELAMONT, SARA, *Interaction in the Classroom*, London: Methuen Books, 1976.

DEUTSCH, M. (ed.), *The Disadvantaged Child*, New York: Basic Books, 1967.

DILLARD, J. L., *Black English*, New York: Random House, 1972.

DILLARD, J. L., *Perspectives on Black English*, The Hague: Mouton, 1975.

EDWARDS, A. D., *Language in Culture and Class*, London: Heinemann Educational Books, 1979.

EDWARDS, JOHN R., *Language and Disadvantage*, London: Edward Arnold, 1979.

EDWARDS, V. K., *The West Indian Language Issue in British Schools*, London: Routledge and Kegan Paul, 1979.

EDWARDS, V. K., 'Patterns of Language Use in the Black British Community', *English World-Wide* 2.2, pp. 154–64, 1981.

FISHMAN, J. A. et al., *The Spread of English. The Sociology of English as an Additional Language*, Rowley, Mass: Newbury House, 1978.

GEERTZ, CLIFFORD, *Interpreting Cultures*, New York: Basic Books, 1973

GILES, H. and POWESLAND, P., (eds), *Speech Style and Social Evaluation*, London: Academic Books, 1975.

GILES, H. AND ST CLAIR, R. (eds), *Language and Social Psychology*, Oxford: Blackwell, 1979.

HALL, ROBERT A. JR, *Pidgin and Creole Languages*, Ithaca: Cornell University Press, 1966.

HALL, S. AND JEFFERSON, T. (eds) *Resistance Through Rituals: Youth Sub-Cultures in Post-War Britain*, London: Hutchinson, 1976.

HANCOCK, I. F., *Romani Sociolinguistics*, The Hague: Mouton, 1979.

HANCOCK, I. F., 'Romani and Anglo-Romani', in P. Trudgill (ed.) *Languages in the British Isles*, 1982.

HANCOCK, I. F., 'Land of pain: five centuries of Gypsy slavery', *Roma,* VI *(3–4)*, pp. 7–21, 1982.

HARRISON, D. AND TRABASSO, T. (eds), *Black English: A Seminar,* Hillsdale, NJ: Erlbaum, 1976.

HIRO, DILIP, *Black British, White British,* Harmondsworth: Penguin, 1973.

JOYCE, P. W., *English As We Speak It In Ireland,* Dublin: M. H. Gill and Son, Ltd, 1910.

KENRICK, DONALD, 'Anglo-Romani today', in T. A. Acton (ed.) *Current changes amongst British Gypsies and their place in international patterns of development,* Oxford, 1971.

KOLERS, PAUL, 'Bilingualism and information processing', *Scientific American,* Vol. 218, No. 3, pp. 78–86, 1968.

LABOV, W., *Language in the Inner City; Studies in the Black English Vernacular,* Philadelphia: University of Pennsylvania Press, 1972.

LABOV, W., 'The study of language in its social context in Pride, J. and J. Holmes (eds) *Sociolinguistics,* Harmondsworth: Penguin, pp. 180–202, 1972.

LABOV, W., *Sociolinguistic Patterns,* Philadelphia: University of Pennsylvania Press, 1977.

LAZAR, IRVING, *Lasting Effects After Pre-School,* Washington: Office of Human Development Services, Dept. of H. E. and Welfare, 1978.

LEPAGE, R. B. (ed.), *Jamaican Creole,* London: Macmillan, 1960.

LEPAGE, R. B. (ed.), *Caribbean Connections in the Classroom,* Pamphlet printed by the University of York, 1981.

MAZRUI, ALI A., *The Political Sociology of the English Language: An African Perspective,* The Hague, Mouton, 1975.

MOULTON, W., 'The Nature of Language' in E. Haugen and M. Bloomfield (eds) *Language as a Human Problem,* London: Lutterworth Press, pp. 3–21, 1975.

O'DONNELL, W. R. AND TODD, LORETO, *Variety in Contemporary English,* London: Allen and Unwin, 1980.

OECD, *Reviews of National Policies for Education: US Federal Policies for the Education of the Disadvantaged,* Paris: Organisation for Economic Co-operation and Development, 1980.

Ó MUIRITHE, D. (ed.) *The English Language in Ireland,* Dublin: Mercier, 1977.

PLATT, J. AND WEBER, HEIDI, *English in Singapore and Malaysia: Status: Features: Functions,* Kuala Lumpur: Oxford University Press, 1980.

POLLARD, VELMA, 'The Social History of Dread Talk', Paper presented at the Third Biennial Conference of the Society for Caribbean Linguistics, Aruba, 1980.

PRIDE, J. B. (ed.), *The New Englishes,* Rowley, Mass.: Newbury House, 1982.

RAMPTON, A. (Chairman), *West Indian Children in our Schools*, London: HMSO, 1981.

RICKFORD, J. R. AND RICKFORD, ANGELA, 'Cut-eye and Suck-teeth: African Words and Gestures in New World Guise', *Journal of American Folklore*, 89, pp. 294–309, 1976.

ROSEN, H. AND BURGESS, T., *Languages and Dialects of London School Children: An Investigation*, London: Ward Lock Educational, 1980.

RUBINSTEIN, D, *Education and Equality*, Harmondsworth: Penguin, 1979.

SALKEY, ANDREW, *Riot*, London: Oxford University Press, 1973.

SCARMAN, THE LORD, *The Brixton Disorders 10–12 April 1981*, London: HMSO, 1981.

SMITH, LARRY (ed.), *English for Cross-Cultural Communication*, London: Macmillan, 1980.

SPOLSKY, B. (ed.), *The Language Education of Minority Children*, Rowley, Mass.: Newbury House, 1972.

STONE, MAUREEN, *The Education of the Black Child in Britain*, Glasgow: Fontana, 1981.

STUBBS, M., *Language, Schools and Classrooms*, London: Methuen, 1976.

SUTCLIFFE, DAVID, *British Black English*, Oxford: Blackwell, 1982.

TODD, LORETO, *Tortoise the Trickster*, London: Routledge and Kegan Paul, 1979.

TODD, LORETO, *Some Day Been Dey: West African Pidgin Folktales*, London: Routledge and Kegan Paul, 1979.

TRUDGILL, PETER, *Sociolinguistics*, Harmondsworth: Penguin, 1974.

TRUDGILL, PETER, *Accent, Dialect and the School*, London: Edward Arnold, 1975.

TWITCHIN, J. AND DEMUTH, CLARE, *Multicultural Education*, London: BBC, 1981.

TURNER, L. D., *Africanisms in the Gullah Dialect*, Chicago: University of Chicago Press, 1949.

WARD, MARTHA C., *Them Children: A Study in Language Learning*, New York: Holt, Rinehart and Winston, 1971.

WATKINS, RICHARD, 'A Review of Language, Culture, Intelligence and Expectation in the Education of Ethnic Minorities and Low Socio-Economic Students', Leeds: unpublished PDESL dissertation, 1981.

WELLS, JOHN, *Jamaican Pronunciation in London*, Oxford: Blackwell, 1973.

WELLS, JOHN, *Accents of English*, Vol. 1 *An Introduction*, Vol. 2 *The British Isles*, Vol. 3 *Beyond the British Isles*, Cambridge: University Press, 1982.

WILLIAMS, F., *Explorations of the Linguistic Attitudes of Teachers*, Rowley, Mass.: Newbury House, 1976.

YAWNEY, CAROLE, 'Remnants of all Nations: Rastafarian Attitudes to Race and Nationality', in F. Henry (ed.) *Ethnicity in the Americas*, The Hague: Mouton, 1976.

CHAPTER 6

Conclusions

𒀭𒀭𒀭𒀭𒀭𒀭

6.1 ASSESSMENT

We have, in the course of the previous five chapters, looked at the English-related pidgins and creoles which have developed over the past four hundred years. We have discovered how pidgins evolved to facilitate rudimentary linguistic contact, and then how people, separated from their own cultures, have taken these makeshift systems and forged them into languages capable of expressing all their communicative needs. We have become aware that creoles and expanded pidgins are not linguistic freaks but flexible, expressive languages created from impoverished input by the exploitation of linguistic common denominators. And finally we have seen that these languages tend to evoke negative social evaluations. Simplicity is confused with inadequacy and creole speakers are often judged to be speaking bad English rather than efficient creole.

There are many inferences to be drawn from our study of English-related pidgins and creoles, some linguistic and others sociological. On the linguistic side, their very existence should cause us to question the widely-held notion that language change is 'slow' (Swadesh, 1972: 31),[1] 'regular and systematic' (Anderson, 1973: 9). If the languages we have studied are to be considered varieties of English, then extensive changes occurred, often within one generation,[2] changes that cannot be captured by traditional linguistic models. If we choose to deny that they are varieties of English and argue that, in spite of their vocabularies, in spite of their word order, and in spite of their syntactic patterning, they are relexifications of African, Asiatic or Pacific languages, we are no nearer a solution that accords with orthodox linguistic theory. Instead we are faced with the problems of how and why languages separated by thousands of miles should be so alike structurally or should behave so similarly when in contact with English. The simple fact is that pidginised Englishes cannot easily be assigned to any family tree. Their vocabulary is certainly English but their lack of morphology[3] makes it impossible to assign them unambiguously to any specific language or group of languages. This fact suggests two interesting corollaries: first, that morphologically distinctive features are linguistically redundant and second, that the study of pidgins and creoles will provide more immediate access to deep structure similarities than can be achieved by the study of standardised, morphologically complex languages. To put the matter some-what simplistically, the time depth for the development of any of the pidgins and creoles referred to is much shorter than for Standard English. Before 1600 they did not exist.[4] In addition, because they have only recently undergone *official* rather than *natural* standardisation, we can more readily see in them the structures that are essential to easy communication.

On the non-linguistic side our study has shown that language change cannot be considered in isolation from relevant, albeit variable, sociological and psychological factors. Language use is only one of the strands in a fabric of interaction among people. Of prime importance in an analysis of contact Englishes, therefore, is information on such factors as the nature and the intimacy[5] of the contact, the perceived worth of the peoples and cultures in contact,[6] the need for, and the benefits accruing to, the acquisi-tion of a new language. Perhaps most important of all, considera-tion should be given to the extent of the social disruption following in the wake of the contact. Where the disruption is extensive, as it was with both slavery and blackbirding, the normal conditions for the transmission of language can be destroyed. And in such circumstances, the English language has undergone massive modifications.

6.2 LANGUAGE CHANGE: PAST, PRESENT AND TO COME

Traditionally linguists have looked at language change in terms of two processes: the separation of linguistically homogeneous communities and the consequent proliferation of related dialects which, through time, become increasingly divergent; and the coming together of people speaking different languages, often with the consequent absorption or modification of some of the languages concerned. It seems likely, however, that many languages, English included, have changed due to both processes, but whereas it is the latter process which triggers off radical changes,[7] it is the former which has received most scholarly attention. Our knowledge of the history of English-related pidgins and creoles allows us to extrapolate back into the past and offers us an algorithm for computing the type and extent of language change possible, especially in situations where one group of people has marked dominance over others.

An examination of the English language from about 1600 clearly indicates the different types of changes that can occur within the same language over the same period of time. Within Britain the language has been modified mainly due to internal pressures such as regularising due to analogy – *dive* and *dived* rather than *dive* and *dove* – and because of the need to describe new objects, from a potato to a daisy wheel,[8] or new concepts from colonialism to computerisation. Outside Britain such internally motivated changes have been accelerated and extended because of the influence of other languages. And the speed and extent of change have been greatest where the contact has been of the kind that produces pidgin and creole Englishes. Such Englishes differ from Standard English and from each other because they reflect different cultures, and yet they have much in common. They share with SE a core vocabulary, a tendency for the verb phrase to be analytic, a fixed word order where subjects precede and objects follow the verb and where adjectives go before the nouns they modify. What we have seen happening to English, in Britain and, more especially abroad, suggests that Anderson may be right in claiming that:

> Languages pass from one general type to another, as from a highly inflected type of language to an uninflected or analytic type.
>
> (1973: 163)

His second claim, however, that:

> From an analytic structure they tend towards a synthetic structure.
>
> (1973: 163)

250

is questionable. It may well have been true in the past, especially where written standards did not exist, but it seems unlikely that modern varieties of English will become increasingly synthetic. And there are two main reasons for this. First, a written standard exists which militates against dramatic syntactic change. The syntax of SE has changed less in the past four hundred years than in any previous four centuries for which we have records. And the written standard also affects all other varieties of world English. Social forces such as education and media entertainment work for convergence towards SE. In pidgin- and creole-speaking areas the convergence may not be as rapid as the divergence but evidence from all areas studied in this book shows that it is already taking place. A second and related force is also at work and this relates to what might be termed the internationalisation of English. Over the past one hundred years in particular, English has become the lingua franca of the world and so international mutual intelligibility has become an effective deterrent to even small-scale, unofficial change. The only changes permitted are those related to facilitating communication. In other words, they are related to the processes of pidginisation. Steiner (1975: 470) was clearly aware of this possibility when, after discussing the negative aspects[9] of the use of English as the world's lingua franca, he commented:

> It would be ironic if the answer to Babel were pidgin and not Pentecost.

Our study has shown that this solution would be much less ironic than Steiner believed. Pidgins arose specifically to counter babels. They were the natural language choice in multilingual plantations in Africa, the Americas and the South Pacific because they utilised structures common to all languages and to all speakers.

6.3 THE LEGACY OF PIDGINS AND CREOLES

The more we study English-related pidgins and creoles, the more they speak to us of the suffering inflicted on one branch of humanity by another. They speak of the disruption of societies and the creation of non-homogeneous communities where parents could not transmit their own mother tongues to their children. But they also speak of the human need to communicate and the human ability to take the most unpromising linguistic material and mould it into a structure capable of expressing dreams and hopes as well as orders and complaints. In 1802 Wordsworth wrote a sonnet in honour of a creole-speaking ex-slave, Toussaint L'Ouverture,[10] which ended with the lines:

Though fallen thyself, never to rise again,
Live, and take comfort. Thou hast left behind
Powers that will work for thee; air, earth, and skies;
There's not a breathing of the common wind
That will forget thee; thou hast great allies;
Thy friends are exultations, agonies,
And love, and man's unconquerable mind.

Wordsworth's pathetic fallacy could not alter the fact that Toussaint L'Ouverture died, an apparent failure, in a Paris jail; but the creole languages lived on and they certainly reveal the 'agonies' and the 'exultations' and the human ability to create, mould and modify languages that are a living testimony to 'man's unconquerable mind'.

NOTES

1. Swadesh expresses this widely-held view as follows:
   One general rule applies to all forms of linguistic change: It goes on slowly . . . whilst linguistic change is always slow, its rate of change varies with social, economic, political and geographical factors; furthermore, some portions of language change less slowly than others.
2. The English-related creoles of Suriname seem to have crystallised within a period of thirty years and yet, in this time, they were sufficiently well established to have been able to withstand other influences for three hundred years. (See p. 60.)
3. One can, for example, point out that all Indo-European languages make use of mutation:
   Eng.   foot feet
   Gaelic fear fir.
   Similarly, all languages belonging to the Niger-Congo family make use of a noun class system where nouns are classified and marked

according to whether or not they are human or animate or liquid or combustible or abstract, etc. Nouns in one category are distinguished from nouns in another by the affix taken, e.g. a, e or n. Neither of these morphologically distinctive features occurs in the English-related pidgins and creoles of West Africa.

4. This is not, of course, the same as claiming that they developed *ex nihilo* but, because of their relatively recent development, we are in a much better position to study their history than we are with Standard English.

5. An examination of the vocabularies of CP and TP suggests that the contacts were non-intimate. Words connected with work, punishment and produce are from English but the words relating to local culture tend to be either from local languages or are realised as calques.

6. It seems clear from the vocabulary of TP that the local people were disparaged by their overseers. We might note, for example, the use of:

as	ass/arse	to mean	'source'
as ples			'native village'
baga	bugger	to mean	'person' and 'wreck'
bagarapim			'ruin, destroy'
lesbaga			'lazy person'
bulsitim	bullshit	to mean	'deceive, cheat'
kan/bokis	can/box	to mean	'female genitals'
sit	shit	to mean	'residue'
sit bilong faia			'ashes'
sit bilong lam			'soot'.

7. One can compare the different rates of change of mother-tongue English in Britain and the United States in the past three hundred years. The latter has changed much more dramatically, especially with regard to vocabulary and idiom. The main reason for these different rates of change is the extensive contact in the States between people of different mother tongues, the so-called 'melting-pot syndrome'.

8. A 'daisy wheel' is a gadget used for printing the letters in word processors.

9. Steiner pointed out that the use of English as a world language was having two ill effects. First, English was eroding the autonomy of local languages, particularly in the third world, thus reducing the linguistic diversity in the world and second, the role of English as the world's esperanto was causing 'negative feedback':

As it spreads over the earth, 'international English' is like a thin wash, marvellously fluid, but without adequate base. One need only converse with Japanese colleagues ... whose technical proficiency in English humbles one, to realise how profound are the effects of dislocation. So much that is being said is correct, so little is right. (1975:470)

10. Toussaint L'Ouverture was a creole-speaking ex-slave who became the governor of St Domingo. He resisted Napoleon's edict to re-establish slavery on the island and was arrested and sent to prison in Paris in June 1802. He died there in April 1803. Wordsworth's sonnet was written shortly after Toussaint L'Ouverture's arrest and published in the *Morning Post* on 2 February 1803.

REFERENCES AND SUGGESTIONS FOR FURTHER READING

ANDERSON, J. M., *Structural Aspects of Language Change*, London: Longman, 1973.

GREENBERG, J. H., *Languages of West Africa*, The Hague: Mouton, 1966.

HERSKOVITS, F. S. (ed.), *The New World Negro. Selected Papers in Afro-American Studies*, New York: Minerva Press, 1969.

STEINER, GEORGE, *After Babel*, London: Oxford University Press, 1975.

SWADESH, M., *The Origin and Diversification of Language*, London: Routledge and Kegan Paul, 1972.

WELMERS, W. E., *African Language Structures*, Berkley: University of California Press, 1973.

WESTERMANN, D. AND BRYAN, M., *The Languages of West Africa*, London: International African Institute, 1970.

Appendix

Here the reader is presented with samples of pidgins and creoles from different periods and from different parts of the world. The texts are divided into three. Section A contains texts that were written before the beginning of the twentieth century. In these the pidgin or creole was employed for literary purposes and was not intended to be read by speakers of the language. Section B contains contemporary texts, many written specifically for pidgin and creole speakers. Section C provides a number of narratives in CP and TP to enable the reader to extend his knowledge of these varieties of English.

SECTION A

1. This comes from Daniel Defoe's *Colonel Jack* which was first published in 1722. Among the features that may be noticed are
    i. the tendency to put 'ee' at the end of a word which ends in a consonant, e.g. ll. 1, 21, 40, etc.
       This '-ee' which became a convention for stereotyping pidginised English may have had factual roots. Many West African languages had CVCV structures and speakers of these languages might well have added a vowel to English words that ended in a consonant. CP, for example, still retains *arata* 'rat', *wɛti* 'what' and *witi* 'with'. In addition, in CP, there is a tendency to recapitulate the third person pronoun *i* after commonly used verbs, thus:

    i go i – he went off
    i kam i – he came
    i ran i – he runs/ran.

    This tendency may have been more widespread in earlier varieties of Atlantic pidgins and creoles.
    ii. the occurrence of serial verbs, l. 5 and l. 41
    iii. the tendency to use unmarked verb forms, l. 47, a reduced set of pronouns l. 40 and to avoid the copula, l. 35
    iv. the use of *no* as a general negator, l. 31ff
    v. the tendency to use items multifunctionally, see l. 40 where 'true' is used as a noun.

HE shook his Head, and made Signs that he was *muchee sorree*, as he call'd it, and what will you say or do, said I, if I should prevail with the Great Master to pardon you? I have a Mind to go and see if I can beg for you: He told me he would lie down, let me kill him, me will, says he, run, go fetch, bring for you as long as me live: This was the Opportunity I had a Mind to have, to try whether as *Negroes* have all the other Faculties of reasonable Creatures, they had not also some Sense of Kindness, some Principles of natural Generosity, which in short, is the Foundation of Gratitude; for Gratitude is the Product of generous Principles.

You please me with the beginning of this Story, says he, I hope you have carried it on.

YES Sir, says I, it has been carried on farther perhaps than you imagine, or will think has been possible in such a Case.

BUT I was not so arrogant as to assume the Merit to my self; No, no, said I, I do not ask you to go or run for me, you must do all that for our Great Master, for it will be from him entirely that you will be pardon'd if you are pardon'd at all; for your Offence is against him, and what will you say, will you be grateful to him, and run, go, fetch, bring, for him as long as you live, as you have said you would for me.

YES *indeed*, says he, *and muchee do, muchee do, for you too* (he would not leave me out) *you ask him for me.*

WELL, I put off all his promis'd Gratitude to me from my self, as was my Duty, and plac'd it to your Account, told him I knew you was *muchee good, muchee pitiful*, and I would perswade you if I could; and so told him I would go to you, and he should be Whipp'd no more till I came again; but hark ye, *Mouchat*, says I, that was the *Negroe's* Name, they tell me when I came hither, that there is no showing Kindness to any of you *Negroes*, that when we spare you from Whipping you laugh at us, and are the worse.

HE look'd very serious at me, and said, O, that no so, the Masters say so, but no be so, no be so, indeede, indeede, and so we parly'd.

Jack. Why do they say so then? To be sure they have tried you all.

Negroe. No, no, they no try, they say so, but no trye.

Jack. I hear them all say so.

Negroe. Me tell you the True, they have no Merciee, they beat us cruel, all cruel, they never have show Mercie. How can they tell we be no better?

Jack. What do they never spare?

Negroe. Master, me speakee the True, they never give Merciee, they always whippee, lashee, knockee down, all cruel: *Negroe* be muchee better Man, do muchee better Work, but they tell us no Merciee.

Jack. But what, do they never show any Mercy?

Negroe. No, never, no never, all whipee, all whipee, cruel, worse than they whippee de Horse, whippee de Dog.

Jack. But would they be better if they did?

Negroe. Yes, yes, *Negroe* be muchee better if they be Mercie; when they Whippee, Whippee, *Negroe* muchee cry, muchee hate, would kill if they had de Gun; but when they makee de Merciee, then *Negroe* tell de great Tankee, and love to Worke, and do muchee Worke; and 50 because be good Master to them.

Jack. They say no, you would laugh at them, and mock when they shew Mercy.

Negroe. How! they say when they shew Merciee, they never shew Merciee, me never see them shew one Mercie since me live.

(*Colonel Jack*, Oxford: Basil Blackwell, pp. 163–5, 1927)

2. This passage is taken from *Negro Myths from the Georgia Coast*, 1888, p. 41. Among the features that may be examined are:

    i.   the use of verbal auxiliaries, *bin* (l. 2), *blan* (l. 2), *kin* (l. 6) *a* (l. 7), *guine* (l. 7), *done* (l. 10) and *yent* (cf. 'aint' l. 13)

    ii. the use of *dem* as third person plural pronoun\(l. 2)

    iii. the use of *fuh* meaning 'in order to' (l. 7)

    iv. the use of 'b' for 'v' (l. 2). Many Africans seem to have used a bilabial fricative instead of a labio-dental fricative and this probably accounts for the different spellings of words like *savi/sabi, palava/palaba, evri/ebri, giv/gib* (l. 13)

    v.   the 'eh' is probably an orthographic device to reproduce /i/.

BUH ELEPHANT AN BUH ROOSTER.

Buh Elephant, him bin know Buh Rooster berry well. Dem blan roam togerrur, an Buh Rooster blan wake Buh Elephant duh mornin, so eh kin hunt eh bittle befo de jew dry.

Dem bin a talk togerrur one day, an Buh Elephant, him bet Buh 5 Rooster say him kin eat longer ner him. Buh Rooster, him tek de bet, an dem tun in nex mornin, wen de sun jis bin a git up, fuh see who guine win de bet. Buh Elephant, him gedder leaf an grass, an eat an eat tel eh full an cant eat no mo. Buh Rooster, him sarche de grass fuh seed an wurrum, an eh pick an eat. Wen Buh Elephant done full, an der tan onder de tree 10 duh flop eh yez, eh see Buh Rooster, dist es spry, duh walk bout an der swaller seed an grasshopper an wurrum same luk eh dis biggin fuh eat. Buh Elephant gib up. Eh fine eh yent de man wid de bigges belly wuh kin eat de longes.

257

3. This passage comes from *Cunnie Rabbit, Mister Spider and the Other Beef* which did not appear in print until 1903, but the stories were collected in Sierra Leone in the nineteenth century by Florence Cronise. Among the features which may be noticed are:

   i. the use of auxiliaries, *bin* (l. 2), *able* (l. 5), *go* (l. 8), *done* (l. 10)
   ii. the use of *dem*, a third person plural pronoun as a marker of plurality, (l. 2, l. 7 etc.)
   iii. the use of adjective verbs, l. 3
   iv. the use of *too much* (l. 3) and *plenty* (l. 10)
   v. the use of *Bimeby* as an indicator of fertility (l. 9)
   vi. the use of *sotay* (l. 4) meaning 'until'
   vii. the use of *cunnie* from 'cunning' meaning 'intelligent, sharp'
   viii. the use of *say* after verbs of mental processes, (l. 7).

Cunnie Rabbit and his Well

Long tem, Cunnie Rabbit en all dem beef bin gadder. Den meet up to one place fo' talk palaver, because de country dry too much. Dey no get one grain (drop) wattah sotay (until) all man wan' fo' die. Dey all get word fo' talk, f'om de big beef to de small, but nobody no able fo' fine sense fo' pull dem f'om dis yeah (here) big trouble. Cunnie Rabbit he no bin say notting, he jus' listen wey dem beef talk; he t'ink say: 'Wey ting I go do fo' get wattah?'

Bimeby he grap (get up), he go home, he begin fo' dig well. He dig, he dig, he *dig*. De wattah come plenty. He drink sotay (until) he done satisfy.

Now dem beef hearee dat Cunnie Rabbit get well. Spider he grap fo' go walker to Cunnie Rabbit. He say:

'Fren', we no get one grain wattah fo' drink, we go die. Make yo' gi we.'

(Swan Sonnenschein & Co., London and New York, 1903, pp. 80–82)

4. This passage in anglicised China Coast Pidgin English appeared in *The Leisure Hour* of 1873. Among the features which we may notice are:

   i. the use of 'ee' mainly as a verb ending (ll. 2ff) but also occasionally appended to nouns, l. 3 \and l. 29. \'o' is also used as an ending, ll. 29–30 \although this is not a frequently used convention for indicating pidginised English. It is similar to the occurrence of '-o' in such Australianisms as:

afto 'afternoon', *beddo* 'bed', *cobbo* 'friend' and *Commo* 'communist'.
  ii. the occurrence of serial verbs, e.g. l. 3 and l. 15
 iii. the tendency to use *piecee* as an adjectival marker, l. 3 and l. 21. This tendency resembles the use of 'fellow' as an adjectival marker in TP. A further similarity to TP occurs in the use of *belong* as a preposition, see l. 9 and l. 10.

Only the CCPE text is numbered but the rest of the article is included to give the reader an idea of the attitudes towards pidginised languages.

PIGEON ENGLISH

WITH a parcel of tea which we lately purchased there came a curious piece of Chinese advertising. It is a native tea merchant's bill or circular, printed on red paper sprinkled with gold leaf. It bears the announcement in "pigeon English," that "Tong-Wo-Sun-Kee never makes or ships LIE TEA." Below this announcement, intended for the information of foreigners, there is a longer statement in Chinese, informing his countrymen that he sells nothing but teas of the purest quality. Now this "lie tea" is not so much an adulteration of other than tea leaves, as it may be a mixture of good fresh leaves with what have been already infused. The latter are chiefly bought for a mere trifle at the large tea-drinking establishments, and dried in the sun. The writer has seen acres of ground in the vicinity of Canton, Macao, Shanghai, and other places, where the leaves were spread, sometimes on mats, and sometimes on the bare soil, to shrivel up under his torrid rays. When mixed with fresh tea this "lie tea" is shipped at a much lower price than usual, but very little of it is consumed in England. Germany has been its principal destination; but since the arrival there of the "Maloo mixture," the authorities have prohibited its importation under heavy penalties.

But we have taken up our Chinese tea bill, not to tell about tea and the tea trade, but to say a few words about the strange language of which the expression "Lie tea" is an example.

"Pidgin," or, as it is sometimes spelled, "pigeon" English, originated at Canton during the early days of our relations with China, when the East India Company monopolised the trade with the Hong merchants. In their intercourse neither took the trouble to learn the language of the other properly, but confined their conversation to the fewest number of English and Chinese words necessary for bargaining and dealing in their merchandise. Hence the greater portion of this *patois* is made up of words used in commerce, and its incongruous appellation is a corruption of the word "business." At first John Chinaman found this a difficult word to pronounce, rarely making a

259

nearer approach than "bidjinish." In time he softened it down to "pidgin," which is now universally used by natives and foreigners, so that the title of this paper means literally "Business" English.

Of course the diplomatic interpreters attached to the consulates and legations speak and write both languages correctly, while most of the missionaries are qualified to discourse in Chinese. But the vocabulary in use between the Chinese and British residents, as well as visitors at the treaty ports, is almost wholly of this bastard language. Some of the words, such as the salutation *chin-chin*, are adopted by foreigners, but generally the attempt is on the part of the natives to use English words, with a pronunciation more or less like that of their own language, especially where the speaker has a difficulty in enunciating the letters. Sometimes they add terminations of their own, to give euphony, in their estimation, to the words of the "barbarian" tongue. On the other hand, to our ears these sound very much like the talk of our nurses to children, such as "Georgy peorgy will have a ridy pidy in a coachy woachy."

From its direct business meaning the term "pidgin" is applied to many other acts of persons, but always alludes to what work or engagement they have on hand. For instance, if one calls to inquire for the master, his servant may reply that "he have makee chow-chow pidgin," that is, he may be at dinner, or if on Sunday the answer might be "he have go church pidgin." Then, as to termination syllables, double e is the most common, such as *makee, talkee, walkee, muchee, showee, piecee* etc. This last corruption of our word piece is very commonly used, and derived from a piece or bale of calico, which is the staple import of British manufactured goods. As these are of different qualities, the trader endeavours to impress upon the Chinese buyer that his shirtings are number one, or A 1. Hence remarks of quality have advanced from "numpah wan piecee silk" to "numpah wan piecee man" (a rich or honest trader), or "numpah wan piecee woman" (a beautiful woman). Then the word "pay" is commonly used like "show," evidently from the money paid for goods being shown, such as, "makee pay two piecee boot," meaning "show me a pair of boots." In like manner, the word "fashion" is used to convey very different meanings from its mercantile sense, such as "my no belong that fasun," or "I am not of that opinion." Besides English and Chinese words, other foreign words occur, such as "savee," from the Portuguese verb expressing to know, or the Malay interjection *maskee*, signifying "never mind." The following dialogue between a British resident at Shanghai and his personal servant, or "boy," as he is termed, will give the reader some idea of the incongruous manner in which the Queen's English is distorted, in defiance of Lindley Murray's grammar. The master seated at his table has rung the bell, and his servant enters.

PIGEON ENGLISH	ENGLISH PROPER	
BOY. You makee ling?	Did you ring, sir?	
MAS. Yes, sendee catchee one piecee tailor-man.	Yes, send for a tailor.	
BOY. Just now hab got bottom side.	He is below at present.	5
MAS. Showee he come top side.	Tell him to come up.	
Exit boy, and re-enter with tailor.		
MAS. You belong tailor-man?	Are you a tailor?	
TAI. Es, sah, my belong tailor-man.	Yes, sir, I am a tailor.	
MAS. Belong what name?	What is your name?	10
TAI. Any man callee my Stultz.	They call me Stultz.	
MAS. Foreigners talkee so fashion, how fashion that Chinaman talkee?	The foreigners call you so, but what is your real Chinese name?	
TAI. Po-hing.	Po-hing.	
MAS. My boy makee pay you what thing my makee wanchee; more better you go bottom side askee he. He makee pay you what thing.	My boy will show you what I want done. You had better go downstairs, and he will show you the article.	15
BOY. What thing you wanchee?	What do you want?	
MAS. Showee he makee mend that more olo piecee coat, and spose he can makee clean my thinkee more better.	Tell him to mend that very old coat, and if he can clean it so much the better.	20
BOY. Jus now teefin hab leddy.	Luncheon is ready.	
MAS. Belong what time?	Why, what time is it?	25
BOY. Wanchee one halp belong catchee that two.	It wants half an hour to two o'clock.	
MAS. What thing hab got?	What have you?	
BOY. Feesantee, colo loso beefo, cully.	Pheasant, cold roast beef, curry.	
MAS. I go chop chop; pay he allo man no makee wait.	I'll go directly; tell them all not to wait.	30

From this example it will be seen that pidgin English is not easy to acquire, especially with foreign residents of different nationalities than the United Kingdom and the United States. Indeed, in some instances, as much time and trouble is spent in picking it up verbally, as would serve to learn sufficient of Chinese, under a native teacher, for transacting all ordinary business. Nevertheless, it is an important vocabulary for merchants, bankers, and their *employés* to acquire; for with few exceptions, all transactions in imports and exports between foreigners and natives are conducted in it, and these amount to not less than fifty millions sterling per annum at the fifteen treaty ports.   S. M.

SECTION B

Passages 5a to 5c are gospel translations into Cameroon Pidgin English, Tok Pisin and the Bislama Pidgin English of Vanuata. A copy of the same passage in SE is provided for comparative purposes.

5a.

1. Di fos tok fo di gud nyus fo Jesus Christ God yi Pikin. 2. I bi sem as i di tok fo di buk fo Isaiah, God yi nchinda (Prophet), "Lukam, mi a di sen ma nchinda fo bifo yoa fes weh yi go fix yoa rud fan." 3. Di vos fo som man di krai fo bush: "Fix di ples weh Papa God di go, mek yi rud tret." 4. John di Baptist bi de fo bush, an yi bi di tok sey baptas bi som nomba fo shu sey God dong chus di bad fo di man wey yi dong chen yi hat. 5. Ol pipu fo Judea weti ol di pipu fo Jerusalem bi go fo yi, an yi bi baptas dem fo Jordan wata, an dem bi di gri sey dem bi bad pipu. 6. Fo dat tam John yi krus bi bi biabia fo camel weti nkanda wey yi bi di taiam fo yi wes, den yi chop bi bi lukos weti honi. 7. Den yi bi tok fo dem ol sey, "Som man di kam fo ma bak weh yi pas mi, weh yi shus mi a no koret fan fo ben daun an lusinam. 8. Mi a dong baptas wuna weti wata, bot yi go baptas wuna weti di Holy Spirit."

(*Di Gud Nyus Hawe St Mark Bi Ratam*,
Société Biblique, Cameroun, 1966, p. 5)

5b. *Jon Bilong Baptals em I autim tok*

Dispela em i gutnius bilong Jisas Kraist, Pikinini bilong God.

Dispela gutnius em I kamap pastaim olsem profet Aisaia I raitim:

"Harim, mi salim man bilong bringim tok bilong mi, na em I go paslain long yu.

Em bai i redim rot bilong yu. / Long graun i no gat man, maus bilong wanpela man i sing-aut, i spik.

'Redim rot bilong Bikpela. Stretim oi rot bilong en.' "

Jon, man bilong givim baptais, em i kamap long graun i no gat man, na em i telimautim tok long ol manmeri i mas tanim bel na kisim baptais, na bai God i tekewe sin bilong ol. / Na olgeta Judia na olgeta manmeri bilong Jerusalem ol i go long Jon. Na ol i autim sin

5c *Jon Baptaes I stap long drae ples, I stap prij*

IHemia gud nyus blong Jisas Kraes, Pikinini blong God. ²Hem i stat olsem we profet Aesea i raetem bifo, we God i talem se

"Hemia man blong karem tok blong mi.

Mi mi sanem hem blong hem i go fastaem, yu biaen.

Hem bambae i mekemrere ol rod blong yu."

³"Wan man i stap singaot long drae ples, i se

'Yufala i mekemrere rod blong Hae God*,

we hem i Masta* blong yumi,

Yufala i stretem ol smosmol rod blong hem.' "

4 Ale biaen, nao Jon, hem i kamtru long drae ples, i stap baptaesem ol man mo i stap prij. Hem i talem se "Yufala i mas tanem tingting blong yufala from

bilong ol, na Jon i baptaisim ol long wara Jodan.

Na Jon i save putim klos ol i bin wokim long gras bilong kamel, na em i pasim let long namel bilong en. Na em i save kaikai grasop wantaim hani bilong bus. / Na em i autim tok, i spik, "Wanpela man i kam bihain long mi, na strong bilong em i winim strong bilong mi. Mi no gutpela man inap long mi lindaun na lusim rop bilong su bilong em. / Mi baptaisim yupela long wara. Tasol em bai i baptaisim yupela long Holi Spirit."

(*Nupela Testamen Long Tok Pisin*, BFBS, p. 120, Canberra, 1969)

ol sin blong yufala, mo yufala i mas tekem baptaes, nao bambae God i tekemaot ol sin blong yufala." [5]Olgeta man blong ol velej long Judia wetem olgeta blong Jerusalem oli stap go lesin long hem. Oli stap talemaot ol sin blong olgeta, nao Jon i stap baptaesem olgeta long Jodan Reva.

6 Jon i no putum flas klos. Kot blong hem oli wokem long hea blong kamel nomo, mo strap blong hem oli wokem long skin blong buluk. Mo kakae blong hem, lokis wetem eg blong sugabag blong bus. [7]Hem i talemaot long olgeta, i se "Biaen long mi i gat wan man i stap kam we i hae moa long mi. Mi mi no stret, mi no naf blong tekemaot sandel blong hem. [8]Mi mi stap baptaesem yufala long wora, be hem bambae i baptaesem yufala long Tabu Speret."

(*Nyutesteman, Long Bislama*, Bible Society, p. 72, Suva, Fiji, 1980)

The Gospel According to St Mark

The beginning of the gospel of Jesus Christ, the Son of God; 2. As it is written in the prophets, Behold, I send my messenger before thy face, which shall prepare thy way before thee.

3. The voice of one crying in the wilderness, Prepare ye the way of the Lord, make his paths straight.

4. John did baptize in the wilderness, and preach the baptism of repentance for the remission of sins.

5. And there went out unto him all the land of Judaea, and they of Jerusalem, and were all baptized of him in the river of Jordan, confessing their sins.

6. And John was clothed with camel's hair, and with a girdle of a skin about his loins; and he did eat locusts and wild honey;

7. And preached, saying, There cometh one mightier than I after me, the lachet of whose shoes I am not worthy to stoop down and unloose.

8. I indeed have baptized you with water: but he shall baptize you with the Holy Ghost.

(*The Holy Bible*, BFBS, London, p. 1001, n.d.)

Passages 6a to 6e possibly owe more to expatriates than to indigenous speakers of pidgins or creoles. They all relate to the creation of Eve. The first comes from the *Nigerian Gazette*, 4 March 1926; b. is from Crocker (1936: 167–8); c., which is extremely similar to b., was recorded by me in Cameroon in 1970; d. was sent to me as an example of Liberian English, but I have not been able to trace its precise origins; e. was recorded for me in 1973 by a Solomon Islander.

6a.

Then He began, He make all thing, He make eny kind beef, He make bush, He make farm, too. After wats He say 'How, I no get people?' Then He take some ground for hand, He mass him, He make him turn op like man. He col him, say 'be Kruboy!' Before he put him for some
5   big big garden; plenty chop live there inside, plenty planten, plenty makabo, plenty fruits, plenty palmoil, eny kind beef too he live, das oll; work no live! so them place be fine too much.

Then He tok for them Kruboy 'I give you this fine place for sit down, oll thing I dash you.' So them Kruboy, he sit down for them garden, he
10   waka there, he waka so oll for him self, he waka so-o-o-te-e-e, he tired.

One day he come for God, he say 'Massa, I com for You, I get some p'lava for tell You; no be You, You make me? No be You, You don't[1] put me for that garden? You no luk out for me, becos You be massa for me? Them garden, You don't put me, he fine too much, I like him bad;
15   plenty chop live, but all them chop he live for spoil, becos I no get woman for cook him; I think better You dash me some.'

1. The writer obviously thought that /dɔn/ which signals recently completed acts derived from 'don't'.

6b.

Dem first time, you savvy, nothing to live. No other thing, no ground, no wata for himself, all he be mixed like so so potapota. Then God he begin. He part him, some place he put some ground, some place he put dem wata, but mem he no fit look him, because so so dark.
5   By and by God he say:

'Better I make some lantern.' Then he hang him one big one, he call him say 'Moon,' and after dat he fix plenty small one for up, call him say 'Star.'

Then he begin to make all thing, he make any kind beef, he make

some bush, he make farm too. After that He say: 'How I no get some   10
people?' Then he some ground for hand, he mash him. He make him
turn up like a man. He call him say he 'Crooboy.' Before He put him
for some big big garden, plenty chop he live for inside, plenty
plaintains, plenty makabo, plenty fruits, plenty palm-oil, any kind
beef he live, dis be all work no live, so dem place be fine too much.   15
Then he call for dem Crooboy: 'I give you this fine place for sit-down,
all ting I dash you.' So dem Crooboy he sit down for dem garden, he
waka there, he waka das all for himself, he waka so t-e-e-e-e-e-e he
tired.

One day he come for God, he say, 'Massa I come for you, I get some   20
P'lava for tell you, no be you, who make me, no be you, who done put
me for dis garden? You no look out for me? Because you be Massa for
me? Dem garden you done put me, he fine too much, I like him, plenty
chop he day, but all dem chop he live for spoil because I no get woman,
for cook him, I better think you dash me one. God he say: "All right,   25
no p'lava, I go give you one, make you sit down, you wait . . ."'

6c.

Dɛn Gɔd bin bigin. I mek ɔl ting. I mek ɛni kain bif. I mek bush. I mek
fam tu. Afta, i tɔk sei: 'Hau a no gɛt pipul e?' Dɛn i tek sɔm graun fɔ
han. I masham. I mekam tɔn laik man. I kɔl i sei karia [i.e. 'carrier' or
'porter'].Dɛn i put i fɔ sɔm big big gadɛn. Plɛnti chɔp bin dei dei, plenti
planti, plenti makabu, plenti pamɔya. ɛni kain bif tu bin dei. Wɔk no   5
dei, so di plɛs bin fain tumɔch. Dɛn i tɔk fɔ di karia sei: 'A gif yu dis fain
plɛs fɔ stei dei. A dash yu ɔl ting dɛm.' So di karia stei fɔ di gadɛn. I
waka dei; i waka dei soso i wan. I waka sotei i taia. Wan dei i kam fɔ
gɔd. I sei: 'Masa, a kam fɔ yu. A gɛt sɔm palava fɔ tɔk fɔ yu. No bi na yu
mek mi? No bi yu dɔn put mi fɔ dat gadɛn? No bi yu di lukɔt fɔ mi   10
fɔseka yu bi ma masa? Dat gadɛn wei yu dɔn put mi fɔ insai, i fain
tumɔch. Plɛnti chɔp dei dei bɔt ɔl dat chɔp i di spɔil fɔseka a no gɛt
wuman fɔ kukam. A tink sei i bɛta mek yu dash mi sɔm wuman.'

6d.

For de first time, noting been de only de Lawd, He be.[2]

An' de Lawd, He done go work hard for make dis ting day call 'um
Earth. For six day de Lawd He work an' done make all ting – everyting
He go put for Earth. Plenty beef, plenty yam, plenty mango, plenty
guinea corn, plenty ground-nut – everyting. An' for de water He put   5
plenty fish, an' for de air He put plenty kinda bird.

After six day de Lawd He done go sleep. An' when He sleep, plenty
palaver start for dis place day call 'um Heaven. Dis Heaven be place
where we go live after we done die, if we no been so-so bad for dis
Earth. De angel day live for Heaven an' play de banjo an' get plenty   10
fine chop an' plenty palm-wine. De headman of dem angel day call'um

Gabriel. When dis palaver start for heaven, there be plenty humbug by bad angel, day call 'um Lucifer. An' Gabriel done catch Lucifer an' go beat 'um an' palaver stop, one-time. An de Lawd tell Gabriel he be 15 good man too much, an' He go dash Gabriel one trumpet an' hit drum for Heaven. An' Lucifer go for Hellfire, where he be headman now.

After de Lawd go look 'um dis ting day call 'um Earth and He savvy dat no man be for seat. So de Lawd take small piece Earth an' He go breathe – an' man day.

20 An' de Lawd He go call dis man Hadam. De Lawd He say "Hadam". An' Hadam he say "Yessah". De Lawd He say "Hadam, you see dis garden? Day call 'um Paradise. Everyting for dis garden be for you – but dem mango tree dat be for middle of dem garden, dat be no for you. Dat tree be white man chop. You no go chop 'um, or you 25 get plenty pain for belly, you savvy?" An Hadam he say "Yessah, Lawd I savvy".

De Lawd He done go back for Heaven to hear Gabriel play dem trumpet, an' Hadam he go walka walka for garden, where everyting be fine too much. Byme-by de Lawd He come back for Earth an' go 30 look 'um see see Hadam. An' He say, "Hadam, everyting be alright? You like 'um?" An' Hadam he say "Yessah, everyting no' be bad, but." An' de Lawd say: "Whassa matta, Hadam? You done get small trouble?" An' Hadam he say, "No, I no get trouble Lawd, Sah – but I no get woman." An' de Lawd He go make Hadam sleep for one place, 35 an' He go take small piece bone from Hadam side – dey call 'um wish-bone. He go breathe – an' woman day. An' de Lawd call dis woman Heva. De Lawd wake Hadam an' He say "Hadam, you see dis woman?" An' Hadam he say, "Yessah, I see 'um, she be past stinkfish." Den de Lawd go 'way for up to Heaven an' Hadam an' 40 Heva go walka walka for garden where dey go play plenty. One day when Hadam done go catch baracuta, Heva done take small small walk an' she meet shanake. An' shanake say, "Hail, Heva, Ekabbo!" An' Heva say, "Hallo, Shanake, Kushayo!" Shanake he say: "Whassa matta, Heva – why you no go chop dem fine mango from for middle of 45 garden?" An' Heva, she say: "A--ha! dat be white man chop, dat no be black man chop. Hadam done told me we get plenty trouble, plenty pain for belly, if we go chop 'um." An' shanake, he say: "Ah! Hadam be blood' fool. Dat chop be good for black man. You go chop 'um, you like 'um". An' Heva she done chop 'um, an' she done like 'um too 50 much. She put dem mango for Hadam ground-nut-stew – den dere be plenty trouble for Paradise one-time.

Hadam an' Heva day savvy day be naked, day get no cloth, so day go put 'um hat for head. Byme-bye, one man day call 'um Noah come for garden – Noah be headman for Elda Demsta boat an' he done take 55 Heva for sail on lagoon an' day go make plenty humbug for Hadam.

Den de Lawd come back for earth an' He go call "Hadam." But Hadam he no be for seat – he go fear de Lawd an' done go for bush one-time. Again de Lawd call: "Hadam". An' Hadam, he say with small voice, "Yessah, Lawd?". An' de Lawd say: "Close me, Hadam, close me." An' Hadam close de Lawd. De Lawd say, "Whassa matta, 60 Hadam, why you go for bush?" An' Hadam say: "I no get cloth, Lawd, an' I no want day you done see me naked." An' de Lawd He vex too much. He say: "A--ha! you done chop dem mango from tree for middle garden." An' Hadam say, "I no chop 'um Lawd. Dem woman you done make for me, she go put 'um for ground-nut-stew". 65

Den de Lawd make plenty palaver an' He done drove Hadam an' Heva from Paradise!

2. This passage was given to me as an example of Liberian English but W. Peters, British High Commissioner in Malawi, wrote to me as follows on 10 May 1982:

Thank you very much for your letter of 19 April, and its enclosure. The latter is indeed the text I have been looking for. It has always been presented to me as a Gold Coast version, rather than Liberian. I speak several Ghanaian languages, but do not recognise the words 'Ekabbo' and 'Kushoyo'. Nor would I expect in Ghana to hear a snake described as 'Shanake'; rather the word is 'Senek'. The truth is probably that this basic account has been converted into several different versions.

6e.
Taim Adam em i stap long gaden bilong Idan, em i lukim olabaut em. Em i lukim everi kain animal. Ol gatim em i misis. Baimbai em sori tumas, woswe em i se: 'Mi no gatim misis.' So em i tingting fo go lukim God. Em i go kachim God haus bilong God. God em i sindaun long insait. Em i se: 'E, monania, wonem yu laikim Adam?' Adam em i se: 5 'Mi lukim olgeta animal, God. Mi sori tumas man mi no gatim misis.' God em se: 'Yu no wori, man. Yu go slip litil bit. Bihain mi kam lukim yu. Mi stretim.' Adam em i go slip insait long gaden. Bihain God em pinisim wonem em duim. Em go lukim Adam. Adam em slip gutpela. Adam em slip. God em kachim em. Em i redi everi kastim bilong em. 10 Adam em slip yet. Go, go, go, God em i tekaut wanpela rib bilong lef sait bilong Adam. Adam em slip yet. Em sori. Bihain God em tekim dispela bun bilong Adam insait long bus. Em i wokim kastim. Go, go, go, wanpela wuman em kamap. God em se: 'Gut tumas.' Em i go bek long Adam. Em i raisim Adam. Em i se: 'E, we misis bilong mi?' God 15 em se: 'Em stap hia.'

Passages 7a to 7c all illustrate pidginised languages being used for official and/or formal purposes. The first passage is part of the

Budget speech made by the Minister of Finance to the Papua New
Guinea parliament in August 1973. The second is part of the
Constitution of Vanuatu, drawn up in 1980 and the third is from the
Solomon Islands' paper *Waswe?* (< which + way) and discusses the
effects of independence in 'Hao fo barava stanap seleva' (i.e. How to
really (< proper) stand on our own (< self).

7a.

BASET TOKTOK

Givim aut long 28th long Augas, 1973 ikam long Minista bilong
Finans, Mista Julius Chan.

Long dispela taim long Namba Tu Riding bilong Apropriasin Bil
1973/74

Mista Spika, Mi muv –
Olsem bai Bil ol iridim long namba tu taim (Namba tu riding long
dispela Bil).

Taim mi bringim namba wan Baset bilong mi long yia igo pinis,
Nesenol Koalisin Gavman ibin stap insait long ofis long sampela mun
tasol. Mi bin tok long dispela taim olsem mipela ibihainim planti ol
tingting Gavman bilong bipo ibin putim insait, na long taim mipela
oraitim olgeta, mipela isave olsem bai mipela inap senisim. Long
dispela taim mi bin stap long ofis long arapela Baset ikam inap nau, na
olsem mi no ken poret long kisim ol samting ikamap stret o nogut long
polisi bilong moni bilong yumi tude.

Yumi mas tanim ol dispela ol tingting long stretim sindaun bilong
yumi igo kamap ol polisi, bai ihalivim yumi long kisim ol dispela ol
samting; na yumi mas lukim olsem bai ol dispela ol polisi yumi mas
mekim bai ikamap. Yumi wok long go long pinisim wok bilong kantri
bilong taim bihain. Pasin bilong Baset em iwanpela bikpela samting
long kirapim wok bilong kantri, long wanem Baset em itoktok long
olgeta wok bilong Gavman long ekonomik na pasin bilong tromoim
moni – olsem ol isave mekim long ol sampela ol bikpela wok.

Ating ol Honorobol Membas bai ol iorait, olsem dispela taim nau
igat bikpela senis moa ikamap, na bikpela tingting moa long kantri
bilong yumi long taim bihain na long ol rot bai yumi go long en. Insait
long wok bisnis (ekonomik) yumi bin tok klia long ol tingting, em
Chip Minista ibin bringim ikam insait long dispela Haus long
Disemba igo pinis, na Haus ibin adoptim (bihainim) long Februari.
Gavman igat tupela wok long mekim.

7b.

Konstitusin Blong Ripablik Blong Vanuatu (Niu Hebrides) 1980
Fas Tok Blong Hem [Preamble]
Yumi ol man Nyuhebrides [We the people of the New Hebrides]
Yumi stap praod from we yumi bin faet strong bilong kam friman
[Proud of our struggle for freedom]

Mo tingting blong yumi i stap strong yet blong yumi lukaot gud
long olgeta samting ya we yumi winim long faet ya [Determined to
safeguard the achievements of this struggle]
Yumi stap holemtaet fasin ya we yumi gat ol naranarafala kala mo ol
naranarafala lanwis mo ol naranarafala kastom [Cherishing our   10
ethnic, liguistic and cultural diversity]
Be yumi save gud we long fyuja bambae yumi evriwan i wokbaut long
wan rod nomo [Mindful at the same time of our common destiny]
Nao yumi talemaot we naoia yumi stanemap Ripablik Blong Nyuhebrides, we tingting blong yumi man ples i wan nomo mo yumi ol   15
friman. Kantri ya blong yumi i stanap long ol gudgudfala fasin blong
ol bubu blong yumi bifoa wetem fasin blong bilif long God mo ol fasin
Kristin man [Hereby proclaim the establishment of the united and free
Republic of the New Hebrides founded on traditional Melanesian
values, faith in God, and Christian principles]   20
Mo blong stanemap Ripablik ya blong yumi olsem, yumi olgeta man
ples evriwan, yumi agri blong stap aninit long Konstitusin ya, blong
hem i holem gud laef blong yumi. [And for this purpose give ourselves
this Constitution.]

Japta Wan [Chapter One]   25
Kantri Ya Mo Paoa Blong Rul Long Hem [The State and Sovereignty]
1. Ripablik blong Hyuhebrides, hem i wan kantri we olgeta man ples
   blong hem i holim paoa blong gavman, nao gavman blong olgeta
   nomo i rul long hem. [The Republic of the New Hebrides is a
   sovereign democratic state.]   30
2. Konstitusin ya, hemia ol loa we i stampa blong ol narafala loa
   blong Nyuhebrides. [The Constitution is the supreme law of the
   New Hebrides]
3. (i) Lanwis blong Ripablik blong Nyuhebrides, hemia Bislama.
   Trifala lanwis blong mekem ol wok long kantri ya, i gat Bislama   35
   mo Inglis mo Franis. Tufala big lanwis blong edukesen long
   kantri ya, i gat Inglis mo Franis. [The national language of the
   country is Bislama. The official languages are Bislama, English
   and French. The principal languages of education are English
   and French.]   40
   (ii) Ol netif lanwis blong Nyuhebrides oli haf blong ol gudgudfala
   samting blong bifo long kantri ya, mo gavman blong Ripablik
   bambae i lukaot gud long olgeta blong oli no lus. Sipos gavman
   ya i wantem mekem olsem, bambae hem i save jusumaot wan
   long ol langwis ya blong i jenisim Bislama, i kam lanwis blong   45
   Ripablik blong Nyuhebrides. [The Republic shall protect the
   different local languages which are part of the national heritage
   and may declare one of them as a national language.]

Hau Fo Barava Stanap Seleva

7c.

Iumi save tu hem mas duim wanem o raetem wanem nao bos ia hemi talem hem fo duim. Hem mas waka falom taem tu ia. Hem
5 mas stat waka long seven klok an finis tuel klok. Hem stat waka moa long wan klok an barava finis waka long foa klok long ivining. So iumi save hemi no
10 save duim enikaen waka nomoa wea hemi save tingim seleva fo duim. An hem kanduit falom taem blong hem seleva. So long saet blong waka, bos hem nao
15 mas talem evrisamting fo duim. Oraet. Narafala man moa hemi stap long vilij blong hem nomoa. Disfala man ia nem blong hem nao Jimi. Nao Jimi hemi go-go
20 long skul tu wetem Jon. An tufala ia tufala kasem wanfala levol long ediukeson nomoa ia, tufala ia i barava wanklas nao. Bat iu save, taem Jon hemi waka
25 long taon long ofis blong Praem Minista, Jimi hemi gobaek long vilij blong hem an hemi mekem wanfala bikfala plandesin long kokonat. Hemi barava waka had
30 nao long disfala plandesin koko-nat blong hem.

Bihaen, taem olketa kokonat blong hem ia i garem frut, Jimi hemi stat fo wakem kopra nao.
35 Fastaem, hemi mekem samfala baeg kopra nomoa, bat long bihaen hemi mekem plande baeg long kopra nao. Evritaem hemi salem kopra blong hem, hemi garen plande moa dola nao. An 40 hemi garen moa dola winim Jon nao. Bat waswe, hemi baebae pei fo haos, wata, an ravis tin tu? Nomoa ia. Hemi baem nomoa inaf kaleko fo hem, waef blong 45 hem an olketa pikinini blong hem nomoa, an lelebet karasin laet blong olketa nomoa an sam-fala samting fo kaikai long hem nomoa. An hemi baebae baem 50 nomoa samfala tul fo waka long hem nomoa olsem naef, akis an fael.

Waswe? Jimi hemi mas weitem bos fo talem waka long hem? 55 Maekrangge! Nomoa ia! Bikos hemi seleva nao i bos long waka blong hem seleva ia. Waswe long taem fo waka? Hu nao fo talem hem taem fo waka? Iu tingse hu 60 nao ia? Hem seleva nao fo save watkaen taem fo hem fo waka ia.

Iumi mas save Jimi seleva nao hemi bos, hemi seleva nao fo save wanem nao fo duim, hemi seleva 65 nao fo save haomas mani nao baebae hemi garem. Waswe?

Go moa long pej foa . . .

Waswe? 21 & 22 1981

Passages 8a to 8d are translations of Shakespeare. The first two are Antony's speech from *Julius Caesar*, Act III, Scene ii, in Krio and Tok Pisin. The second two are Hamlet's soliloquy, Act III, Scene i, in the Pidgin Englishes of Cameroon and the British Solomon Islands.

8a.

> ANTONI: Padi dem, kohntri, una ohl wey dey
> na Rom. Meyk una ohl kak una yeys.
> A kam ber Siza, a noh kam preyz am.
> Dem kin memba bad wey pohsin kin du
> Lohng tem afta di pohsin kin dohn dai.   5
> Boht plenti tem di gud wey pohsin du
> kin ber wit im bon dem. Meyk i bi so
> wit Siza. Bra Brutohs dohn tel una
> sey Siza na bin man wey want pas mak.
> If i tohk tru, na badbad ting dis ya.   10
> En Siza dohn get im bad pey foh dat.
> A teyk pamishohn frohm Bra Brutohs dem
> foh kam tohk na Bra Siza im berin.
> En Bra Brutohs na ohnareybul O!
> Dem ohda wan sef na ohnareybul.   15
> Siza na bin mi fren; I gud en treyt.
> Boht Brutohs sey na man wey want pas mak;
> en Bra Brutohs na ohnareybul O!
> Siza dohn bring plenti prizna kam Rom,
> di kohpoh wey dem pey foh dem bil ohp   20
> di reveniu. Na want-want pas mak dat?
> Wen po man ala, Siza kin bohs krai.
> Man wey want-want pas mak foh get trohng at;
> boht Brutohs sey na man wey want pas mak
> En Bra Brutohs na ohnareybul O!   25
> Na una ohl bin si sey na bin tri tem
> a bin want foh kraun am boht i noh gri.
> Na so man wey want-want pas mak kin du?
> Boht Brutohs sey na man wey want pas mak.
> En Brutohs na ohnareybul O!   30
> A noh want pwel weytin Bra Brutohs sey.
> A kam na ya foh tohk weytin mi no.
> Una bin lek Siza; na sohmtin meyk.
> Weytin du una noh foh krai foh am?
> Mankain dem noh no au foh tink eygeyn.   35
> Una bia wit mi ya; mi at dey
> insai di kohfin dey wit Siza.
> A go tap fohs tey i kam bak to mi!

(Thomas Decker, *Sierra Leone Language Review* 4 (1965: 74).
Decker uses 'ey' to represent /e/ and 'oh' to represent /ɔ/.)

b.

Pren, man bolong Rom, Wantok, harim nau. Mi kam tasol long
olantim Kaesar. Mi noken beiten longen. Sopos sampela wok bolong

(fragments from overlapping pages)

n
on

n bi fain
bin di slip
am waka i.
Dis big man

givam sɔm big
n plenti fɔ dis
usi tɔk sei i beta
dɔn chɔp plenti
dem kip di fish fɔ

ata tɔk sei: 'Fɔseka
i kipam fɔ taim wei
kuk ɔda kain chɔp.'
p daso smɔl fɔseka sei
t Pusi no sabi usai i go.

en i kuk   10
pikin dem.

wampela man I stret; sampela i no stret; na ma... ...ng
wok i no stret tasol. Gutpela wok bolong... ...g
5 giraun wantaim long Kalopa. Fesin b...
tu, gutpela wok i slip.
  Brutus ia tokim yu long K...
pekato tru. Tasol Kaes...
Tru, Brutus, na ol...
10 orait long mi t...
  Kaesar...
em n...

30

35

8c.

Foh bi foh...
plenti hamb...
Wehda na so...
Foh di shap st...
5 man foh dis gra...
Oh foh kari wow...
Foh dai – na foh sl...
Nohting i dei agehn;
Di wohrinehs foh wi h...
10 Wei dehm di mek man...

An i di soso hala fɔ haus. Ɛni smol smol ting i go hala sotei man fit tink
sei na sɔm big big ting.
  Kanak i mama an i papa dem kam tɔk fɔ Kanak sei i no bi so dem di
15 du. I get wuman an tri fain pikin, tu man an wan wuman. An i wuman
sabi wɔk fɔ fam plenti. An di wuman no di hambɔk[1] i laik ɔda wuman
dem sabi hambɔk dem man. Dem tel i sei dat kain fashɔn no gud. An
dem hala Kanak plenti.
  Taim wei i papa an i mama dem dɔn go, Kanak i bit i wuman. I
20 draivam mek i go fɔ i papa i taun. I hala i sei i bin go kɔnggosa fɔ i papa
an i mama. I draiv Koko wit i pikin dem ɔl, mek dem go fɔ i papa i
taun. So Koko an i pikin dem bin go fɔ i papa i taun an dem shidɔng fɔ
dei.
  Wan wik nɛva pas, Kanak dɔn mari sɔm ɔda wuman, sɔm wuman
25 pikin wei i fain fain. Dis wuman bin fain sotei ɔl man pikin dem tɔk sei
fɔ tru na wuman dat! An di wuman sɛf bin sabi kuk chɔp. If pipul dem kam
An i no bin sabi wɔk fɔ fam an i no bin sabi kuk chɔp, dem go shem. Smol taim ɔl man
fɔ haus an i kuk chɔp, dem go chɔpam daso fɔ shem. Smol taim ɔl man
30 bigin tɔk sei dat Kanak i wuman i fain daso fɔ ai. I no fit kuk chɔp an i
no fit wok fam. . . .

1. *hambɔk* from 'humbug' – annoy, worry, complain
2. Koko was driven back to her own father's compound. This actio...
   was tantamount to divorcing Koko.
3. *mek nyanga na dai* – really knew how to dress herself up, to pu...
   airs and graces.

Fɔseka wɛti pusi di soso kash arata kilam
(Why cats always chase and kill rats)

9b.

Fɔs taim, Pusi an Arata dem bin laik dem sɛf fain. Dem b...
kɔmbi. Ɛni ples wei yu si Pusi yu go si Masa Arata. An dem...
fɔ wan haus. Sɔm dei nau, sɔm big man bin kɔl dem fɔ k...
Dem wash dem skin fain an dem go fɔ dis man i haus.
5 gifam plenti chɔp, witi bif sotei dem no fit chɔp ɔl sɛf.
  Taim wei dem wan go bak fɔ dem haus, dis big man...
big fish mek dem go kuk sup. Dem tank di big ma...
wandaful ting wei i du. Wɛn dem kam rish fɔ haus, p...
mek dem kuk di fish wan taim.[1] Arata tɔk sei dem...
10 ɔredi.[2] Dem lɔkam. Pusi kip ki.[3] Arata tɔk sei dem kuk dat fish. A...
stoa.[3] Dem lɔkam. Pusi kip ki,[4] Pusi tɔk sei mek dem kuk dat fish? I bɛta mek y...
  Dei klin,[4] Pusi tɔk sei mek dem kuk dat fish? I bɛta mek y...
wɛti yu di soso wori fɔ dat fish so? I bɛta mek y...
hɔngri go kam. Jɔsnau, wi get plenti chɔp. Wi fi...
15 So dem bin kuk yam chɔpam. Arata bin ch...
hɔngri no di du i. Afta chɔp, Arata wikɔp go b...

Wɛn i dɔn ritɔn bak, Pusi asam usai i bin dei. Arata tɛl i sei i bin go fɔ ples wei dɛm di baptais pikin. Pusi asam sei na wich man i pikin dɛm 20 bin baptaisam. Arata tɔk sei na Masa Wi-ɔl[5] i pikin. Pusi as sei hau dɛm bin kɔl di pikin. Arata tɔk sei di pikin i nem na 'Dɛm-dɔn-bigin'. Pusi di laf. I tɔk fɔ Arata sei: Pipul dɛm di gif pikin wandaful nem!' . . .

1. *wan taim* from 'one time' — immediately, on the double
2. *ɔredi* from 'already' — already
3. *stoa* from 'store' — a storing cupboard, a fridge
4. *dei klin* from 'day clean' — at dawn, at daybreak
5. *Wi-ɔl* from 'We-All' — All-of-us. Naming is extremely important in Cameroon society and in their folktales the trickster hero often wins by assuming a name.

9c. *Dis smɔl swain . . .*
(This little piggy)

Dis smɔl swain i bin go fɔ makɛt.
Dis smɔl swain i bin stei fɔ haus.
Dis smɔl swain i bin chɔp sup witi fufu. 5
Dis smɔl swain i no bin chɔp no nɔting.
An dis smɔl swain i bin go wi, wi sotei fɔ haus.

10a. *Bikpela longlong man*
(The Foolish Giant)

Long bipo bipo tru, em i gat wanpela bikpela man i bin sindaun insait long maunten Kuvui bilong hap san i kamap i go olsem long Choiseul Island long Solomon Group. Wanpela samting i mekim dispela 5 bikpela man em wanem i no klia gut long rot bilong painim gutpela kaikai olsem mit na pis.[1]

Dispela pasin em mekim bikpela man hia i wokabaut na askim ol pipel long givim kaikai sapos em i bungim[2] ol na pasim. Sapos ol i givim kaikai long em i kaikai pinis, bai kirap na askim ol long ol i bin 10 kisim olsem wanem na mekim olsem wanem na kukim gut long mekim swit.

Long wanpela de, dispela bikpela man i bin kirap wokabaut i go kamap long wanpela ples na i bungim fopela yangpela man sindaun raunim paia na i wok long kukim ol pis i stap. Em i lukim olsem na 15 wokabaut i go klostu tru long ol na askim long givim sampela na em i kaikai. Ol fopela man hia i bin mekim gutpela pasin na givim sampela pis long em i kaikai, na ol i kirap givim sampela moa gen na kaikai. Bihain long kaikaim ol pis pinis em i wok long toktok wantaim ol na

20   askim ol long rot bilong kisim ol pis. 'Yupela i bin kisim ol dispela pis
          we na yupela i bin mekim olsem wanem na kukim?'
           Wanpela long ol i bin kirap bekim tok bilong em: 'Mipela i bin
          kisim ol dispela pis insait long wara na kukim insait long pot.' 'O, mi
          lukim. Long narapela taim bai mi traim olsem yupela i bin mekim. Ol
25   mit bilong pis i swit gut tru,' em i tokim ol.
           Bihain nau em i go bek long ples bilong em na traim wokim wanpela
          liklik umben[3] bilong kisim ol pis insait long wara. Em i bin kisim
          planti na bihainim toktok bilong ol fopela man na kukim long pot na
          kaikaim.[4]
30   Long narapela de dispela bikpela man i go kamap long narapela
          ples. Insait long dispela ples em i bin painim tripela man i wok long
          kukim wanpela kapul long paia i stap. . . .

Jennifer Boseto

     1. *mit na*   –   meat and fish. 'Mit' is beginning to oust 'abus' in
              pis   the TP of educated and urban speakers.
     2. *bungim*   –   meet
     3. *umben*   –   comes from the local vernaculars of New Britain
                         and means a fishing net.
     4. *kaikai*   –   normally does not take the transitive marker 'im'
                         although there is a growing tendency among
                         young speakers to regularise it. This narrator
                         invariably does do. She also makes more systema-
                         tic use of 'bin' than I have found in other
                         narratives.

10b.   *Rat na Pusi*
                             (The Rat and the Cat)

Bipo tru, em i gat wanpela Rat i stap long bus. Em i gat save nogut tru.
Wanpela de, ol abus ol i kam lukim Rat na wanpela abus em i tokim
5   long Rat em i se: 'Pusi em i wokabaut long bus em i painim yu. Sapos
     em i painim yu, bai em i kaikai yu.'
       Rat em i tok: 'I orait. Mi no guria. Mi gat save plenti. Bai mi painim
     Pusi na bai mi kilim em.'
       Bihain, Rat i go wokabaut long bus na em i lukim wanpela bikpela
10   Pusi. Pusi i wokabaut isi isi na em i kamap long Rat na em i tok: 'Yu
     mekim wanem, Rat'?'
       Rat em i bekim: 'Mi go long painim kaikai.' Pusi i tok: 'Mi inap
     helpim yu. Mi inap kilim olgeta abus i dai'. . . .

10c.   *Tripela liklik pik*
                         (The three little pigs)

Bipo tru,[1] tripela liklik pik ol i stap long bush. Ol i no gat haus na ol i laikim wokim haus.

I gat wanpela wail dok em i stap long dispela bus. Em i bikpela bikpela na em i laikim kaikai pik. Em i save kilim plenti pik long bus na em i save kaikai ol.

Wanpela liklik pig em i wokabaut long bus. Em i lukim wanpela man i karim kunai.[2]

1. *bipo tru* from 'before true' – long ago
2. *kunai* – a type of sword grass used for matting and for making baskets.

Index

๑๑๑๑๑๑